Burnout at Work

The psychological concept of burnout refers to long-term exhaustion from, and diminished interest in, the work we do. It is a phenomenon that most of us have some understanding of, even if we have not always been affected directly. Many people start their working lives full of energy and enthusiasm, but far fewer are able to maintain that level of engagement.

Burnout at Work: A psychological perspective provides a comprehensive overview of how the concept of burnout has been conceived over recent decades, as well as discussing the challenges and possible interventions that can help confront this pervasive issue. With contributions from the most eminent researchers in this field, the book examines a range of topics including:

- the links between burnout and health
- how our individual relationships at work can affect levels of burnout
- the role of leadership in mediating or causing burnout
- the strategies that individuals can pursue to avoid burnout, as well as wider interventions.

The book will be required reading for anyone studying organizational or occupational psychology, and will also interest students of business and management, and health psychology.

Michael P. Leiter is Professor and Canada Research Chair in the Psychology Department at Acadia University, Canada.

Arnold B. Bakker is Professor in the Department of Work and Organizational Psychology at Erasmus University Rotterdam, the Netherlands, and Adjunct Professor in the Department of Applied Psychology at Lingnan University, Hong Kong.

Christina Maslach is Professor of Psychology at the University of California, Berkeley, USA.

Current Issues in Work and Organizational Psychology
Series Editor: Arnold B. Bakker

Current Issues in Work and Organizational Psychology is a series of edited books that reflect the state-of-the-art areas of current and emerging interest in the psychological study of employees, workplaces and organizations.

Each volume is tightly focused on a particular topic and consists of seven to ten chapters contributed by international experts. The editors of individual volumes are leading figures in their areas and provide an introductory overview.

Example topics include: digital media at work, work and the family, workaholism, modern job design, positive occupational health, and individualized deals.

A Day in the Life of a Happy Worker
Edited by Arnold B. Bakker and Kevin Daniels

The Psychology of Digital Media at Work
Edited by Daantje Derks and Arnold B. Bakker

New Frontiers in Work and Family Research
Edited by Joseph G. Grzywacz and Evangelia Demerouti

Burnout at Work: A Psychological Perspective
Edited by Michael P. Leiter, Arnold B. Bakker and Christina Maslach

Burnout at Work

A psychological perspective

**Edited by Michael P. Leiter,
Arnold B. Bakker
and Christina Maslach**

Ψ Psychology Press
Taylor & Francis Group

LONDON AND NEW YORK

First published 2014
by Psychology Press
27 Church Road, Hove, East Sussex BN3 2FA

and by Psychology Press
711 Third Avenue, New York, NY 10017

Psychology Press is an imprint of the Taylor & Francis Group, an informa business

© 2014 Michael P. Leiter, Arnold B. Bakker and Christina Maslach

British Library Cataloguing in Publication Data
A catalogue record for this book is available from the British Library

Library of Congress Cataloging in Publication Data
Burnout at work : a psychological perspective / [edited by] Michael P Leiter,
Arnold B Bakker, Christina Maslach. — 1 Edition.
    pages cm
    Includes bibliographical references and index.
  1. Burn out (Psychology) 2. Job stress. 3. Psychology, Industrial. I. Leiter,
Michael P., editor of compilation. II. Bakker, Arnold B., editor of
compilation. III. Maslach, Christina, editor of compilation.
BF481.B8677 2014
158.7'32—dc23   2013044971

ISBN: 978-1-84872-228-6 (hbk)
ISBN: 978-1-84872-229-3 (pbk)
ISBN: 978-1-315-84941-6 (ebk)

Typeset in Times
by Keystroke, Station Road, Codsall, Wolverhampton

FSC
www.fsc.org   MIX
Paper from
responsible sources
FSC® C013056

Printed and bound in Great Britain by
TJ International Ltd, Padstow, Cornwall

Contents

List of contributors   vii

1. **The contemporary context of job burnout**   1
   MICHAEL P. LEITER, ARNOLD B. BAKKER, AND
   CHRISTINA MASLACH

2. **Burnout and health**   10
   KIRSI AHOLA AND JARI HAKANEN

3. **Individual strategies to prevent burnout**   32
   EVANGELIA DEMEROUTI

4. **The good and bad of working relationships:
   implications for burnout**   56
   ARLA DAY AND MICHAEL P. LEITER

5. **Daily burnout experiences: critical events and
   measurement challenges**   80
   DESPOINA XANTHOPOULOU AND LAURENZ L. MEIER

6. **The influence of constructive and destructive
   leadership behaviors on follower burnout**   102
   KIMBERLEY BREEVAART, ARNOLD B. BAKKER,
   JØRN HETLAND, AND HILDE HETLAND

7. **Multilevel models of burnout: separating group level
   and individual level effects in burnout research**   122
   JONATHON R. B. HALBESLEBEN AND MATTHEW R. LEON

8. Interventions to prevent and alleviate burnout   **145**
MICHAEL P. LEITER AND CHRISTINA MASLACH

Index   168

List of contributors

Kirsi Ahola, Finnish Institute of Occupational Health, Finland

Arnold B. Bakker, Erasmus University Rotterdam, Netherlands

Kimberley Breevaart, Erasmus University Rotterdam, Netherlands

Arla Day, Saint Mary's University, Canada

Evangelia Demerouti, Eindhoven University of Technology, Netherlands

Jari Hakanen, Finnish Institute of Occupational Health, Finland

Jonathon R. B. Halbesleben, University of Alabama, USA

Hilde Hetland, University of Bergen, Norway

Jørn Hetland, University of Bergen, Norway

Michael P. Leiter, Acadia University, Canada

Matthew R. Leon, University of Alabama, USA

Christina Maslach, University of California, Berkeley, USA

Laurenz L. Meier, University of Friborg, Switzerland

Despoina Xanthopoulou, Aristotle University of Thessalonkiki, Greece

1   The contemporary context of job burnout

Michael P. Leiter, Arnold B. Bakker, and Christina Maslach

The contemporary context of job burnout

Job burnout was first identified in the 1970s as a career crisis of professionals working with people in some capacity. Subsequent research has established that burnout was neither a passing phase of baby boomers' entry into the workforce nor a minor problem easily resolved. Instead, burnout has persisted.

Burnout as a human challenge

Despite a considerable body of knowledge about the nature of job burnout, its causes, and its consequences, burnout continues as a major career crisis in the twenty-first century. The persistence of burnout over time and its prevalence around the world support the idea that burnout reflects a fundamental challenge of working life (Maslach et al., 2001; Schaufeli et al., 2008). People do not simply shrug off frustrations at work, but react in ways that are reflected in their energy (exhaustion), involvement (cynicism), and efficacy. That quality of people was not specific to late twentieth-century America, but was a pervasive, widespread phenomenon.

Complementing this enduring quality of people were enduring qualities in the nature of workplaces. In 2013, many people work in situations that are conducive to burnout. Some struggle to address intense demands with inadequate resources. Some feel alienated from their employers' espousal of lofty values for which their employers evidence no meaningful commitment. Some do tedious, joyless, meaningless work for meagre pay. These and other changes in the nature of work have implications for employees' vulnerability to burnout (Ten Brummelhuis et al., 2012).

The social and economic context of work

The information/service economy that dominates the post-industrialized world has increased the proportion of the economy that is devoted to providing services to people. It has also increased the proportion of work that is done with people through various sorts of workgroups. Working with people enhances employees' experience of work life by increasing opportunities for pleasant social contact and access to the knowledge, skills, and social capital of their colleagues and clients. Working with people also increases the amount of uncertainty employees encounter in their jobs. The interdependencies in the work of team members can make work more interesting but can also increase distress when the contributions of others to a shared project arrive late or lack the expected quality. Working with others requires employees to have the capacity to collaborate, to lead, and to follow. Technical or analytical skills provide only part of the solution to an effective worklife. Social skills increase in importance in the context of contemporary work. As a result, the increasingly social nature of work brings with it both additional resources and additional demands.

Another challenge inherent in team-based work is that job feedback becomes more complex. Clear feedback has been long established as an important contributor to employees' experience of motivating, fulfilling work (Hackman & Oldham, 1976). With many people contributing to a patient's treatment or an application's design, the line from an individual's contribution to a specific outcome becomes blurred. Further, much of contemporary work is inconclusive: people contribute to complex projects that rarely have clear-cut outcomes. Large-scale projects in international finance, information technology, or communications rarely produce a definitive product. For example, agencies constantly update information on unemployment rates, and computer operating systems regularly execute updates. In contrast to a crafts model that permits a concentrated focus on producing a complete, refined product, employees attend meetings, analyze data, and contribute to reports of no apparent consequence.

Furthermore, contemporary work has become increasingly portable. A variety of gizmos carry information along with the capacity to analyze. Maintaining a clear boundary between work and personal life requires deliberate action from employees. Communication technology not only enables employers or clients to contact employees anywhere, it also allows employees to continue working on unresolved projects when they would be better served by a complete break from work (Derks et al., in press). People can become trapped in a continuous cycle attempting to address the inherent lack of closure in contemporary work (Derks & Bakker, in press).

Another strain in contemporary worklife is uncertainty. Since the financial crisis of 2008, job security feels more tenuous (Burke, 2012). Beyond short-term concerns, there are challenges to the financial viability of private pension funds, municipal governments, or even national governments to meet their obligations to retired workers. As pension plans shift from defined benefit plans to defined contribution plans, employees face increasing uncertainty (Broadbent et al., 2006). (Defined benefit plans commit the pension to a certain payment to retirees while defined contribution plans only designate the employees' pension contributions, leaving the eventual payment to be defined by the pension fund's eventual earnings.) With high levels of youth unemployment, families have greater uncertainty about their future aspirations. Austerity programs are immediate in delivering short-term pain and slow to convey long-term gain. In the USA and Europe, state and municipal governments have taken positions that show antipathy against public sector employees, challenging their job security, compensation, and pensions (Befort, 2012). The change in the psychological contract of employees with their employers generates uncertainty for employees' future wellbeing, productivity, and career development (Burke, 2012).

Financial challenges and greater uncertainty are not the only unintended consequences of organizational restructuring. As upper-level managers strive to address steady or growing demands with shrinking resources, they often resort to restructuring organizations or departments (Ashman, 2013; McKenzie, 2012; Teo et al., 2012). The demands of adjusting to a restructured work environment, including the uncertainty inherent in such changes, have been linked to job burnout in various countries (Allisey, Rodwell, & Noblet, 2012; Carter et al., 2013; Raftopoulos et al., 2012). In addition to their demands on employees' overall energy, restructuring initiatives often challenge employees' professional values. Despite assurances that changes will maintain or even enhance service quality, employees experience the changes as steps towards reducing service quality.

In sum, this brief overview of the challenges facing employees at the time of writing (September, 2013) identifies factors with a potential for engendering career crises among employees worldwide. As international and national political/ economic systems adjust to system-level strains, they create tensions on organizations and workgroups that eventually affect individuals.

A call for action

Research reports on burnout have consistently called for action to develop strategies to prevent and alleviate the syndrome. Despite both reasoned and impassioned calls for action, progress has been modest. The progress that has occurred provides a solid foundation for future work, but much remains to be accomplished.

Work engagement

Work engagement has provided a positive target for burnout interventions. The simple goal of eliminating burnout fails to specify what will take its place. When people recover from burnout, will they experience a state of calm indifference or of energetic enthusiasm? It is likely that most employees and all employers would prefer the latter outcome.

Maslach and Leiter (1997) identified engagement with work as a positive alternative to burnout. First, they noted that surveys of health care organizations showed a full range of experiences from constant exhaustion on the burnout end of the continuum to a complete lack of exhaustion on the other end. Second, the distributions were skewed towards the positive end of the scale. Third, they noted that the distribution did not show a clear cut-off indicating a distinct state of burnout: did the term, burnout, apply to the top 50 percent on the exhaustion scale or the top 1 percent?

They proposed that it was more constructive to identify a positive alternative to burnout than to simply divide the world into those who were experiencing burnout and those who were not. The concept of work engagement has been elaborated extensively since that time (e.g., Schaufeli & Bakker, 2004), including the development of the Utrecht Work Engagement Scale (Schaufeli et al., 2006). The Job-Demand Resources model (JD-R; Bakker & Demerouti, 2007; 2014) has articulated a framework for identifying distinct and shared qualities of burnout and engagement.

A positive target for intervention makes such initiatives more appealing to employers and focuses intervention design on constructive results. A constructive target for interventions reduces the risk inherent in organizational change. Although participants may agree on the importance of reducing burnout and its unfortunate impact on health, fulfillment, and productivity, participants appreciate knowing that the intervention will promote constructive qualities as well.

This book explores some of the core issues in burnout intervention. As Leiter and Maslach (2000) have argued, effective intervention is furthered by knowing the leverage points (Maslach & Leiter, 2008). These are aspects of organizational life, management practices, or working relationships that have a close relationship to burnout. Changing the leverage points imposes an imbalance in the network of relationships that maintains the status quo for people experiencing distress at work. For example, changing the extent to which employees experience improvements in a manageable workload or meaningful recognition is likely to reduce feelings of exhaustion or increase efficacy. Background research in burnout helps to identify effective leverage points. The second feature of effective intervention is focusing on what can be changed. For example, an organization undergoing a sharp increase in client demands may lack ways of making workload more manageable but may be able to increase recognition for employees' extraordinary efforts.

Knowledge translation

An ongoing issue for applied psychology is the process of translating research findings and the research process to accommodate the interests and concerns of the general working public. Job burnout is not solely an academic topic, it is also a practical concern for working people, managers, and the larger community. Meaningful field research and intervention testing require an enthusiastic and sustained cooperation both within and beyond the academic world.

One level of knowledge translation is a communication strategy that includes messages directed toward research participants and their counterparts in their industry. Through writing, speaking, and media interviews, researchers convey their findings in accessible language to a broad audience outside of the world of academic journals and conferences.

A deeper level of knowledge translation begins with conversations before the research begins. For example, the research discussed in this book about the CREW intervention (see Chapter 8) had its beginning in conversations that included researchers with chief nursing officers of hospitals who identified the problem.

Hospitals had units characterized by poor collegiality and their efforts to address this problem were not having the desired impact. They actively sought help in developing a new approach that would address relationship problems and inspire greater engagement with work. Having organizational leaders involved from the problem definition through the process of defining the methodology, implementation, analysis, and reporting assures that knowledge will transfer. Researchers learn from the practitioners and practitioners learn from the researchers. Progress toward making a change in burnout requires such partnerships to thrive.

Overview of the book

A noteworthy theme across the contributions in this book is the sophisticated level of research conducted on job burnout. The field clearly reflects progression from general questions to focused explorations of processes. Research on job burnout has evolved beyond linking the syndrome with antecedents and consequences. The three major foci of burnout research in the early twenty-first century are: (1) delving into the processes through which burnout changes over time, (2) the role of social relationships in the burnout process, and (3) the processes through which the syndrome can be alleviated. These three streams of research focus have multiple branches that are reflected in the chapters of this book.

In Chapter 2, "Burnout and health," Kirsi Ahola and Jari Hakanen begin with conclusive evidence of burnout's relationships to health problems. The authors go beyond acknowledging the connection between burnout and health to review prospective studies designed to untangle the pathways underlying this relationship. They identify studies that have supplemented self-report measures of health with independent sources of institutional or health system data. Their review confirms the value of a multi-dimensional burnout construct in that exhaustion has a more clear-cut relationship with health outcomes than do the other two dimensions of burnout. A one-dimensional measure would miss this nuance. Another important issue within their review is the complex causal framework of burnout and health. They supplement the more common structure of burnout leading to health problems with research that has considered the potential of health problems contributing to the subsequent development of burnout. The growing evidence for both directions of influence (burnout to health problems and health problems to burnout) suggests that the field can move beyond evaluating "reversed causality" to considering complex models with reciprocal relationships over time. That is, the phrase, "reversed causality," implies processes that run contrary to an established unidirectional causal path. Increasingly, evidence supports models in which multi-directional influences maintain balance among elements. Within this context it is clear that reporting a simple correlation between exhaustion and health problems would no longer be considered an advancement of knowledge. Progress calls for deeper explorations on the mechanisms through which health problems and exhaustion influence one another.

The chapter by Despoina Xanthopoulou and Laurenz Meier, "Daily burnout experiences: critical events and measurement challenges," examines burnout processes with the close lens provided through daily diary studies. The authors argue that the long-term stability of burnout permits considerable within-person variation within and across workdays. The multiple assessments within a diary format permit researchers to test complex models of reciprocal causation that put aside a structure of antecedents and consequences to depict ongoing sequences of events and experiences that characterize employees' experience of their worklife. They point out that the burst design that encompasses a series of daily diaries separated by longer periods have a potential for placing short-term fluctuations within long-term processes. An important message in the authors' in-depth consideration of research methods is that researchers must critically examine constructs and their operationalization in measures to articulate similarities and differences inherent in their distinct time scales.

The second major theme in this book is the social context of burnout. The chapter by Jonathan Halbesleben and Matthew Leon, "Multilevel models of burnout: separating group level and individual level effects in burnout research," approaches the social context from the perspective of multi-level analysis. This approach strives to separate the extent to which employees' experience of their worklife reflects qualities shared by members of workgroups in contrast to individual characteristics or experiences. Members of workgroups share a management environment with common experiences of job demands and common access to shared resources. Despite these commonalities, individuals differ in their resiliency to withstand demands and their capacity to make effective use of available resources. A comprehensive model of job burnout would encompass both of these levels.

The chapter by Kimberley Breevaart, Arnold Bakker, Jørn Hetland, and Hilde Hetland, "The influence of constructive and destructive leadership behaviors on follower burnout," shifts the focus from the overall workgroup to a critical workgroup relationship. Employees' relationship with organizational leaders has implications for the challenges and hindrances that they encounter in the course of their work. Their capacity to build constructive relationships with leaders may influence employees' access to organizational resources that are critical to their success at their jobs or in their careers. The chapter also covers potential for emotional contagion or other processes in which employees share their leaders' experiences of exhaustion, cynicism, or inefficacy. The chapter provides further evidence that burnout goes beyond an individual experience of distress to reflect something essential about a social group.

The chapter by Arla Day and Michael Leiter, "The good and bad of working relationships: implications for burnout," considers social encounters from the micro-level of day-to-day social encounters with coworkers and supervisors. This work builds on a growing body of research on workplace civility and incivility (Cortina, 2008; Leiter, 2012; Lim et al., 2008) that has explored the impact of low intensity displays of disrespect or rudeness on employees' experience of worklife. Essentially, humans have developed a refined sensitivity to the extent to which others regard them with respect. Evidence of disrespect in social encounters signals a risky social environment that will challenge employees' self-respect and sense of belonging.

Both of these themes – describing the burnout process and its social context – contribute to the third theme: preventing and alleviating burnout. The chapter by Evangelia Demerouti, "Individual strategies to prevent burnout," considers ways in which individuals manage their connections with work to avoid burnout. When functioning well, these strategies further active engagement with work. The chapter considers reactive coping to address demanding aspects of jobs as well as proactive approaches to developing resources to address anticipated demands. A section on job crafting provides a fresh approach to employees' creative and constructive behavior to make the most of their current situation while striving to evolve it into a more fulfilling situation.

In the final chapter, "Interventions to prevent and alleviate burnout", Michael Leiter and Christina Maslach review the current state of work on burnout interventions. They describe a thin body of work on demonstrating meaningful change in burnout. The paucity of output runs contrary to the interests of both managers and researchers. However, it does directly reflect the challenges in designing, funding, implementing, and publishing systematic, controlled research on deliberate change. The chapter ends by integrating the three themes in describing an intervention approach designed to reverse the burnout process by improving the quality of social relationships among people at work.

Conclusion

Throughout the book, the authors reflect on the research formats that have been developed to address each of three themes: the burnout process, its social context, and preventing or alleviating burnout. The authors recognize the challenges inherent in conducting research on burnout processes that develop over time, on social interactions, and on strategies for organizational change. Significant advances in burnout research require sophisticated research formats. Ongoing working relationships of researchers with organizational leaders provide the foundation for more ambitious projects. Finding the balance of scientific rigor and practical application is essential for maintaining the active participation of employees and leaders necessary to gain a greater understanding of burnout and an ability to deal effectively with it.

Acknowledgment

The editors wish to thank Stephanie Gumuchian for her thorough and cheerful work in the preparation of this manuscript.

References

Allisey, A., Rodwell, J., & Noblet, A. (2012, July). *Officer wellbeing, satisfaction and commitment: job conditions of Australian law enforcement personnel*. Presentation in AIRAANZ 2008: Workers, corporations, and community: Facing choices for a sustainable future: proceedings of the 22nd conference of the Association of Industrial Relations Academics of Australia and New Zealand, Melbourne, Australia.

Ashman, I. (2013). The face-to-face delivery of downsizing decisions in UK public sector organizations. *Public Management Review*, (ahead-of-print), 1–21. Online version: http://www.tandfonline.com/doi/abs/10.1080/14719037.2013.785583#.Uc7WmfnCa-0 (accessed 19 December 2013).

Bakker, A. B., & Demerouti, E. (2007). The job demands-resources model: State of the art. *Journal of Managerial Psychology, 22,* 309–328.

Bakker, A. B., & Demerouti, E. (2014). Job demands – resources theory. In C. Cooper & P. Chen (Eds.), *Wellbeing: A complete reference guide* (pp. 37–64). Chichester, UK: Wiley-Blackwell.

Befort, S. F. (2012). Public-sector employment under siege. *Indiana Law Journal, 87,* 231–238.

Broadbent, J., Palumbo, M., & Woodman, E. (2006). *The shift from defined benefit to defined contribution pension plans–implications for asset allocation and risk management.* Reserve Bank of Australia, Board of Governors of the Federal Reserve System and Bank of Canada.

Burke, R. (2012). Economic recession, job insecurity and employee and organizational health. In C. L. Cooper & A. G. Antoniou (Eds), *The Psychology of the recession on the workplace* (pp. 143–152). London: Edward Elgar.

Carter, B., Danford, A., Howcroft, D., Richardson, H., Smith, A., & Taylor, P. (2013). 'Stressed out of my box': Employee experience of lean working and occupational ill-health in clerical work in the UK public sector. *Work, Employment & Society.* Online Version: http://wes.sagepub.com/content/early/2013/05/20/0950017012469 064.abstract, doi: 10.1177/0950017012469064 (accessed 19 December 2013).

Cortina, L. M. (2008). Unseen injustice: Incivility as modern discrimination in organizations. *Academy of Management Review, 33,* 55–75.

Derks, D., & Bakker, A. B. (in press). Smartphone use, work-home interference, and burnout: A diary study on the role of recovery. *Applied Psychology: An International Review.*

Derks, D., Ten Brummelhuis, L. L., Zecic, D., & Bakker, A. B. (in press). Switching on and off . . . Does smartphone use obstruct the possibility to engage in recovery activities? *European Journal of Work and Organizational Psychology.*

Hackman, J. R., & Oldham, G. R. (1976). Motivation through the design of work: Test of a theory. *Organizational Behavior and Human Performance, 16,* 250–279.

Leiter, M. P. (2012). *Analyzing and theorizing the dynamics of the workplace incivility crisis.* Amsterdam: Springer.

Leiter, M. P., & Maslach, C. (2000). *Preventing burnout and building engagement: A training package.* San Francisco: Jossey Bass.

Lim, S., Cortina, L. M., & Magley, V., J. (2008). Personal and workgroup incivility. Impact on work and health outcomes. *Journal of Applied Psychology*, *93,* 95–107.

Maslach, C., & Leiter, M. P. (1997). *The truth about burnout.* San Francisco: Jossey Bass.

Maslach, C., & Leiter, M. P. (2008). Early predictors of job burnout and engagement. *Journal of Applied Psychology, 93,* 498–512.

Maslach, C., Schaufeli, W. B., & Leiter, M. P. (2001). Job burnout. *Annual Review of Psychology, 52,* 397–422.

McKenzie, C. R. (2012). *Economic and public sector restructuring in Japan.* Osaka University Knowledge Archive. Online version: http://hdl.handle.net/11094/11983 (accessed 19 December 2013).

Raftopoulos, V., Charalambous, A., & Talias, M. (2012). The factors associated with the burnout syndrome and fatigue in Cypriot nurses: A census report. *BMC Public Health, 12,* 457, doi:10.1186/1471-2458-12-457.

Schaufeli, W. B., & Bakker, A. B. (2004). Job demands, job resources, and their relationship with burnout and engagement: A multi-sample study. *Journal of Organizational Behavior, 25,* 293–315.

Schaufeli, W. B., Bakker, A. B., & Salanova, M. (2006). The measurement of work engagement with a brief questionnaire: A cross-national study. *Educational and Psychological Measurement, 66,* 701–716.

Schaufeli, W. B., Leiter, M. P., & Maslach, C. (2008). Burnout: Thirty-five years of research and practice. *Career Development International, 14*, 204–220.

Ten Brummelhuis, L. L., Bakker, A. B., Hetland, J., & Keulemans, L. (2012). Do new ways of working foster work engagement? *Psicothema, 24,* 113–120.

Teo, S., Newton, C. J., Pick, D., Yeung, M., & Salamonson, Y. (2012). *Negative change and job outcomes: the impact of subjective fit in public sector health care organization.* In Proceedings of: 16th Annual Conference of the International Research Society for Public Management (IRSPM XVI): Contradictions in Public Management Managing in Volatile Times. Rome, Italy.

2   Burnout and health

Kirsi Ahola and Jari Hakanen

Introduction

According to the World Health Organization's definition (1946), health is more than the absence of diseases. It is "a state of complete physical, mental, and social well-being." Partly because this concept is difficult to operationalize in research designs, there is a long tradition of studying the effects of work life using emerging health problems as the outcome rather than indicators of well-being.

According to the Global Burden of Disease Study in 2010, the diseases that cause the most disability-adjusted life years in Western Europe and high-income North America, calculated as the sum of years of life lost and years lived with disability, are heart and cerebrovascular diseases, low back pain, and major depressive disorder (Murray et al., 2012). These disease groups, i.e., mental, musculoskeletal, and cardiovascular disorders, also cover the most common causes for work disability in Northern European countries (Järvisalo et al., 2005). In this chapter, we will focus on the diseases causing the major disease burden and decrease in work capacity in Western countries, as related to job burnout.

When studying the relationship between burnout and ill-health, the nature and quality of the samples, designs, and methods used have special relevance in the interpretation of results. The majority of burnout research has, due to many practical reasons, been conducted in particular organizations or professions, for example in a hospital or among teachers, and among those employees who are currently at work. Most burned-out employees are missing from these samples because they are most likely not present at work (the healthy worker effect; see for example Li & Sung, 1999). In addition, confining the research to only certain work places or professional groups introduces the possibility of selection bias (Ellenberg, 1994), and poses problems regarding the interpretability of the results: Do the health problems relate to exposure in general or are they somehow typical of the vulnerabilities of people working in these sectors, branches, or jobs? Therefore, from the generalizability perspective the most valuable studies regarding the relationship between burnout and health are those using population-based samples representing the whole working population.

Another important requirement in order to be able to infer conclusions regarding causality in the relationship between burnout and health is the use of prospective designs (Shapiro, 2008). In a cross-sectional design, it is impossible to determine whether the observed association between burnout and health problems is a result of a situation in which burnout has predisposed the employee to, for example, a heart disease or whether the heart disease and its subclinical phases have decreased the employee's resources to meet the demands of the job, therefore increasing the risk of burnout. At the moment, most studies on burnout and health do not fulfill both of these criteria, i.e., the population-based sample and the prospective design. Therefore, we first present the results from studies using population-based samples and then those from studies with a prospective design. As a special case, we also review the redundancy of burnout and depression, as whether or not these two negative mental health states can be distinguished from each other is one of the most debated issues in the burnout literature.

Finally, the assessment of burnout using self-report questionnaires increases the risk of common-method bias (Lindell & Whitney, 2001) when health is also assessed using self-reports of symptoms or illnesses. The use of more independent sources of information, such as clinical health examinations or employers' and health care institutions' registers help to overcome this problem. Therefore we prefer to review studies using independent sources of information regarding illnesses whenever possible.

Co-occurrence of burnout and mental and physical disorders

To our knowledge, the only published population-based study that includes burnout and the independently assessed diagnosed illnesses of the participants is the Finnish Health 2000 Study which was conducted in 2000–2001 (Aromaa & Koskinen, 2004). Therefore, we will first focus on studies that have used this dataset. The sample was representative of the Finnish mainland population aged 30 or over. The data was collected via interviews, questionnaires, and a clinical health examination. The health examination began with a symptom interview and a questionnaire, after which a research physician took a medical history and performed a standard 30-minute clinical examination including tests and measurements. The diagnostic criteria of the physical illnesses were based on current clinical practice. The health examination also included the computerized version (M-CIDI) of the Composite International Diagnostic Interview, which is a fully standardized diagnostic interview for the assessment of mental disorders for research purposes (Andrews & Peters, 1998; Wittchen et al., 1998). Burnout was assessed with the Maslach Burnout Inventory – General Survey (MBI-GS; Schaufeli et al., 1996). An averaged weighted sum score was calculated to assess the burnout syndrome (Kalimo et al., 2006; Kalimo et al., 2003). Exhaustion, cynicism, and diminished professional efficacy had different weights in the sum score (Burnout = $0.4 \times$ Exhaustion + $0.3 \times$ Cynicism + $0.3 \times$ Diminished professional efficacy). This syndrome indicator had been constructed with the help of a discriminant function analysis, in which various health-related indicators were used as dependent variables (Kalimo & Toppinen, 1997). In some analyses, burnout was categorized as no burnout (scores 0.0–1.49), mild burnout (scores

1.50–3.49), and severe burnout (scores 3.50–6.0). In severe burnout, symptoms are experienced approximately weekly, and in mild burnout approximately monthly. The data was later also linked to several national independent registers.

Mental disorders

Among the sample of 3,276 working Finns, burnout was found to co-occur with depressive disorders including major depressive disorder, dysthymic disorder (American Psychiatric Association, 1994), and minor depression (a depressive episode with two to four symptoms) (Ahola et al., 2005). Altogether 53 percent of all employees with severe burnout (odds ratio 14.1, 95% confidence interval 9.2–21.7), and 20 percent of all employees with mild burnout (OR = 3.2, 95% CI 2.6–4.0) fulfilled the criteria of depressive disorders compared to 7 percent of employees without burnout. Possible confounding factors were not controlled for in these analyses.

When analyses were stratified by sex, burnout was related to depressive disorders among both men and women. However, mild burnout was more strongly related to depressive disorders among men (OR = 4.8, 95% CI 3.26–7.0) than among women (OR = 2.5, 95% CI 1.7–3.26). When analyzed separately, the exhaustion, cynicism, and diminished professional efficacy sub-scales were all significantly related to depressive disorders. When minor depression was left out and the depressive disorders included only the International Classification of Diseases diagnoses (the ICD-10; American Psychiatric Association, 1994), the prevalence of depressive disorders was 3 percent among those without burnout, 11 percent among those with mild burnout, and 45 percent among those with severe burnout (Ahola, 2007). In other words, burnout was related to depressive disorders in a dose-dependent manner. Still, only about half of the employees with severe burnout had a depressive disorder, even when depressive disorders were broadly conceptualized to also include minor depression.

Burnout also co-occurred with anxiety disorders (n = 3,209) and alcohol dependence (n = 3,251) in the Health 2000 Study (Ahola, 2007). Anxiety disorders included panic disorder, generalized anxiety disorder, social phobia, agoraphobia, and phobia not otherwise specified (American Psychiatric Association, 1994). Altogether 21 percent of employees with severe burnout and 8 percent of those with mild burnout fulfilled the criteria of an anxiety disorder compared to 2 percent of employees without burnout. When treated as a continuous variable, a one-unit increase in the burnout sum score was related to an adjusted (for socio-demographic factors) odds ratio of 2.3 (95% CI 1.8–2.9) for an anxiety disorder among men and 2.1 (95% CI 1.7–2.5) among women. Altogether, 10 percent of employees with severe and 8 percent of those with mild burnout fulfilled the criteria of alcohol dependence (American Psychiatric Association, 1994) compared to 3 percent of employees without burnout. When treated as a continuous variable, a one-unit increase in the burnout sum score was related to the adjusted (for socio-demographic factors) odds ratio of 1.5 (95% CI 1.3–1.8) for alcohol dependence among men and of 2.1 (95% CI 1.5–2.8) among women.

Physical illnesses

In the Health 2000 Study (n=3,368), burnout was related to musculoskeletal and cardiovascular disorders but not to respiratory diseases or a mixed group of other diseases (Honkonen et al., 2006). Of the employees with severe burnout, 47 percent had a musculoskeletal disorder. The corresponding figure was 36 percent among those with mild burnout and 28 percent among those without burnout. The association was significant among both sexes when adjusted for socio-demographic factors and health behavior but after adjustment for depressive symptoms, the association remained significant only among women. The odds ratio for a one-unit increase in burnout was 1.2 (95% CI 1.1–1.4). When the burnout sub-scales were analyzed separately, exhaustion, cynicism, and diminished professional efficacy were all associated with musculoskeletal disorders.

Of the employees with severe burnout, 28 percent had a cardiovascular disease (Honkonen et al., 2006). The corresponding figure was 20 percent among the employees with mild burnout and 14 percent among those without burnout. The unadjusted association was significant among both sexes but when adjusted for socio-demographic factors, the association remained significant only among men. The fully adjusted odds ratio for a one-unit increase in the burnout sum score was 1.4 (95% CI 1.1–1.6). When the burnout sub-scales were analyzed separately, exhaustion, cynicism, and diminished professional efficacy were all associated with cardiovascular diseases.

Morbidity in general

When burnout was dichotomized as no burnout versus mild or severe burnout, it overlapped with both physical illnesses (musculoskeletal, cardiovascular, respiratory, or other) and common mental disorders (depressive, anxiety, or alcohol-related) (n=3,211) (Ahola, 2007). When the focus was on employees with severe burnout (weekly symptoms) nine out of every ten employees had a disease or disorder. The most common of the disorders were musculoskeletal (47 percent) and depressive disorders (45 percent).

In summary, it seems that when burnout is severe, i.e., the symptoms are experienced often, it is almost always related to a disease or disorder in the working population. The manifesting health problem may take alternative forms, mental or physical, or probably even both, depending on the individual predisposing factors of the employee ("the Achilles heel").

Burnout as a predictor of health problems

Somatic health problems

As regards somatic health problems, burnout has been studied in relation to heart disease, diabetes, common infections, and musculoskeletal pain in prospective designs. In these epidemiological studies, the question has been whether burnout, assessed at the beginning of the study, is related to new cases of future health problems after known risk factors are taken into account.

In an eight-year prospective study among Israeli workers (n=8,838), burnout predicted new cases of coronary heart disease (Toker et al., 2012). The apparently healthy employees participated in an annual routine health examination in a medical center. The protocol included filling out the Shirom-Melamed Burnout Measure (SMBM; Shirom, 1989; Shirom & Melamed, 2006) to assess burnout. Coronary heart disease, which included acute myocardial infarction, diagnosed ischemic heart disease, and diagnosed angina pectoris, was assessed during the visits to the medical center or followed via e-mail, land mail, or telephone among those who did not return. The illness was confirmed by hospitalization date and a discharge diagnosis. A relationship was found between burnout and the risk of heart disease. Burnout was found to be an independent risk factor for heart disease but the risk was not linear. Instead, the risk of a new heart disease was pronounced in the upper quintile of the burnout sum score. Such a high level of burnout was related to a 1.8-fold risk (95% CI 1.1–3.0) of future heart disease after adjustment for socio-demographic factors, psychosocial factors at work, behavioral health risk factors, and depressive symptoms. The researchers proposed that high burnout could be associated with a dysregulation of the hypothalamic-pituitary-adrenal axis, which is a key stress-responsive endocrine system, as well as proinflammatory cytokine levels, inflammation biomarkers, and higher allostatic load. The results also suggested that burnout might be a stronger predictor of heart disease than job characteristics, such as subjective work load.

In a prospective Israeli study using two different samples (altogether n=677), burnout, assessed using the SMBM, predicted the onset of type 2 diabetes (Melamed et al., 2006a). The first sample comprised apparently healthy employees who took part in a health checkup at their work place and the second comprised employees recruited for a study on job strain and burnout. The occurrence of diabetes was assessed using a self-report of diagnosed and treated disease in the follow-up questionnaire. During the follow-up period which lasted from three to five years, each one-unit increase in the burnout sum score was related to 1.8-fold odds ratio (95% CI 1.2–2.9) of the onset of type 2 diabetes after adjustment for socio-demographic factors and behavioral health risk factors. The risk of diabetes was even higher (OR=4.3, 95% CI 1.8–10.6) in a sub-sample in which the blood pressure of the employees was also controlled for. This suggests that the link between burnout and diabetes was not mediated by hypertension. Burnout scores were found to be relatively consistent over the follow-up. The researchers argued that prolonged burnout may set the stage for various pathophysiological processes, such as chronic acute phase response, inflammatory processes, and metabolic events, which may culminate in health impairment.

In a one-year prospective study using the Maastricht Cohort (n=12,140 at baseline, response rate 45%), burnout assessed using the MBI-GS predicted new infections among employees from various professions and organizations (Mohren et al., 2003). Burnout was operationalized as complaints and as clinical burnout. Burnout complaints were indicated by the exhaustion sum score in the upper quantile and either the cynicism sum score in the upper quantile or the professional efficacy sum score in the lowest quantile (the Ex + 1 rule; Brenninkmeijer & van Yperen, 2003). Clinical burnout was indicated by the exhaustion sum score in the 95th percentile and either the cynicism sum score in the 95th percentile or the professional efficacy sum score in the 5th percentile of the scale. Three common infections (the common cold, flu-like illness, and gastroenteritis) were inquired about every four months with a brief description of the symptoms, using a questionnaire. Burnout complaints were related to a 1.6-fold increase in the risk of subsequent gastroenteritis (95% CI 1.3–1.9), a 1.3-fold risk of future flu, and a 1.2-fold risk of a new cold (95% CI 1.02–1.3) after socio-demographic factors and self-reported longstanding somatic illnesses were taken into account. Of the sub-scales of burnout, exhaustion and diminished professional efficacy predicted all types of infections while cynicism predicted flu-like illness and gastroenteritis. Clinical burnout (and only the exhaustion sub-scale) was related to an increased risk of future gastroenteritis (RR=2.1, 95% CI 1.1–4.0), commonly related to stress in general, but not to other infections. The results indicate that the immune system of the employees with burnout may be less effective. Burnout may thus act as a co-factor in the pathogenesis of common infections.

No prospective studies have been published that have analyzed the relationship between burnout and musculoskeletal disorders in a prospective design. Instead, elevated levels of burnout, assessed with the SMBM, were found to predict new cases of musculoskeletal pain in an Israeli study among apparently healthy employees (n=601) taking part in a periodic health examination three times in three years (Armon et al., 2010). Musculoskeletal pain was indicated by self-reported pain for which medical care was sought in the neck, shoulder region, or lower back over the past 12 months. An increase in burnout during the first 18 months was related to an increased risk of musculoskeletal pain during the next 18 months (OR=2.1, 95% CI 1.1–4.10) after adjustment for socio-demographic factors, obesity, symptoms of depression and anxiety, and baseline burnout. The possibility of reversed causation was also considered, but musculoskeletal pain did not predict burnout after adjustment for baseline level of burnout. According to the authors, the elaborated mechanisms via which burnout might cause musculoskeletal pain include: 1) Job demands and high mental load increase muscle tension and decrease micro-pauses in muscle activity, leading to muscle fatigue; 2) work stress impedes one's ability to unwind, i.e., to reduce physiological activation, during breaks and after work; 3) stress induces adverse changes in the immune and inflammatory systems which may increase vulnerability to bodily disorders; and 4) stress increases the activation of the sympathetic-adrenal medullary system which in turn leads to secretion of norepinephrine which further heightens muscle activity.

To conclude, burnout has been found to relate to heart disease, diabetes, common infections, and musculoskeletal pain in prospective studies lasting from three to eight years after adjustment for some of the other known risk factors of these health problems. Existing studies indicate that burnout at baseline is related to a 1.2–2.1-fold risk of a new illness. The results concerning heart disease and musculoskeletal pain are in accordance with those obtained regarding the co-occurrence of burnout and these diseases.

Depressive symptoms

No prospective studies have been reported in which the temporal relationship between burnout and depressive disorders (e.g., depression as a disease based on psychiatric assessment) would have been investigated. Instead, many studies have used depressive symptoms as an approximation of depression. However, symptoms may fluctuate and be more temporary. Therefore they constitute a less severe outcome regarding health. In the studies using depressive symptoms as an approximation of depression, burnout has been shown to relate to an increased risk of depressive symptoms.

In a three-year Finnish study (Ahola & Hakanen, 2007) using the Maslach Burnout Inventory (the MBI; Maslach & Jackson, 1996) to assess burnout among dentists (n= 2,555), burnout (monthly or more frequent symptoms) predicted new cases of depressive symptoms assessed with the short form of Beck's Depression Inventory (Beck & Beck, 1972). The odds ratio of burnout for new cases of depressive symptoms was 2.6 (95% CI 2.0–3.5) after socio-demographic factors were taken into account. This association was replicated in the study's next, seven-year follow-up (n=1964) with structural equation modeling. Burnout, assessed at the beginning of the study, predicted depressive symptoms in the first follow-up three years later and no reversed effects were found when assessed at the second measurement point and again during the third measurement point four years later (Hakanen & Schaufeli, 2012).

In a prospective Israeli study among employees attending a routine health checkup three times in six years (n=1632), the relationship between burnout (assessed using the SMBM) and depressive symptoms (assessed using the Personal Health Questionnaire; Kroenke et al., 2009) was demonstrated using change scores of the symptoms (Toker & Biron, 2012). An increase in the burnout score between the first and the second measurement point predicted an increase in the depressive symptoms between the second and the third measurement point.

Based on the results of the studies reviewed above, burnout is clearly related to future depressive symptoms. When work stress is prolonged, the symptoms may eventually generalize and affect life in general instead of just work. It has been suggested that work stress could affect mental health through a psychological pathway of injured self-esteem via erosion of the feelings of mastery in an adverse work situation (Stansfeld & Candy, 2006). However, the obtained results are limited for two reasons. First, depressive symptoms alone do not define depressive disorders, i.e., depression as a disease. The length and severity of the symptoms need to be taken into account in order to reach a medical diagnosis. Second, both burnout and depressive symptoms are based on self-reports which poses the possibility of common method bias (Lindell & Whitney, 2001). These and other notions have led to the question of how distinctive burnout and depression phenomena really are.

Overlap of burnout and depression

Similarities and differences between burnout and depressive symptoms

The relationship between burnout and depression has been one of the most widely studied topics in the area of burnout and health. The main question has been whether burnout and depression are manifestations of the same phenomena or two distinct indicators of ill-being. This question has been explored by studying their co-occurrence, qualitative features, and mutual relationship.

Conceptually and on the basis of many studies, it can be said that burnout and depression are clearly related to each other. On the basis of the inventories measuring them (Beck et al., 1961; Schaufeli et al., 1996), they share similar symptoms, for example loss of energy, lowered self-esteem, and negative attitudes. The exhaustion dimension of burnout, in particular, has been found to correlate strongly with depressive symptoms and burnout and depression share a large amount of common variance (Schaufeli & Enzmann, 1998; Shirom & Ezrachi, 2003).

However, burnout and depression do not always co-occur, either on an individual level (Ahola, 2007; Ahola et al., 2005) or on a statistical level (Bakker et al., 1994). In the population-based Finnish Health 2000 Study, only about half of those with severe burnout (weekly symptoms) fulfilled the criteria of a depressive disorder (Ahola, 2007). Further, when the items of the Maslach Burnout Inventory and a depression inventory (Beck Depression Inventory; Beck et al., 1961 or Center for Epidemiological Studies Depression Scale CES-D; Radloff, 1977) were pooled and factor-analyzed together, one high-order factor of negative affectivity would have supported the idea of burnout and depression being indicators of the same phenomenon. However, the two-factor solution (burnout and depression) was statistically superior to the one-factor solution, supporting the distinction of burnout from depressive symptoms (Bakker et al., 2000; Leiter & Durup, 1994).

In the theoretical models of both burnout and depression, the interaction between individual vulnerability and environmental challenges, familiar to the stress theoretical paradigm, play a relevant role (Billings & Moos, 1982; Schaufeli & Enzmann, 1998; Semmer et al., 2005). However, the main difference between the concepts is that burnout, in most of the models, is work-related whereas depression is context-free, i.e., it can develop in any domain of life (Warr, 1987).

Burnout could also be viewed as a special case of depression, i.e., work-related depression. Indeed, in a Dutch study using the MBI to assess burnout among teachers (n=154), lack of reciprocity in the work-context (i.e., with students) was related to burnout while lack of reciprocity in the non-work context (i.e., with one's spouse) was related to depressive symptoms (Bakker et al., 2000). The cross-sectional results were in accordance with the possibility that burnout leads to depression. Therefore it seems that burnout and depression might share a similar social exchange process that takes place in different domains. According to the researchers, depression could be a direct result of a lack of reciprocity in one's private life and an indirect result (through the development of burnout) of a lack of reciprocity at work.

However, qualitative differences have been detected in the processes of burnout and depression which support the idea of different phenomena. For example, another Dutch study using the MBI to assess burnout among teachers (n=190) found that a reduced sense of superiority was more characteristic of depression than of burnout (Brenninkmeijer et al., 2001). Depressive symptoms (assessed using the CES-D) were related to burnout when the teachers experienced low superiority compared to their colleagues. According to the researchers, burned-out teachers seemed to still consider themselves potentially successful whereas depressed teachers seemed to have given up.

Burnout and depression were also differently related to the characteristics of employees and their work environment in a French study (n=536) using the MBI to assess burnout among health care professionals (Martin et al., 1997). For example, burnout was more prevalent among women with unconventional work hours, young employees, and employees who had instrumental work motivation. Depressive symptoms (assessed using the CES-D), however, were more prevalent among senior workers and employees lacking social support at work. Results on other factors relating differently to burnout and depression suggest that they are separate entities.

Differences have even been found on a neurobiological level. In an Israeli study using the SMBM to assess burnout in a medical examination (n=1563), burnout and depressive symptoms were differently related to inflammation biomarkers (Toker et al., 2005). Among women, a high level of burnout was related to increased concentrations of C-reactive protein and fibrinogen, whereas a high level of depressive symptoms was not. Among men, the opposite was found. Depressive symptoms were related to C-reactive protein and fibrinogen concentrations. The fact that burnout and depression were differentially related to inflammation biomarkers in men and women supports the contention that burnout is not redundant to depression. The results also shed light on the possible mechanisms between burnout and health which might, according to this study, be different among the sexes. Despite the associations between burnout and depression, only partial overlap and observed differences in the relationships with other factors demonstrate that burnout and depression are not redundant phenomena.

Temporal association between burnout and depressive symptoms

A two-year prospective North American study, using the MBI to assess burnout among nurses (n=100), could not establish a temporal sequence between burn-out and depressive symptoms, assessed using the BDI (McKnight & Glass, 1995). Instead, the analysis of change scores and strength of associations of burnout and depression showed that the scores of exhaustion symptoms of burnout and depressive symptoms in particular changed concurrently. These results led the researchers to conclude that the shared variance of burnout and depression could be attributed to their co-development. It seemed that burnout and depression might develop "in tandem."

However, a three-year prospective Finnish study using the MBI to assess burnout among dentists (n=2,555) found a reciprocal relationship between burnout and depressive symptoms (Ahola & Hakanen, 2007). Of those dentists who had burnout (monthly or more frequent symptoms) at baseline but who were free from depressive symptoms, 23 percent reported depressive symptoms after the three-year follow-up (odds ratio of 2.6 with 95% CI of 2.0 to 3.5 after adjustment for socio-demographic factors). Similarly, of the dentists who had depressive symptoms but no burnout at baseline, 63 percent had burnout (severe or mild symptoms) after three years (odds ratio of 2.2 with 95% CI of 1.4 to 3.4). A reciprocal association was also found in an Israeli study using SMBM to assess burnout among employees (n=1632) attending a routine health checkup three times in six years (Toker & Biron, 2012). An increase in the burnout scores between the first two checkups predicted an increase in the depressive symptoms between the last two checkups, and an increase in the depression scores between the first two checkups similarly predicted an increase in the burnout scores between the last two checkups. It seems that burnout may predispose to depressive symptoms and that depressive symptoms may increase the risk of burnout.

However, in the second follow-up of the Finnish dentists (n=1964), using the whole sample and structural equation modeling to analyze the cross-lagged longitudinal relationships between burnout and depressive symptoms, burnout predicted depressive symptoms, but the same was not true in reverse (Hakanen & Schaufeli, 2012; Hakanen et al., 2008). This model also included the positive side of work-related and mental well-being, i.e., work engagement and life satisfaction. The results showed that burnout and engagement predicted depressive symptoms and life satisfaction, albeit in opposite directions, indicating that specific, work-related affective states (burnout and work engagement) generalize and spill over to extensive, context-free experiences (depression and life satisfaction).

The primary importance of the "from burnout to depressive symptoms" path compared to the other "from depressive symptoms to burnout" path was also noticed in the first follow-up of the study (Ahola & Hakanen, 2007). When burnout and depressive symptoms were analyzed in regard to job strain, it was found that burnout always mediated the path from job strain to depressive symptoms while depression only partly mediated the path from job strain to burnout (Ahola & Hakanen, 2007). In addition, using the whole sample of dentists with a full two-wave design to test the job demands-resources model, burnout appeared to mediate the impact of different job demands and the lack of job resources on depressive symptoms, providing robust support for burnout as an antecedent rather than a consequence of depressive symptoms (Hakanen et al., 2008). In other words, burnout was always a phase in the development of job strain-related depression while depression may or may not relate to future burnout.

The "from job strain via burnout to depressive symptoms" path presented above has been also shown to be strong in regard to depressive disorders, but only in a cross-sectional study (Ahola et al., 2006). In the Finnish Health 2000 Study, burnout fully mediated the association between job strain and depressive disorders, whereas depressive disorders only partly mediated the association between job strain and burnout. The results supported the relative importance of the "from burnout to depression" sequence compared to the other way around.

All in all, the results have shown that burnout is related to depressive symptoms over time. It seems possible that burnout is a phase in the development of work-related depression. However, it is also possible that burnout exists without depression, and that depression can exist without burnout. Because burnout is always assessed using self-reports, study designs using independent measures to assess health outcomes would be valuable. Studies linking questionnaire data to independent register data offer a more objective way to assess the health status of employees.

Burnout as a predictor of work disability and severe health problems

Health-related registers cover, for example, work disability benefits (compensated sickness absence and disability pension) and some severe health consequences, such as hospital admission and mortality. In northern European countries, for example, Finland, Sweden, the Netherlands, and Germany, compensation benefits reimburse the loss in income due to work disability that has resulted from medically diagnosed illness, handicap, or injury (Järvisalo et al., 2005). These grants are recorded in national registers according to the personal identification code which is given to citizens at birth and used in all contacts with health care institutions. When personal information is collected, it is possible to later link the questionnaire data to the register data. The national registers are complete but some registers are limited, for example, sickness absence registers which are kept by organizations or insurance companies.

Sickness absence

Among the Finnish employees (n=3,895) of a multinational forest industry cor-poration, burnout assessed using the MBI-GS predicted all-cause company-registered medically certified sickness absence periods lasting over three days during a period of three years (Toppinen-Tanner et al., 2005). A high level of burnout, i.e., the upper tertile in the weighted sum score (Kalimo et al., 2006), was related to an 8 percent increase in the risk of absence (95% CI 1.01–1.15) when adjusted for age, sex, occupation, and baseline absence. Analyses by disease group revealed that burnout predicted absences based on mental and behavioral disorders, circulatory diseases, respiratory diseases, and musculoskeletal diseases, but it did not predict absences based on digestive or a mixed group of other diseases. Of the sub-dimensions of burnout, exhaustion was related to all-cause absence but cynicism or diminished professional efficacy was not. In addition, all burnout sub-dimensions predicted absences based on mental and musculoskeletal disorders. Exhaustion also predicted absences based on circulatory and other diseases, while cynicism predicted absences based on digestive and other diseases.

In the Finnish Health 2000 Study, sickness absences lasting for at least two weeks in the two-year time frame (2000–2001) were extracted from a complete national register. Burnout was assessed using the MBI-GS and the weighted sum score (Kalimo et al., 2006) was categorized as none, mild (monthly symptoms), or severe (weekly symptoms). Among employees aged 30–60 years from various branches and sectors (n=3151), severe burnout was related to having at least one long (over ten days) absence during the two-year period (Ahola et al., 2008). The odds ratio of having such an absence with severe burnout was 2.1-fold (95% CI 1.1–4.0) among women and 6.9-fold (95% CI 2.7–17.8) among men after socio-demographic factors and baseline health were taken into account. Among women, mild burnout was also related to such absence, while among men the absence, had there been such, was longer.

There probably are several reasons for the observed high risk for work disability among men with burnout. The stigma and social consequences of having psychological problems at work may be worse for men than for women due to cultural role expectations and actual job demands. Men also tend to seek help for strain to a lesser degree than women (Oliver et al., 2005). Missing professional advice and social support may lead to accumulating problems and longer time needed for recovery. All in all, burnout-related absences were long even though burnout as such was not a valid cause for sickness absence. The number of excess absence days related to severe burnout was 55 among men and 41 among women over two years, compared to eight excess days related to mental disorders and 23 excess days related to physical illnesses.

In a Swedish study among female health professionals (n=3,976), a high score on the exhaustion dimension of burnout predicted an increased risk of long medically certified sickness absence (of at least 90 days) extracted from an insurance company's register during a 44-month follow-up (Peterson et al., 2011). Burnout was assessed using the Oldenburg Burnout Inventory (Demerouti et al., 2010). In addition to predicting all-cause absence, a high score on exhaustion also predicted absences based on mental and musculoskeletal disorders.

Disability pension

Among a representative sample of Finnish employees aged 30 to 60 from various branches and sectors (n=3,125), burnout assessed using the MBI-GS predicted all-cause disability pension during a four-year follow-up period (Ahola et al., 2009a). The grants were extracted from a complete independent national register. A one-unit increase in the weighted burnout sum score (Kalimo et al., 2006) was related to a 49 percent increase in the risk of disability pension (95% CI 1.2–1.8) after socio-demographic factors and health status at baseline were taken into account. Disability pensions were most often granted on the basis of mental and musculo-skeletal disorders among those with burnout, as is also the case in the whole Finnish population (Järvisalo et al., 2005). Of the sub-dimensions of burnout, cynicism as well as exhaustion among men predicted disability pension after adjustments.

Among Finnish employees from a multinational forest industry corporation (n=7,810), burnout assessed using the MBI-GS predicted all-cause disability pension during an eight-year follow-up period (Ahola et al., 2009b). Severe burnout (weekly symptoms) was related to an un-adjusted hazard ratio of 3.8 (95% CI 2.7–5.4) for disability pension but the risk attenuated to 1.6-fold (95% CI 1.1–2.3) after adjustment for socio-demographic factors, registered medication use, and self-reported chronic illnesses at baseline. Of the sub-dimensions of burnout, severe exhaustion, cynicism, as well as diminished professional efficacy among women predicted disability pension after adjustment for socio-demographic factors and registered medication use. After additional adjustment for self-reported chronic illnesses, cynicism did not predict disability pension.

Hospital admission

Among the Finnish employees (n=7897) of a multinational forest industry corporation, burnout assessed using the MBI-GS predicted future hospital admissions due to mental and cardiovascular disorders during a ten-year follow-up period (Toppinen-Tanner et al., 2009). Socio-demographic factors, physical work environment, and previous hospitalization periods and medication for the related disorders were taken into account in the analyses. A one-unit increase in the weighted sum score of burnout (Kalimo et al., 2006) was related to a 1.4-fold hazard ratio (95% CI 1.2–1.6) for hospital admission due to mental disorders and to a 1.1-fold hazard ratio (95% CI 1.02–1.2) for hospital admission due to cardiovascular disorders. Burnout was not related to hospitalization due to musculoskeletal or other disorders when fully adjusted. Of the sub-dimensions of burnout, exhaustion and cynicism sub-scales predicted hospitalization due to mental and cardiovascular disorders but diminished professional efficacy was not related to future hospitalization.

Psychotropic drug use

In Finland, the national sickness insurance scheme covers the entire population and reimburses the costs of prescribed medication for virtually all outpatients. The purchase of prescriptions is recorded in the National Prescription Register, which is maintained by the Social Insurance Institution of Finland. A study among Finnish forestry workers (n= 4356) indicated that changes in burnout predict a future risk of psychotropic (e.g., antidepressants) drug use (Leiter et al., 2012). Inconsistency in the levels of the MBI subscales (e.g., a high score in exhaustion and a low score in cynicism or vice versa) at baseline was likely to lead to a change in burnout (towards either high or low on both symptoms) four years later. In turn, the change toward high scores in both exhaustion and cynicism predicted the use of psychotropic drugs during the next eight years.

Mortality

Among the Finnish employees (n=7,396) of a multinational forest industry corporation, burnout assessed using the MBI-GS predicted all-cause mortality during a ten-year follow-up period (Ahola et al., 2010). A one-unit increase in the weighted burnout sum score (Kalimo et al., 2006) was related to a 31 percent increase in the odds ratio of premature death among employees under 45 years of age at baseline. Socio-demographic factors and health problems requiring registered medication use were taken into account in the analyses. Among older employees over 45 years of age, burnout was not related to mortality. The inclusion of older employees may have diluted the association between burnout and mortality as a result of healthy worker survivor bias (Kivimäki et al., 2008). Of the sub-dimensions of burnout, only exhaustion was related to mortality.

Burnout seems to predict a decrease in work capacity as well as severe health consequences. Register-linking studies are considered reliable because the outcomes are not based solely on the subjective assessment of the employees and are therefore considered independent of the predictor. The benefits are granted on the basis of medical diagnosis because burnout as such is not, in most countries, a diagnosis and therefore justifiable as grounds for disability benefit (Järvisalo et al., 2005). Burnout probably affects the onset and prognosis of the accompanying illness as well as decreasing energetic resources of the employee to cope with the demands of work and with the consequences of the illness (the cause for benefit).

Conclusions

A comprehensive review covering the first 25 years of burnout research (Maslach et al., 2001) noticed that some attention had been paid to the health outcomes of burnout. However, the authors warned that these results had to be interpreted with caution because they were mainly based on self-reported and cross-sectional data. During the last decade, the focus in burnout research has at least partly shifted from identifying the antecedents to recognizing the consequences. According to a considerably voluminous amount of studies reported in this chapter, it can now be fairly reliably stated that burnout is indeed related to many kinds of health problems as well as decreased work capacity. Therefore it poses a heavy burden on both individuals and society.

The health problems related to burnout do not seem to be restricted to any particular domain but can be either physical or mental in nature or even both, most likely depending on the individual vulnerabilities of the employee. Despite consistent evidence supporting the temporal sequence of burnout predisposing to illnesses, burnout and health problems most probably form negative spirals that reciprocally influence each another. Research in the area of stress and health problems support the view on these interlinked connections (de Lange et al., 2005; Kivimäki et al. 2006). The mechanisms between burnout and health most probably include direct, indirect, and reversed relationships. That is, burnout may predispose to illnesses directly and via, for example, adverse health behaviors. In addition, sub-clinical or acute health problems may decrease employees' energetic resources and increase the risk of burnout.

Of the burnout dimensions, exhaustion is most consistently and most strongly related to the health outcomes but there are also robust associations between other dimensions of burnout and health problems. In some studies, the burnout syndrome has shown a little stronger or different kind of association with health problems (Ahola et al., 2005; Mohren et al., 2003; Toppinen-Tanner et al., 2005) than the exhaustion sub-scale alone. Therefore it seems that exhaustion is the key aspect of burnout and the most relevant in regard to health. However, it does not capture the complete burnout concept and people's relationship with their work.

Even though the results concerning burnout and health are obtained from prospective designs, they cannot fully prove causality, and the possibility of reversed causality remains. The sub-clinical phases of illnesses may decrease workers' possibilities for meeting the demands of their work and thus predispose them to burnout and later to the incidence of illness leading to the spiral-like developments between health and burnout. For example, in a Swedish study using a self-made index to assess burnout among consecutive female patients and controls (n = 97 and n = 97), women who had a cardiovascular disease reported more burnout than women without cardiovascular disease (Hallman et al., 2003).

Many studies have tried to establish a direct link between burnout and health problems by identifying the biological or physiological risk factors of illnesses. Individual studies have found associations between such risk factors and burnout (see for example, Kitaoka-Higashiguchi et al., 2009; Melamed et al., 2006b) but a systematic review, which identified 31 studies analysing 38 different biomarkers, found no potential biomarker for burnout (Danhof-Pont et al., 2011). One hypothesized reason for this was the incomparability of the studies: burnout was, for example, assessed in a variety of ways in the included studies.

Some health consequences of burnout may be due to behavioral health risk factors as mediators. In the representative Finnish Health 2000 Study (n = 3264), burnout was shown to associate with risky health behaviors (Ahola et al., 2012a). Low physical activity and obesity in particular were associated with burnout. In an Israeli study among employees in medical checkups (n=1632), an increase in burnout also led to an increase in depressive symptoms among the employees with low physical activity (Toker & Biron, 2012).

Upcoming studies will hopefully deepen our understanding of the mechanisms between burnout and health in the future. New pathways may emerge. For example, high exhaustion was found to relate to similar changes in the DNA-protein complexes that cap chromosomal ends in cells, as those detected in normal aging (Ahola et al., 2012b). When cells divide, the end of the cell is not fully replicated because of the limitations of the DNA polymerase in completing the replication, leading to shortening with every replication. Further, in the search for individual vulnerability to burnout a recent genome-wide study found a weak regulating effect in one gene variant (an intron of the uronyl-2-sulfotransferase) situated in chromosome six which has also shown a functional connection with the genes related to depression (Sulkava et al., 2013). Also, twin studies have shown that the association between burnout and anxious depression is due to overlapping genetic and shared environmental factors (Middeldorp et al., 2006). In addition to these innovative research frames, there is also a need for a high-quality multidimensional design which would produce a comprehensive model of burnout and total health in which the variance is explained by both individual and environmental factors at the same time instead of the focused studies conducted so far.

This qualitative review suggests that burnout with its many potential negative health consequences becomes expensive for organizations and for society at large. Although research has not found very strong direct associations between burnout and job performance (Swider & Zimmermann, 2010; Taris, 2006), burnout is likely to have indirect negative effects on overall productivity. Health problems with following sickness absences and disability pensions are likely to be associated with decreased innovativeness and productivity in organizations. Therefore, from both the humane and economic perspective, preventing burnout and increasing employee engagement are of utmost importance.

Proposal for future research

The understanding of the relationships between burnout and various indicators of ill-health has considerably increased during the past decade. However, many open questions still remain. One important challenge relates to the mechanisms explaining the relationship between burnout and ill-health, i.e., what links burnout to morbidity. An important research challenge concerns planning a longitudinal study design with several time points. In this multi-wave design, the key individual and environmental risk and protective factors would be assessed at the same time and combined with the data on all kinds of health outcomes, i.e., total worker health. This kind of study design could yield a comprehensive model of burnout and help to explore whether or not the antecedents of burnout and ill-health would differ from each other. The essential antecedents would include job and home demands and resources and factors related to organizational and even societal factors as well as critical meaningful life events, health behaviors, and personal characteristics of the employee.

Parts of the above mentioned antecedents of burnout could actually be in turn also possible consequences of burnout in the long run. Therefore, the bidirectional associations between burnout and related factors should be analyzed in detail in multi-wave longitudinal designs. Also the thus far unsolved question, whether burnout and ill-health reciprocally influence each other leading to vicious circles, could be studied this way. The majority of the longitudinal studies on the relationship between burnout and ill-health still rely only on self-reports concerning symptomalogy. Therefore, it would be valuable to shed more light on the constantly haunting question of the temporal relationships between burnout and ill-health by using, for example, clinical assessments of disorders and diseases in the longitudinal designs to overcome the problems of common method variance. In addition, the possibilities of accompanying the assessment of burnout with some objective evaluation criteria should also be explored.

Further, the inner dynamics of the development of the three dimensions of burnout is still somewhat unclear even after several decades of active research. It would be interesting to combine the analysis of the temporal development of burnout dimensions with the exploration of the mechanisms between burnout and ill-health. The use of repeated measures design that combines measures of burnout and health consequences could shed new light on the specific temporal order of burnout and health outcomes. Different developmental processes can also be possible depending, for example, on the health problem.

Most research on burnout and ill-health has been variable-centered. A variable-centered approach investigates the relative contributions that predictor variables make to an outcome. Instead, a person-centered approach is based on the assumption of heterogeneity of the population in relation to the investigated phenomenon and its change over time (Laursen & Hoff, 2006; Mäkikangas et al., 2011). Therefore, by using person-centered approaches it is possible to identify latent groups of individuals with similar attributes and compare these groups with different developmental trajectories.

So far, we identified only two studies that have used a person-centered approach to investigate relationships between burnout and health. A favorable change was found in the levels of anxiety and depression in a sample of workers who experienced high exhaustion at baseline and had moved towards lower burnout at one-year follow-up, compared to those employees who had moved towards burnout or remained incongruent in their scores (Boersma & Lindblom, 2009). In addition, depression was found to have decreased and job satisfaction was found to have increased among employees whose burnout symptoms had decreased in a Finnish rehabilitation study (Hätinen et al., 2009). Person-centered research is a promising approach to gain a more diversified understanding on the relationship between burnout and ill-health and their temporal development.

Finally, burnout and its positive opposite, work engagement, have shown to be negatively related but distinct constructs (e.g. Schaufeli & Bakker, 2004). A Finnish study showed that both burnout and work engagement had incremental longitudinal effects on depressive symptoms and life satisfaction over and above each other (Hakanen & Schaufeli, 2012). In addition to studies on burnout and negative health consequences, studies showing work engagement to predict subsequent positive health consequences would strengthen the evidence regarding the importance of burnout to health consequences. We call for future research to investigate how these two work-related mental states, burnout and work engagement, may jointly affect individual health.

References

Ahola, K. (2007). *Occupational burnout and health.* People and Work Research Reports 81. Helsinki: Finnish Institute of Occupational Health.

Ahola, K., & Hakanen, J. (2007). Job strain, burnout and depressive symptoms: A prospective study among dentists. *Journal of Affective Disorders, 104,* 103–110.

Ahola, K., Honkonen, T., Isometsä, E., Kalimo, R., Nykyri, E., Aromaa, A., & Lönnqvist, J. (2005). The relationship between job-related burnout and depressive disorders – results from the Finnish Health 2000 Study. *Journal of Affective Disorders, 88*, 55–62.

Ahola, K., Kivimäki, M., Honkonen, T., Virtanen, M., Koskinen, S., Vahtera, J., & Lönnqvist, J. (2008). Occupational burnout and medically certified sickness absence: A population-based study of Finnish employees. *Journal of Psychosomatic Reseach, 64*, 185–193.

Ahola, K., Gould, R., Virtanen, M., Honkonen, T., Aromaa, A., & Lönnqvist, J. (2009a). Occupational burnout as a predictor of disability pension: A population-based cohort study. *Occupational and Environmental Medicine, 66*, 284–290.

Ahola, K., Toppinen-Tanner, S., Huuhtanen, P., Koskinen, A., & Väänänen, A. (2009b). Occupational burnout and chronic work disability: An eight-year cohort study on pensioning among Finnish forest industry workers. *Journal of Affective Disorders, 115*, 150–159.

Ahola, K., Väänänen, A., Koskinen, A., Kouvonen, A., & Shirom, A. (2010). Burnout as a predictor of mortality among industrial employees: Ten-year prospective register-linkage study. *Journal of Psychosomatic Research, 69*, 51–57.

Ahola, K., Pulkki-Råback, L., Kouvonen, A., Rossi, H., Aromaa, A., & Lönnqvist, J. (2012a). Burnout and behavioral-related health risk factors – Results from the population-based Health 2000 Study. *Journal of Occupational and Environmental Medicine, 54*, 17–22.

Ahola, K., Sirén, I., Kivimäki, M., Ripatti, S., Aromaa, A., Lönnqvist, J., & Hovatta, I. (2012b). Work-related exhaustion and telomere length: A population-based study. *PLoS ONE, 7*, e40186.

American Psychiatric Association. (1994). *Diagnostic and Statistical Manual of Mental Disorders* (4th edn). Washington: American Psychiatric Association.

Andrews, G., & Peters, L. (1998). The psychometric properties of the Composite International Diagnostic Interview. *Social Psychiatry and Psychiatric Epidemiology, 33*, 80–88.

Armon, G., Melamed, S., Shirom, A., & Shapira, I. (2010). Elevated burnout predicts the onset of musculoskeletal pain among apparently healthy employees. *Journal of Occupational Health Psychology, 15*, 399–408.

Aromaa, A., & Koskinen, S. (2004). *Health and functional capacity in Finland. Baseline results of the Health Examination Survey*. Helsinki: National Public Health Institute.

Bakker, A. B., Schaufeli, W. B., Demerouti, E., Janssen, P. P., van der Hulst, R., & Brouwer, J. (2000). Using equity theory to examine the difference between burnout and depression. *Anxiety, Stress, and Coping, 13*, 247–268.

Beck, A. T., & Beck, R. W. (1972). Screening depressed patients in family practice. A rapid technic. *Postgraduate Medicine, 52*, 81–87.

Beck, A. T., Ward, C. H., Mendelson, M., Mock, J., & Erbaugh, J. (1961). An inventory for measuring depression. *Archives of General Psychiatry, 4*, 561–571.

Billings, A. G., & Moos, R. H. (1982). Psychosocial theory and research on depression: An integrative framework and review. *Clinical Psychology Review, 2*, 213–237.

Boersma, K., & Lindblom, K. (2009). Stability and change in burnout profiles over time: A prospective study in the working population. *Work & Stress, 23*, 264–283.

Brenninkmeijer, V., & van Yperen, N. W. (2003). How to conduct research on burnout: advantages and disadvantages of a unidimensional approach in burnout research. *Occupational and Environmental Medicine, 60*, i16–i20.

Brenninkmeijer, V., van Yperen, N. W., & Buunk, B. P. (2001). Burnout and depression are not identical twins: Is decline of superiority a distinguishing feature? *Personality and Individual Differences, 30,* 873–880.

Danhof-Pont, M. B., van Veen, T., & Zitman, F. G. (2011). Biomarkers in burnout: A systematic review. *Journal of Psychosomatic Research, 70,* 505–524.

de Lange, A. H., Taris, T., Kompier, M. A. J., Houtman, I. L. D., & Bongers, P. M. (2005). Different mechanisms to explain the reversed effects of mental health on work characteristics. *Scandinavian Journal of Work, Environment & Health, 31,* 3–14.

Demerouti, E., Mostert, K., & Bakker, A. B. (2010). Burnout and work engagement: A thorough investigation of the independency of both constructs. *Journal of Occupational Health Psychology, 15, 209–222.*

Ellenberg, J. H. (1994). Cohort studies. Selection bias in observational and experimental studies. *Statistics in Medicine, 13,* 557–567.

Hakanen, J. J., & Schaufeli, W. B. (2012). Do burnout and work engagement predict depressive symptoms and life satisfaction? A three-wave seven-year prospective study. *Journal of Affective Disorders, 141,* 415–424.

Hakanen, J. J., Schaufeli, W. B., & Ahola, K. (2008). The Job Demands-Resources model: A three-year cross-lagged study of burnout, depression, commitment, and work engagement. *Work & Stress, 22,* 224–241.

Hallman, T., Thomsson, H., Burell, G., Lisspers, J., & Setterlind, S. (2003). Stress, burnout and coping: Differences between women with coronary heart disease and healthy matched women. *Journal of Health Psychology, 8,* 433–445.

Hätinen, M., Kinnunen, U., Mäkikangas, A., Kalimo, R., Tolvanen, A., & Pekkonen, M. (2009). Burnout during a long-term rehabilitation: comparing low burnout, high burnout – benefited, and high burnout – not benefited trajectories. *Anxiety, Stress and Coping, 22,* 341–360.

Honkonen, T., Ahola, K., Pertovaara, M., Isometsä, E., Kalimo, R., Nykyri, E., Aromaa, A., & Lönnqvist, J. (2006). The association between burnout and physical illness in the general population – results from the Finnish Health 2000 Study. *Journal of Psychosomatic Research, 61,* 59–66.

Järvisalo, J., Andersson, B., Boedeker, W., & Houtman, I. (Eds.) (2005). *Mental disorders as a major challenge in prevention of work disability. Experiences in Finland, Germany, the Netherlands and Sweden.* Helsinki: The Social Insurance Institution.

Kalimo, R., Hakanen, J., & Toppinen-Tanner, S. (2006). *Maslachin yleinen työuupumuksen arviointimenetelmä MBI-GS* (The Finnish version of Maslach's Burnout Inventory – General Survey). Helsinki: Finnish Institute of Occupational Health.

Kalimo, R., Pahkin, K., Mutanen, P., & Toppinen-Tanner, S. (2003). Staying well or burning out at work: Work characteristics and personal resources as long-term predictors. *Work & Stress, 17,* 109–122.

Kalimo, R., & Toppinen, S. (1997). *Työuupumus Suomen työikäisellä väestöllä* (Burnout among Finnish working population). Helsinki: Finnish Institute of Occupational Health.

Kitaoka-Higashiguchi, K., Morikawa, Y., Miura, K., Sakurai, M., Ishizaki, M., Kido, T., et al. (2009). Burnout and risk factors for arteriosclerotic disease: Follow-up study. *Journal of Occupational Health, 51,* 123–131.

Kivimäki, M., Virtanen, M., Elovainio, M., Kouvonen, A., Väänänen, A., & Vahtera, J. (2006). Work stress in the etiology of coronary heart disease – a meta-analysis. *Scandinavian Journal of Work, Environment & Health, 32,* 431–442.

Kivimäki, M., Theorell, T., Westerlund, H., Vahtera, J., & Alfredsson, L. (2008). Job strain and ischaemic disease: Does the inclusion of older employees in the cohort dilute the association? The WOLF Stockholm Study. *Journal of Epidemiology and Community Health*, *62*, 372–374.

Kroenke, K., Strine, T. W., Spitzer, R. L., Williams, J. B., W., Berry, J. T., & Mokdad, A. H. (2009) The PHQ-8 as a measure of current depression in the general population. *Journal of Affective Disorders*, *141*, 163–173.

Laursen, B., & Hoff, E. (2006). Person-centred and variable-centred approaches to longitudinal data. *Merrill Palmer Quarterly*, *52*, 377–389.

Leiter, M. P., & Durup, J. (1994). The discriminant validity of burnout and depression: a confirmatory factor analytic study. *Anxiety, Stress and Coping*, *7*, 357–373.

Leiter, M. P., Hakanen, J., Toppinen-Tanner, S., Ahola, K., Koskinen, A., & Väänänen, A. (2013). Changes in burnout: A 12-year cohort study on organizational predictors and health outcomes. *Journal of Organizational Behavior*, *34*, 959–973.

Li, C.-Y., & Sung, F.-C. (1999). A review of the healthy worker effect in occupational epidemiology. *Occupational Medicine*, *49*, 225–229.

Lindell, M. K., & Whitney, D. J. (2001). Accounting for common method variance in cross-sectional research designs. *Journal of Applied Psychology*, *86*, 114–121.

Mäkikangas, A., Hyvönen, K., Leskinen, E., Kinnunen, U., & Feldt, T. (2011). A person-centred approach to investigate the development trajectories of job-related affective well-being: A 10-year follow-up study. *Journal of Occupational and Organizational Psychology*, *84*, 327–346.

Martin, F., Poyen, D., Bouderlique, E., Gouvernet, J., Rivet, B., Disdier, P., Martinez, O., & Scotto, J.-C. (1997). Depression and burnout in hospital health care professionals. *International Journal of Occupational and Environmental Health*, *3*, 204–209.

Maslach, C., & Jackson, S. E. (1996). Maslach Burnout Inventory – Human Services Survey (MBI-HSS). In Maslach, C., Jackson, S. E., & Leiter, M. P. (Eds), *Maslach Burnout Inventory Manual* (3rd edn, pp. 3–17). Palo Alto, CA: Consulting Psychologists Press.

Maslach, C., Schaufeli, W. B., & Leiter, M. P. (2001). Job burnout. *Annual Review of Psychology*, *52*, 397–422.

McKnight, J. D., & Glass, D. C. (1995). Perceptions of control, burnout, and depressive symptomology: A replication and extension. *Journal of Consulting and Clinical Psychology*, *63*, 490–494.

Melamed, S., Shirom, A., Toker, S., & Shapira, I. (2006a). Burnout and risk of type 2 diabetes: A prospective study of apparently healthy employed persons. *Psychosomatic Medicine*, *68*, 863–869.

Melamed, S., Shirom, A., Toker, S., Berliner, S., & Shapira, I. (2006b). Burnout and risk of cardiovascular disease: Evidence, possible causal paths, and promising research directions. *Psychological Bulletin*, *132*, 327–353.

Middeldorp, C. M., Cath, D. C., & Boomsma, D. I. (2006). A twin-family study of the association between employment, burnout and anxious depression. *Journal of Affective Disorders*, *90*, 163–169.

Mohren, D. C., Swaen, G. M., Kant, I. J., van Amelsvoort, L. G., Borm, P. J., & Galama, J. M. (2003). Common infections and the role of burnout in a Dutch working population. *Journal of Psychosomatic Research*, *55*, 201–208.

Murray, C. L., Vos, T., Lozano, R., Naghavi, M., Flaxman, A. D., Michaud, C., et al. (2012). Disability adjusted life years (DALYs) for 291 diseases and injuries in 21 regions, 1990–2010: A systematic analysis for the Global Burden of Disease Study 2010. *Lancet*, *380*, 2197–2223.

Oliver, M. I., Pearson, N., Coe, N., & Gunnell, D. (2005). Help seeking behavior in men and women with common mental health problems: Cross-sectional study. *British Journal of Psychiatry, 186*, 297–301.

Peterson, U., Bergström, G., Demerouti, E., Gustavsson, P., Asberg, M., & Nygren, A. (2011). Burnout levels and self-rated health prospectively predict future long-term sickness absence: A study among female health professionals. *Journal of Occupational and Environmental Medicine, 53*, 788–793.

Radloff, L. S. (1977). The CES-D scale: A self-report depression scale for research in the general population. *Applied Psychological Measurement, 1*, 385–401.

Schaufeli, W. B., & Bakker, A. B. (2004). Job demands, job resources, and their relationship with burnout and engagement. *Journal of Organizational Behavior, 25*, 293–315.

Schaufeli, W. B., & Enzmann, D. (1998). *The Burnout Companion to Study and Practice: A Critical Analysis.* London, UK: Taylor & Francis.

Schaufeli, W. B., Leiter, M. P., Maslach, C., & Jackson, S. E. (1996). Maslach Burnout Inventory – General Survey (MBI-GS). In Maslach, C., Jackson, S. E., & Leiter, M. P. (Eds), *Maslach Burnout Inventory Manual* (3rd edn, pp. 19–32). Palo Alto, CA: Consulting Psychologists Press.

Semmer, N. K., McGrath, J. E., & Beehr, T. A. (2005). Conceptual issues in research on stress and health. In Cooper, C. L. (Ed.), *Stress, Medicine & Health* (2nd edn, pp. 2–43). Boca Raton: CRL Press.

Shapiro, S. (2008). Causation, bias and confounding: A hitchhiker's guide to the epidemiological galaxy. Part 1. Principles of causality in epidemiological research: Time order, specification of the study base and specificity. *Journal of Family Planning and Reproductive Health Care, 34*, 83–87.

Shirom, A. (1989). Burnout in work organizations. In Cooper, C. L. & Robertson, I. (Eds), *International Review of Industrial and Organization Psychology* (pp. 25–48). Chichester, UK: Wiley.

Shirom, A., & Ezrachi, Y. (2003). On the discriminant validity of burnout, depression, and anxiety: A re-examination of the burnout measure. *Anxiety, Stress and Coping, 16*, 83–99.

Shirom, A., & Melamed, S. (2006). A comparison of the construct validity of two burnout measures among two groups of professionals. *International Journal of Stress Management, 13*, 176–200.

Stansfeld, S., & Candy, B. (2006). Psychosocial work environment and mental health – a meta-analytic review. *Scandinavian Journal of Work, Environment & Health, 32*, 443–462.

Sulkava, S., Ollila, H. M., Ahola, K., Partonen, T., Viitasalo, K., Kettunen, J., & Paunio, T. (2013). Genome-wide scan of job-related exhaustion with three replication studies implicate a susceptibility variant at the UST gene locus. *Human Molecular Genetics, 22*, 3363–3372.

Swider, B. W., & Zimmerman, R. D. (2010). Born to burnout: A meta-analytic path model of personality, job burnout, and work outcomes. *Journal of Vocational Behavior, 76*, 487–506.

Taris, T. W. (2006). Is there a relationship between burnout and objective performance? A critical review of 16 studies. *Work & Stress, 20*, 316–345.

Toker, S., & Biron, M. (2012). Job burnout and depression: Unraveling their temporal relationship and considering the role of physical activity. *Journal of Applied Psychology, 97*, 699–710.

Toker, S., Shirom, A., Shapira, I., Berliner, S., & Melamed, S. (2005). The association between burnout, depression, anxiety, and inflammation biomarkers: C-reactive protein and fibrinogen in men and women. *Journal of Occupational Health Psychology, 10*, 344–362.

Toker, S., Melamed, S., Berliner, S., Zeltser, D., & Shapira, I. (2012). Burnout and the risk of coronary heart disease: A prospective study of 8838 employees. *Psychosomatic Medicine, 74*, 840–847.

Toppinen-Tanner, S., Ojajärvi, A., Väänänen, A., Kalimo, R., & Jäppinen, P. (2005). Burnout as a predictor of medically certified sick-leave absences and their diagnosed causes. *Behavioral Medicine, 31*, 18–27.

Toppinen-Tanner, S., Ahola, K., Koskinen, A., & Väänänen, A. (2009). Burnout predicts hospitalization for mental and cardiovascular disorders: 10-year prospective results from industrial sector. *Stress and Health, 25*, 287–296.

Warr, P. (1987). *Work, Unemployment and Mental Health.* Oxford, UK: Clarendon Press.

Wittchen, H.-U., Lachner, G., Wunderlich, U., & Pfister, H. (1998). Test-retest reliability of the computerized DSM-IV version of the Munich-Composite International Diagnostic Interview (M-CIDI). *Social Psychiatry and Psychiatric Epidemiology, 33*, 568–578.

World Health Organization. (1946). *Definition of Health.* Preamble to the Constitution of the World Health Organization as adopted by the International Health Conference, New York, 19–22 June, 1946; signed on 22 July 1946 by the representatives of 61 States (Official Records of the World Health Organization, no. 2, p. 100) and entered into force on 7 April 1948.

3 Individual strategies to prevent burnout

Evangelia Demerouti

Burnout was first coined in the 1970s by Freudenberger to describe the gradual emotional depletion and loss of motivation he observed among people who had volunteered to work for aid organizations in New York. On the basis of his observations, Freudenberger (1974) defined burnout as "a state of mental and physical exhaustion caused by one's professional life." During the same time period, Maslach and her colleagues interviewed human service workers in California to find out how they were coping with client-related stressors (Maslach & Jackson, 1981). The human service workers used the term 'burnout,' and indicated that they experienced feelings of exhaustion, had developed negative attitudes towards their clients, and often felt that they lacked the professional competence needed to help their clients (Schaufeli et al., 2009). Although burnout was initially believed to be the result of the provision of services (e.g. Maslach & Jackson, 1981), research in the 1990s suggested that burnout can be found in virtually every job that has a specific constellation of working conditions. Namely, when employees are confronted with high job demands and are provided with inadequate job resources, they are at risk of developing burnout (Demerouti et al., 2001; Lee & Ashforth, 1996). Ample evidence has confirmed this suggestion (overview in Bakker & Demerouti, 2007; Bakker & Demerouti, 2014).

Although there is no doubt that the presence of demanding job characteristics combined with the absence of resources or motivational job characteristics triggers burnout, it is interesting from both a theoretical and practical point of view to examine whether there are strategies that individuals use to minimize burnout and its unfavorable effects. Individual strategies represent methods or plans that people choose to achieve a goal or solve a problem. In the business literature, strategies generally involve some planning or marshaling of resources for their most efficient and effective use. Finding such bottom-up strategies that help individuals deal with their burnout experiences such that they avoid becoming burned out or manage to deal with burnout experiences may be essential to complement the top-down interventions that organizations introduce to reduce the risk of burnout. Specifically, insight into individual strategies can help the development of interventions targeted to guide individuals such that they apply strategies that are more effective and refrain from using non-effective strategies to prevent burnout or minimize its effects.

The current chapter will focus on three categories of strategies that might be relevant to burnout. First, strategies that individuals use to deal directly with diminished resources that come with burnout. Some target the individual's relationship to the job (e.g. coping, selection, optimization with compensation, humor), while others focus on strengthening the individual's internal resources (e.g. recovery) (Maslach & Goldberg, 1998). Second, strategies that individuals apply to change their job characteristics such that the job is less demanding and more motivating. These two categories partly overlap with the two-part scheme for effective approaches to prevent burnout discussed by Maslach and Goldberg (1998): individual-centered and situation-centered. A third category represents strategies that individuals use to manage the interplay between the work and non-work domains. As inter-role conflict represents a situation that increases the risk of burnout (Byron, 2005; Geurts & Demerouti, 2003), inter-role management represents strategies that individuals may use to avoid or deal with interrole conflict and its related effects on burnout. The chapter will end with a conclusion on how successful strategies may be stimulated among employees and some avenues will be suggested for future research related to the issue of individual strategies.

Strategies to deal with diminished resources

Burnout has been defined as a long-term consequence of aversive working conditions characterized by the simultaneous experience of the symptoms of exhaustion and disengagement from one's job (Demerouti et al., 2001; Demerouti et al., 2010; Maslach et al., 2001). Exhaustion is defined as a consequence of intensive physical, affective, and cognitive strain, i.e., as a long-term consequence of prolonged exposure to certain job demands. Disengagement refers to distancing oneself from one's work object, work content, and work in general. From these definitions it becomes clear that inherent in the experience of burnout is the experience of diminished resources in terms of ability and willingness to invest effort into work tasks. Hobfoll (2001) described burnout as a result of the lack of resource gain following significant resource investment of time and energy. Employees who have already invested a substantial amount of time and energetic resources in their jobs may not be able to gain new resources that would help them manage the demands of their work and maintain optimal functioning in the long run. Investing their resources differently and maybe more effectively may protect them against (further) resource loss, help them recover from loss, and even gain new resources (a so-called gain cycle might develop; Hobfoll, 2001). It is not surprising that burnout has been linked to strategies that individuals may use to deal with the diminished resources. The next section will present a brief overview on coping, which represents one of the most known strategies used to deal with stress and burnout. In this context, the following strategies will be presented: recovery from work, Selective Optimization with Compensation, humor, and other strategies derived from qualitative research. All these strategies share a common objective of addressing diminishing time and energetic resources.

Coping strategies

Applying a transactional approach to stress, Lazarus and Folkman (1984) defined coping as "changing cognitive and behavioral efforts developed for managing the specific external and/or internal demands judged as exceeding or surpassing the individual's own resources" (p. 164). In the literature, several classifications of coping strategies can be found, which are made depending on the specific methods used or according to the precise objectives towards which coping strategies are directed. Billings and Moos (1981), for example, identified three methods of coping: a) active-cognitive, i.e. the management of the appraisal of stressful events such that they are less stressful; b) active-behavioral, i.e. the observable efforts aimed at managing a stressful situation; and c) avoidance, i.e. the refusal to face a problematic or stressful situation. On the basis of the objectives of coping, authors have made an essential distinction between coping oriented to the problem and coping oriented to the emotion (Lazarus & Folkman, 1984). Problem-focused coping represents an attempt to respond directly to the stressful situation, while emotion-focused coping consists of attempts to moderate the emotional response to stressful events.

Studies have related coping strategies to burnout in professionals working in various domains. Thornton (1992), for example, found a statistically significant association between avoidance coping and burnout in a sample of workers at a psychiatric clinic. In a longitudinal study with social workers, Koeske (1993) found that active coping strategies provided greater capacity for coping with difficult situations at work. Chan and Hui (1995) found that coping strategies addressed to avoidance were positively related to the three components of burnout in a group of secondary school teachers.

An increasing amount of studies seem to have examined the coping strategies that individuals used in reaction to their burnout experiences. Leiter (1993) posited that outcomes reflecting withdrawal tendencies (e.g., avoidance coping, low job involvement, and desire to quit) are more related to either emotional exhaustion or depersonalization, whereas outcomes reflecting positive self-efficacy (e.g., active coping and favorable work attitudes) are more related to personal accomplishment. Consistent with Leiter's (1993) model, the findings of the meta-analysis of Lee and Ashforth (1996) revealed that the three dimensions of burnout were differentially associated with several of the behavioral and attitudinal correlates. Emotional exhaustion and depersonalization were weakly associated with active coping. In an attempt to explain the findings, Lee and Ashforth (1996) suggested that the weak associations might reflect the underuse of such a coping behavior or its lack of effectiveness and subsequent abandonment. In any case, the lack of an effective coping response might have served to reinforce subsequent feelings of helplessness and futility (Lee & Ashforth, 1993). Conversely, personal accomplishment was strongly related to active coping, suggesting that a problem-focused response and a positive self-appraisal may be mutually reinforcing (Lazarus & Folkman, 1984; Leiter, 1991). The findings of this meta-analysis suggested that outcomes stemming from emotional exhaustion reflect the desire to withdraw.

More recently, in a correlation study, Jenaro and colleagues (2007) found that workers with a higher sense of personal accomplishment tended to use problem-focused coping strategies and refrained from using emotion-focused ones. Workers with high levels of emotional exhaustion are more likely to use emotion-focused strategies as well as some problem-focused strategies. Third, workers with a high sense of depersonalization (i.e., irritability, and negative, cold, and impersonal attitudes toward users) refrain from initiating either problem-focused or emotion-focused strategies. The authors explained the lack of significant correlations between depersonalization and any of the coping strategies by suggesting that depersonalization may be the last resource to use when coping strategies do not seem to work any longer (Wallace & Brinkerhoff, 1991). Namely, once someone has cynical or impersonal feelings toward his or her users, no further efforts are initiated and no coping strategies are used.

Similarly, Yela (1996) reported that the greater the feelings of emotional exhaustion, the more likely these professionals were to use strategies coinciding with a passive form of coping, including strategies based on behavioral and mental disconnection from the situation, concentrating on one's emotions, and venting one's feelings when faced with difficult or stressful events.

Regarding the relationship between coping strategies and burnout, Aluja Fabregat et al. (2003) suggested that the effectiveness of coping depends on the situation. Although it seems evident that strategies oriented to the problem are much more effective for coping with stressful situations than those oriented to the emotion and to avoidance (Hart et al., 1995; Roger et al., 1993), the effectiveness of strategies oriented to the problem has been found to depend on effective control of the potential stressors of the environment and individual emotions (Folkman, 1984; Ito & Brotheridge, 2001). On the other hand, persistent use of problem-focused coping strategies when there are few possibilities of controlling and/or changing the environmental stressors may exacerbate the undesirable effects of work stress (Schaubroek & Merritt, 1997; de Rijk et al., 1998). At the same time, it has been pointed out that in less controllable circumstances, strategies oriented to the problem in combination with strategies oriented to avoidance may be useful for improving adaptation and well-being (Aluja Fabregat et al., 2003). In this way, flexibility in utilized coping strategies would be adaptive rather than maladaptive, that is, coping oriented to the problem would be adaptive in controllable situations, whilst coping oriented to avoidance would be adaptive in situations that are difficult to control (Koeske, 1993; Latack, 1986). In this line, Cheng (2001) concluded that both perception of control and objective controllability of the stressors would play a key role in the achievement of effective coping.

Taken together, burnout seems to be related to different types of coping, but generally avoidance and emotion-focused coping seem to be stronger related to burnout than active and problem-focused coping. More importantly, what seems to matter more is whether the applied coping attempt was effective for the situation that the individual was aiming to deal with. It seems that whether or not the individual has control of the situation seems to determine the effectiveness of the applied coping strategy.

Humor

Humor is suggested to serve as a coping mechanism that helps individuals appraise and restructure stressful situations (Abel, 2002). It has been demonstrated that humor states and associated laughter can improve various health-related outcomes, such as stress, cardiac rehabilitation and pain threshold (Healy & McKay, 2000). Hence, engagement in humorous activities can be expected to result in decreased fatigue and burnout, increased recovery, and higher subsequent work engagement (Demerouti et al., 2009). Nevertheless, not all types of humor are beneficial, and individuals differ in their use of humor (Martin et al., 2003). Martin and colleagues (2003) have distinguished between four types of humor. On the positive side, *self-enhancing humor* pertains to a tendency to be amused by the incongruences of life and by having a genuine humorous outlook, even in times of stress. *Affiliative humor* is expressed to amuse others, facilitate relationships, and reduce inter-personal tensions. On the negative side, *self-defeating humor* pertains to making disparaging jokes at one's own expense while *aggressive humor* refers to a hostile type of humor, aimed to hurt or manipulate others, mostly to defend oneself against threat. Self-enhancing and affiliative humor consistently relate positively to individuals' physical, psychological, and social well-being, while self-defeating and aggressive humor show negative relationships with well-being and optimal functioning (e.g., Greengross & Miller, 2008).

In a study among Belgian employees, Van den Broeck et al. (2012) analyzed the impact of these two interpersonal humor styles on burnout and work engagement. In line with the humor-health hypothesis, results attested to the direct health-enhancing associations of self-enhancing and affiliative humor (Martin et al., 2003): Self-enhancing and affiliative humor associated negatively with burnout and positively with work engagement. Thus, these two humor types can be considered to represent strategies to change one's outlook on one's job, thereby decreasing the risk of burnout.

Recovery from work

Perhaps the most relevant strategy that individuals may use daily to reduce their burnout levels is to recover from work. Recovery occurs after strain when the stressor is no longer present (Sonnentag & Fritz, 2007). It represents the process that repairs the negative strain effects. More specifically, recovery refers to the process during which an individual's functioning returns to its pre-stressor level and in which strain is reduced (Sonnentag & Natter, 2004). Put differently, recovery refers to activities that might reduce fatigue to restore a status of physiological and psychological performance readiness. This makes recovery particularly relevant for regulating the levels of energy and reducing the levels of exhaustion.

According to Meijman and Mulder (1998), effort expenditure at work is unavoidably associated with, in principle adaptive, acute load reactions (e.g., accelerated heart rate, elevated blood pressure levels, and fatigue). Under optimal circumstances, the stress-related acute load reactions return to pre-stressor levels during after-work hours, and recovery is completed before the next working period starts. However, when the stress-related acute load reactions prolong or re-occur during after-work hours (i.e., sustained sympathetic activation), recovery is incomplete (Geurts & Sonnentag, 2006). Consequently, the worker will start the next working period while being in a suboptimal condition, and will have to invest compensatory effort in order to perform adequately at work. Prolonged exposure to work demands (e.g., daily overtime work) that strain the *same* psycho-physiological systems that were already activated on the job also after work may lead to a total breakdown (Geurts & Sonnentag, 2006). Particularly employees at risk of burnout may be willing to work even when they are at home in order to avoid the backlog that may come with their feelings of exhaustion.

What recovery strategies have been found to be successful in reducing the risk of burnout? Among other things, Sonnentag and Fritz (2007) have discriminated between psychological detachment from work during non-work time and relaxation as recovery experiences that may be relevant for burnout. Psychological detachment means that individuals stop thinking about work and disengage themselves mentally from work. Lack of detachment has been associated with higher exhaustion. For instance, Sonnentag et al. (2010) found that pastors who were more able to detach from their work during their spare time had lower levels of emotional exhaustion and a lower need for recovery. Interestingly, psychological detachment mediated the relation between job stressors on the one hand and emotional exhaustion and need for recovery on the other hand. Additionally, in a longitudinal study by Sonnentag et al. (2008), lack of detachment predicted an increase in emotional exhaustion one year later, even when the researchers controlled for the initial level of emotional exhaustion, job stressors, and a broad range of background variables.

Furthermore, Sonnentag and Fritz (2007) found that relaxation is negatively correlated with health complaints, exhaustion, sleep problems, and need for recovery. This indicates that low-effort activities require minimal amounts of effort on the part of the individual and therefore pose no demands on the psycho-biological system (Sonnentag & Natter, 2004); therefore they help individuals reduce their levels of exhaustion on days that these levels are high.

Another recovery activity that has been linked to burnout represents social activities, i.e. time that individuals spend with other people when they finish work (Sonnentag, 2001). Sanz-Vergel et al. (2010) demonstrated that talking to family, colleagues, or friends about positive emotions had a beneficial impact on vitality at the end of the day, and created a positive relationship between work and family life. However, talking about negative issues led to higher levels of exhaustion and work-family conflict.

Thus, recovery experiences like detachment and relaxation as well as social activities are found to be beneficial in diminishing the daily experiences of burnout as well as the risk of burnout over time (particularly detachment from work). The good news found is that paying attention to sufficient recovery on a daily basis represents a clear daily strategy that individuals can apply to diminish their burnout levels.

Selection, optimization with compensation

Demerouti et al. (2014b) suggest that the Selective Optimization with Compensation (SOC) model of Freund and Baltes (1998, 2002) may be applied to specify strategies that individuals may use to keep optimal functioning even when their time and energetic resources are diminished (as is the case with burnout). The SOC model suggests that the use of SOC strategies facilitates optimal allocation of individual resources, maintenance and enhancement of functioning in the face of challenges, and adaptivity to the loss of resources. The SOC model was initially developed to explain how individuals could deal with diminishing resources that come with aging (e.g. illness and physical deterioration etc.). To do so, they apply management strategies of (1) selecting the goals to pursue, (2) optimizing and using goal-relevant means, and (3) using compensatory means to maintain goal attainment when previously employed resources are no longer available or blocked.

Selection involves setting goals and deciding on goal priorities. It can be guided by personal preferences such that employees may focus more on those aspects of their work that they consider the most important (elective selection), or it results from reconstruction of the goal hierarchy, or search for new goals in response to a decline of resources (loss-based selection). For instance, employees might abandon work-related goals that they cannot accomplish any more because of a lack of time or health constraints (Zacher & Frese, 2011). Optimization refers to the obtainment, improvement, and use of personal resources to achieve relevant goals (Freund & Baltes, 2002). Optimization can take the form of learning and practicing new procedures, and investing more time in challenging work tasks (Schmitt et al., 2012). Finally, compensation refers to the organization of substitute means to reach goals and to maintain a given level of functioning in response to actual or anticipated resource losses. Employees can compensate for increases in workload by using external aids or drawing upon the help of colleagues (Schmitt et al., 2012).

To test whether the application of specific SOC strategies by individuals experiencing burnout will enhance optimal functioning despite a reduction in energy, and thus minimize the detrimental effects of burnout on task performance, Demerouti et al. (2014a) collected data among 294 employees and their supervisors. Employees reported their levels of burnout and utilization of SOC while their supervisors rated the employees' task performance. The researchers found that the combined use of selection, optimization, and compensation strategies buffers the unfavorable effect of disengagement on supervisor-ratings of task performance and adaptivity to organizational change. They found that compensation is the most successful strategy in buffering the negative associations of burnout with supervisor-ratings of task performance and adaptivity to organizational change. When time and energetic resources decline or are lost (as with burnout), compensation strategies become necessary to avoid a reduction in self-regulation regarding goals (Freund & Baltes, 2000, 2002; Freund & Riediger, 2001). An individual may compensate by using different external resources, such as the help of others or of technology, but also by increasing his or her efforts or by learning new skills (Ouwehand et al., 2007). In contrast, elective and loss-based selections were found to exacerbate the negative relationship of exhaustion with adaptivity to organizational change. In line with the suggestions of the SOC model, when people select between alternatives or make a new goal hierarchy, they manage to avoid performance decrements (e.g., by setting performance goals high on the hierarchy and ignoring other goals). However, in line with the reasoning of Hockey (1997), in this case they fail to keep their optimal functioning on more peripheral, discretional behaviors such as adaptation to changes (see Dewett & Denisi, 2007).

The SOC model contains strategies that are promising in dealing with burnout. It can be concluded that of the three strategies (i.e. selection, optimization, and compensation) compensation was the most successful strategy for buffering the negative associations of burnout with task performance and adaptivity. In other words, the acquisition and use of alternative means, (i.e., using external aids or drawing upon the help of colleagues) seem to diminish unfavorable effects of burnout. However, selection, i.e. setting priorities and focusing on fewer aspects of one's work, was found to enhance unfavorable effects of burnout on peripheral performance dimensions (such that the task performance remains intact). More empirical evidence is welcome to expand our insights on the role of SOC for burnout.

Other strategies

Beyond coping, recovery, SOC strategies, and humor, other strategies to deal with diminishing resources have been uncovered, mainly through qualitative studies. A notable study is the qualitative study by Swetz and colleagues (2009). The authors conducted interviews among physicians in hospice and palliative medicine, in which they asked them to report ways to minimize stress, to provide advice to young physicians to sustain their energy for the years to come, and to report their own strategies, rituals, habits, etc. that are essential for their survival in the field. On the basis of the interviews, they found several strategies that physicians use to manage their resources. Specifically, the most common strategy for dealing with stress and preventing burnout was promotion of physical well-being. Methods for promoting physical well-being included exercise, proper nutrition, rest, and an increased focus on one's own health. Another common category involved taking a "transcendental perspective," which emphasized what makes us human, aspects of personhood, and how one deals with spirituality and nature. The means that were reported varied from prayer and meditation to structured attendance at religious services.

Conclusion

Taken together, the review presents several strategies that individuals use to deal with diminished resources either by changing their relationship to the job (e.g. coping, selection, optimization, compensation, humor), or by directly strengthening their internal resources (e.g. recovery). As was shown, individuals seem to use coping, humor, and compensation to reduce the impact of work stressors by changing the stressor (in case of problem-focused coping) or how they respond to them. Additionally, individuals seem to offset the negative load effects of stressors and replenish resources by using (daily) recovery, a healthy lifestyle and meditation. Such strategies seem to be beneficial to maintain their time and energetic resources and to avoid the risk of burnout.

Strategies to change job characteristics

To this point, the focus of this chapter was on what individuals do in general to deal with the feelings of diminished resources they are experiencing. Individuals can, however, realize that as burnout experiences are related to work, they should also find ways to change or adjust their work (characteristics) such that they avoid enhanced levels of burnout. This comes close to active coping but differs in that coping represents a reaction to stressors, while the driver of the main strategy presented here, job crafting, is the search for meaning and for a motivating and healthy work environment.

Job crafting

Job crafting (Wrzesniewski & Dutton, 2001) represents actions employees take so as to alter the task boundaries of a job (i.e. type or number of activities), the cognitive task boundaries of a job (i.e. how one sees the job), and the relational boundaries of a job (i.e. whom one interacts with at work). Examples of job crafting could be hospital cleaners starting to interact with patients (Wrzesniewski & Dutton, 2001) or a police officer who organizes a sports event to increase the physical condition of herself and her colleagues. In order to describe in more detail the actions that are performed by job crafters, recent literature (Petrou et al., 2012; Tims et al., 2012) has used the Job Demands-Resources (JD-R) model (Demerouti et al., 2001) and the two-dimensional work stressor framework by Podsakoff et al. (2007) as conceptual frameworks. These two frameworks distinguish job characteristics into hindering job demands (i.e., the demanding aspects of a job which require physical and psychological effort), challenging job demands (i.e., demanding aspects of a job that have the potential to promote employee growth and development), and job resources (i.e., job aspects that are functional for achieving work goals and can eliminate the costs of the demands). Following this stream of literature, job crafting refers to voluntary self-initiated employee behaviors targeted to seeking resources (i.e., asking a manager or colleagues for advice), seeking challenges (i.e., asking for more responsibilities), and reducing hindering demands (i.e., eliminating emotionally, mentally, or physically demanding job aspects). Following Wrzesniewski and Dutton (2001), Petrou et al. (2012) suggested that even in the most stable environments with detailed job descriptions and clear work procedures, individuals can and do adjust the tasks they perform to further mobilize the resources they need to carry out their tasks successfully. In this way, individuals remain healthy and motivated to carry out their tasks successfully.

More specifically, *seeking resources* (e.g., performance feedback, advice from colleagues or the manager, maximizing job autonomy) can be a form of coping with job demands or achieving goals and completing tasks (Petrou et al., 2012). Hobfoll (2001) also suggested that a basic human motivation is directed towards the accumulation of resources, which are important for the protection of other valued resources. At the workplace, this can take the form of proactive behavior with positive outcomes for employee motivation and well-being (Salanova & Schaufeli, 2008). Thus, by successfully seeking job resources, employees accumulate resources and expand their current resource pool.

Seeking challenges may include behaviors such as pursuing new stimulating tasks at work, keeping busy during one's work day, or asking for more responsibilities once assigned tasks have been completed. Csikszentmihalyi and Nakamura (1989) argued that when individuals engage in activities offering opportunities for growth, they seek challenges to maintain motivation and avoid boredom. Job demands do not play an exclusively dysfunctional role (Demerouti et al., 2001). Podsakoff et al. (2007) suggested that there are some demands that have a positive effect on employee job satisfaction and commitment. These demands have been called challenge stressors. Challenge is a central idea in the Job Demands-Control framework (Karasek & Theorell, 1990) that assumes that workers in active jobs (characterized by high job demands and high control) seek challenges that promote mastery.

Reducing job demands represents a way to reduce hindrances, for example, by minimizing the emotionally, mentally, or physically demanding aspects of one's work and reducing one's workload or time pressure (Petrou, et al., 2012; Tims et al., 2012). Unlike challenging job demands, hindering job demands are demanding job aspects that employees appraise as potentially constraining their development and performance (Podsakoff et al. 2007). Reducing job demands is not an extensively studied employee behavior. Avoidance coping techniques, which could involve similar behaviors, are linked with impaired mental health and social functioning (Endler & Parker, 1994), and should relate to individuals' emotional numbness and unawareness of what causes them stress (Roth & Cohen, 1986). Although at work employees may eliminate their demands to avoid stress (Tims & Bakker, 2010), it seems that these employees are not particularly engaged in their work (Petrou et al., 2012).

How do burnout and job crafting relate to each other over time? Job crafting has been examined both as a predictor of burnout (in the sense that it can facilitate or hinder it) and as an outcome of burnout (in the sense that it represents attempts to deal with it). Recently Tims et al. (2013) conducted a longitudinal study to examine whether employees can impact their own well-being by crafting their job demands and resources. On the basis of the Job Demands-Resources model, the authors hypothesized that employee job crafting would have an impact on work engagement, job satisfaction, and burnout through changes in job demands and job resources. Data was collected in a chemical plant at three time points with one month in between the measurement waves. The results of structural equation modeling showed that employees who crafted their job resources in the first month of the study showed an increase in their structural and social resources over the course of the study (2 months). This increase in job resources was negatively related to burnout and positively related to engagement and job satisfaction. More specifically, it was shown that increasing structural job resources (i.e. autonomy, variety, and opportunities for development) as a form of job crafting was negatively directly related to burnout and indirectly through the perception of structural job resources themselves. Additionally, increasing social resources (i.e. social support, feedback, and coaching) as a form of job crafting was indirectly negatively related to burnout through the perception of social job resources. Crafting job demands did not result in a change in job demands, but results revealed direct effects of crafting challenging demands (i.e. workload) on decreases in burnout (and increases in work engagement). In this study, contrary to expectations, crafting hindering demands (i.e. cognitive demands and emotional demands) were unrelated to future burnout. These findings highlight the importance of mobilization of job resources (both structural and social) in order to diminish the risk to burnout.

Partly similar findings are reported by Petrou et al. (2014), who used a longer time frame of one year between the measures and a sample of police officers within a police district that was undergoing organizational change. In this study, seeking resources was unrelated to exhaustion. As in the study by Tims et al. (2013), seeking challenges did have a positive implication; namely it contributed to lower levels of exhaustion. In other words, an approach of actively confronting new demanding aspects of the job is associated with lower rather than higher levels of strain. An active and problem-focused approach to work goals has also been linked with successful employee adjustment during organizational change and low levels of exhaustion (Cunningham et al., 2002; Terry et al., 1996). Employees with such a proactive work orientation are self-efficacious (Somech & Drach-Zahavy, 2000) and resilient (Mallak, 1998) and, therefore, protected from the adverse effects of a demanding job environment. A possible interpretation of the findings of Petrou et al. (2014) is that in order to survive within the demanding context of organizational change, an employee needs to experience the feeling that he or she is efficacious and able to respond to the demands of the change. This feeling develops more efficiently via an active approach of trial and error and direct confrontation of the challenges rather than reliance on others (i.e. for support, feedback etc.).

Petrou et al. (2014) found an interesting pattern of relationships between reducing demands and exhaustion. Employees who attempted to reduce their demands reported higher exhaustion, a state that, in its turn, led to further decreasing demands. This means that exhaustion and decreasing demands are reciprocal over time and strengthen each other. Although one would expect that reducing demands is a successful strategy to reduce exhaustion, our findings show the opposite. This is in line with literature that describes vicious cycles in which burned-out employees can be entrapped (Singh et al., 1994). Exhausted employees are physically and mentally drained and therefore put less effort into their tasks (Banks et al., 2012; Swider & Zimmerman, 2010). By doing so, they increase their workload and time pressure (van Eerde, 2000), which intensifies their feelings of exhaustion.

This latter finding agrees with the findings of a daily diary study conducted by Demerouti et al. (2014a) among employees from various occupations who filled in a short questionnaire for five consecutive days. On the basis of COR theory, the authors suggested that the more employees experience exhaustion, the less likely they will be to invest the limited resources they have, and instead will maintain a defensive posture to protect those resources (Hobfoll, 2001). An exhausted employee's primary motivator becomes protecting whatever scarce resources are left, and he or she may not have the resources needed to invest in completing the tasks, duties, and functions of the job (Halbesleben & Wheeler, 2008). Moreover, exhausted employees will become conservative in where they invest any remaining resources and will only invest those resources in actions that have typically provided the greatest return (Baltes, 1997). Therefore, feelings of exhaustion will make employees less willing to show proactive behaviors in terms of adjusting their work environment, even if doing so would help them to reduce those feelings. Findings support these suggestions as it was found that on days that employees were more exhausted they also reported lower job crafting behavior (i.e. less seeking resources, less seeking challenges and less reducing demands). Perhaps it would have helped them to reduce the elevated feelings of exhaustion on a specific day if they had followed that strategy. The lack of resources experienced by exhausted employees is so distracting that they are unable to craft their job and thus not only to address the disadvantages but also enjoy the benefits of these strategies. Fatigue has also been defined as a subjective phenomenon characterized by tiredness, weakness, lack of energy, lethargy, and depression, all pointing to an inability to act (Winningham et al., 1994).

Other strategies

Next to these general job crafting actions, burnout has been linked to other specific strategies that are directed towards changing work aspects. One of the most common strategies that the physicians in the study of Swetz et al. (2009) used to avoid burnout was to promote supportive and nurturing professional relation-ships with other colleagues, which emphasizes the important role of teamwork, camaraderie and collegiality in the workplace. In a similar vein, participants often reported talking with others, and expressed the need to debrief with colleagues, explaining to them the difficulties that they confronted in their work on a specific day and how they felt. In addition to these social resources, one third of the physicians reported the search for clinical variety. Accordingly, they combined the provision of care, which is more draining, with other less draining activities like research, writing and teaching.

Conclusion

Individuals seem to use bottom-up, job crafting strategies to change their job characteristics such that they become less hindering and more motivating and challenging. The limited empirical evidence seems to suggest that the mobilization of resources and challenges by the individual seems to reduce burnout. In particular, promoting supportive and nurturing professional relationships with colleagues, as well as the search for variety in tasks, seem to represent the use of crafting strategies. When individuals reduce their job demands, they seem to enter into a negative spiral in which reducing demands is related to more exhaustion, which over time is related to more reducing demands. Thus, specific job crafting behaviors seem to diminish burnout. However, burnout does not seem to stimulate job crafting, which shows that individuals need to have the energy and motivation available to adjust their jobs to their preferences.

Strategies for inter-role management

Although burnout is considered a work-related syndrome, the unsuccessful boundary management of work and non-work life has also been found to be related to burnout. This occurs not only in the form of work-related experiences (e.g. exhaustion) that spill over from work to home, but also because an ineffective inter-role management might be another trigger of burnout. Below, the form of inter-role relationships and management will be clarified in order to uncover their effects on burnout.

Spillover vs. segmentation

Classically, the relationship between the work and the non-work domains has been the basis of three different hypotheses (Cohen, 1997). The earliest hypothesis is the *segregation* (or segmentation) hypothesis (Dubin, 1956; Dubin & Champoux, 1977), postulating that there is no relationship between "work" and "non-work." Both domains are considered (psychologically, physically, temporally, and functionally) separate domains, and the activities in each domain are assumed to make unique demands on the individual. This view has been applied more frequently to blue-collar workers, who more often have unsatisfying and uninvolving jobs (Lambert, 1990). Lambert (1990) suggested that segregation does not occur naturally but may be the result of workers' active attempts to let work activities not intrude into their family lives.

Besides the segregation hypothesis, Wilensky (1960) distinguished two major hypotheses about the work and non-work interface. First is the *compensatory* hypothesis, which represents attempts to make up for the deprivations experienced at work. Second is the *spillover* or generalization hypothesis, which posits the carry-over or generalization of alienation from work into alienation from non-work. Both hypotheses are based on a negative view of the work domain, as negative experiences at work are compensated for or carried over to the non-work domain. Both competing hypotheses have received some evidence (Kabanoff & O'Brien, 1980). In some studies (Meissner, 1971; Rousseau, 1978), positive correlations have been found between the sort of work people perform and their non-work activities. Individuals with a repetitive and unchallenging job seemed to have similar routine non-work activities, supporting the spillover (or generalization) hypothesis. Other studies (Mansfield & Evans, 1975) have found negative correlations between work and non-work as individuals with routine and unchallenging jobs seemed to choose varied and challenging non-work activities, supporting the compensatory hypothesis.

Next to these relatively static hypotheses, more recent literature views the issue of inter-role management in a more dynamic and differentiated way. Border theory (Clark, 2000) proposes that each person's role takes place in different domains that are separated by physical, temporal, or psychological borders. It is possible to "cross borders" between domains, and people may differ in the way in which they cross these borders. There are different types of border crossers depending on the degree to which they are peripheral or central participants in either domain. Border crossers are individuals who make frequent transitions between the work and family domains (which may be physical, temporal, or psychological). Whereas peripheral border crossers do not internalize the domain characteristics, central border crossers personally identify with them. Specifically, border crossers who are central participants in one domain feel more motivated to guard the borders of that domain (Clark, 2000). The interruptions (conflict) or positive impact (facilitation) of work aspects on family and personal lives are expected to be more prevalent and frequent than those of family life, because work represents a domain with strong and clear borders that are guarded by border keepers (i.e., the supervisor and colleagues) (Clark, 2000; Demerouti, 2012). Border keepers are those domain members who are especially influential in defining the domain and border, usually a spouse or significant other at home and a supervisor or colleague at work.

Boundary theories generally suggest that creating and maintaining boundaries around life domains represent the attempts of individuals to simplify and order their environment (Ashforth et al., 2000; Clark, 2000; Hahn & Dormann, 2013; Nippert-Eng, 1996). Boundaries may be viewed as helping individuals to structure and delineate the various roles they have in their different life domains (Clark, 2000). Employees vary in their preferences for separating or integrating aspects of work and home domains (Kreiner, 2006). According to Ashforth et al. (2000), their preferences may range on a continuum between complete segmentation on the one hand and complete integration on the other. Depending on their segmentation preferences, people tend to construct more or less permeable boundaries around their work and home domains to get the degree of segmentation or integration that they prefer (Powell & Greenhaus, 2010). When people have a strong segmentation preference, they may use physical, temporal, communicative, and behavioral boundary management strategies to construct impermeable boundaries between work and home (Hahn & Dormann, 2013; Kreiner et al., 2009). For example, employees preferring to segment work and home may prefer not to have an office at home or to use work-related communication technologies at home, they may not talk about work with their partner when at home, or they may avoid displaying work-related mementos at home (Hahn & Dormann, 2013).

A clear segmentation between work and home limits the psychological influence of work on the home domain by preventing the spillover from work aspects such as job-related thoughts and worries into the home domain (Ilies et al., 2009; Park & Jex, 2011). Individuals with cynicism are likely to ruminate about the problems that they may have with customers, colleagues, or supervisors while being at home (Hahn & Dormann, 2013). This behavior will make their feelings of cynicism even worse as they will repeat and re-experience the triggers of their cynicism. Ilies and colleagues (2009) suggested that individuals who segment their work and non-work roles are less likely to think about work while they are at home. As a consequence, employees can experience less frequent intrusive thoughts about their work when they encounter some cues in their environment that are related to their work, even while they are involved in other activities during their off-job time (Hahn & Dormann, 2013).

When employees do not bring their work into their home domain, it is less likely that they will encounter work-related cues that stimulate rumination and prevent detachment from work (Hahn & Dormann, 2013). First, empirical studies support the idea that preferring to segment work and home promotes detachment (Park et al., 2011; Sonnentag et al., 2010). Also, Hahn and Dormann (2013) found in a dyadic study with dual-earner couples that both employees' own and their partners' work–home segmentation preferences were positively associated with employees' detachments from work. The presence of children in the household attenuated the relation of partners' work–home segmentation preferences on employees' detachments. Moreover, employees' and partners' detachments were also positively associated. Again, the relation was weaker when there were children living in the household. The study indicates that employees are more likely to react to their partners' work-related cues when their partners' cues resemble their own work-related cues. Moreover, the presence of children is an important boundary condition for the effects of partners' preferences and experiences on employees' detachments from work.

Inter-role conflict/interference

Conflict theory claims that the work and family environments are incompatible because they have distinct norms and requirements (Zedeck & Mosier, 1990). Specifically, work-family conflict is defined as

> a form of inter-role conflict in which the role pressures from the work and family domains are mutually incompatible in some respect. That is, participation in the work (family) role is made more difficult by virtue of participation in the family (work) role.
>
> (Greenhaus & Beutell, 1985, p. 77)

Although the latter authors explicitly stated that work-family conflict is inherently non-directional (p. 84), most scholars distinguish between two types of inter-role conflict: (1) *work-family conflict*, referring to a situation in which role pressures at work hamper functioning at home; and (2) *family-work conflict*, referring to role pressures at home interfering with functioning at work.

In a similar vein, the role scarcity hypothesis (Edwards & Rothbard, 2000) has been used to explain negative spillover or conflict. Accordingly, people possess limited and fixed amounts of resources (e.g., time and energy). Managing multiple roles (e.g., of employee, spouse, and parent) is problematic as they draw on the same, scarce resources. High job demands require employees to devote more resources (e.g., time, emotions) to work, leaving them with fewer resources to devote to their families (Frone et al., 1997). Employees confronted with work overload and high emotional demands have more problems in combining their work and family lives (Allen et al., 2000; Amstad et al., 2011). In other words, job demands can spill over into the home domain and interfere with family life.

Not surprisingly it has been found repeatedly that job and home demands may lead to burnout because they increase the experience of work-family and family-work conflict, respectively. Specifically, Peeters et al. (2005) found that job demands and home demands appeared to have a direct and indirect effect (through work-family interference and family-work interference, respectively) on burnout. Similarly, with a sample of New Zealand government workers, Haar (2006) found that the two types of conflict (work-family and family-work) were significant predictors of employee burnout. Additionally, Haar (2006) examined the moderating effects of employee coping strategies in the relationship between both types of conflict and burnout. Results showed that active coping intensified the negative relationships for both work-family and family-work conflict, with employees coping through working harder suffering intensified burnout effects.

Conclusion

Taken together, it was shown that when employees manage to create boundaries between the work and non-work domains, it helps them detach from work and avoid the diminishment of energy and thus restrict the negative impact of the job. Additionally, it was shown that confrontation with high job and home demands might lead to burnout because it increases the experience of work-family and family-work conflict, respectively.

Conclusions and future research

The goal of this chapter was to discuss strategies, i.e. methods or plans that people use to minimize burnout and its unfavorable effects. Although there is extensive knowledge on the work or personal characteristics that are linked to the experience of burnout, knowledge on the specific strategies that are used by individuals to deal with burnout is limited. Finding such bottom-up strategies that help individuals to deal with their burnout experiences such that they avoid becoming burned out or manage to deal with burnout experiences may be essential to complement the top-down interventions that organizations introduce to reduce the risk of burnout. The strategies discussed here should not be seen as replacing top-down, organizational approaches (e.g. job redesign, optimization of workflow, reduction of work hazards) that aim to optimize the work environment and working conditions such that the risk of burnout is minimized. Rather, they should be viewed as strategies that occur simultaneously with organizational approaches and are generally spontaneous and unattended, e.g. job crafting. It is essential that organizations and individuals are aware of the effectiveness of the different individual strategies so that more effective strategies can be implemented.

An increasing amount of research is necessary to uncover several unresolved issues regarding individual strategies. Although several strategies were reviewed, it is by no means plausible that individuals use only the presented strategies. Future research should expand the knowledge on what the other possible strategies are that individuals use to avoid burnout or minimize its detrimental effects.

Second, we still do not know how long the effects of these strategies last. Considering the fluctuating character of the utilized strategies as well as the insight that the effectiveness of the applied strategy seems to depend on the situation, it is suggested that specific research designs might be more appropriate for studying individual strategies than others. For instance, diary research that follows individuals daily during several measurement moments close to the natural context in which they operate (Ohly et al., 2010) might be a useful way to study individual strategies. Combining quantitative with qualitative diary designs might also help to uncover other possible strategies that are involved in the experience of burnout.

Third, virtually all studies presented in this review examined the effect of one unique strategy. The critical question is, however, whether it is possible that the combined use of the strategies is more effective than the employment of a single strategy. This is similar to the suggestion of Karanika-Murray et al. (2009) to consider the multivariate impacts of job characteristics on work-related health, as this can potentially convey a more accurate view of effects than one that looks at variables in isolation (Warr, 1994) (synergistic or inhibitory effects). This necessitates a shift beyond the tendency to focus on one-cause-one-effect relationships to examining combinations of predictors (Kahn & Byosiere, 1992).

Fourth, it is essential to know how individuals can be helped to develop or learn the effective strategies. To this end, intervention studies are essential. Such studies have shown that individuals can develop effective coping strategies in terms of stimulating support-seeking behavior, which reduced their burnout symptoms (Peterson et al., 2008). Hahn et al. (2011) developed an intervention on how to recover from job stress, which proved to be beneficial for recovery, experienced stress, and negative affect. Although there is no evidence of the effectiveness of training programs to stimulate SOC at the workplace, Zacher and Frese (2011) provided clear suggestions on what such trainings should look like. There is evidence that individuals can learn to craft their jobs by setting small job crafting assignments for themselves that they can execute per week (van den Heuvel et al.,

2012). The effectiveness of such interventions to minimize the risk to burnout is still not known.

Insight into the effectiveness of individual strategies can be used to help individuals avoid burnout or minimize the detrimental effects of burnout. Organizations, through human resource practices and supervisors, should inform individuals about the importance of such strategies so that they are able to make more effective choices. Organizations should motivate employees to use the effective strategies for their current and future health and well-being, and teach them how to do so by providing them training possibilities. Focusing on individual, in addition to organizational, approaches seems to be a promising means of dealing with burnout and to create more healthy workforces.

References

Abel, M. H. (2002). Humor, stress, and coping strategies. *Humor, 15,* 365–381.

Allen, T. D., Herst, D. E. L., Bruck, C. S., & Sutton, M. (2000). Consequences associated with work-to-family conflict: A review and agenda for future research. *Journal of Occupational Health Psychology, 5*, 278–308.

Aluja Fabregat, A., Blanch Plana, A., & Biscarri Gassió, J. (2003). Burnout syndrome and coping strategies: A structural relations model. *Psychology in Spain, 7*, 46–55.

Amstad, F. T., Meier, L. L., Fasel, U., Elfering, A., & Semmer, N. K. (2011). A meta-analysis of work–family conflict and various outcomes with a special emphasis on cross-domain versus matching-domain relations. *Journal of Occupational Health Psychology, 16*, 151–169.

Ashforth, B. E., Kreiner, G. E., & Fugate, M. (2000). All in a day's work: Boundaries and micro role transitions. *Academy of Management Review, 25*, 472–491.

Bakker, A. B., & Demerouti, E. (2007). The Job Demands-Resources model: State of the art. *Journal of Managerial Psychology, 22,* 309–328.

Bakker, A. B., & Demerouti, E. (2014). Job demands – Resources theory. In C. Cooper & P. Chen (Eds), *Wellbeing: A complete reference guide* (pp. 37–64). Chichester, UK: Wiley-Blackwell.

Baltes, P. B. (1997). On the incomplete architecture of human ontogeny: Selection, optimization, and compensation as foundation of developmental theory. *American Psychologist, 52*, 366–380.

Banks, G. C., Whelpley, C. E., Oh, I. S., & Shin, K. (2012). (How) are emotionally exhausted employees harmful? *International Journal of Stress Management, 19*, 198–216.

Billings, A. G. & Moos, R. H. (1981). The role of coping responses and social resources in attenuating the stress of life events. *Journal of Behavioral Medicine, 4*, 139–157.

Byron, K. (2005). A meta-analytic review of work–family conflict and its antecedents. *Journal of Vocational Behavior, 67*, 169–198.

Chan, D. W., & Hui, E. K. P. (1995). Burnout and coping among Chinese secondary school teachers in Hong-Kong. *British Journal of Educational Psychology, 65*, 15–25.

Cheng, C. (2001). Assessing coping flexibility in real life and laboratory settings: A multimethod approach. *Journal of Personality and Social Psychology, 80*, 814–833.

Clark, S. C. (2000). Work/family border theory: A new theory of work/family balance. *Human Relations, 53*, 747–770.

Cohen, A. (1997). Personal and organizational responses to work-nonwork interface as related to organizational commitment. *Journal of Applied Social Psychology, 27,* 1085–1114.

Csikszentmihalyi, M., & Nakamura, J. (1989). The dynamics of intrinsic motivation: A study of adolescents. In C. Ames and R. Ames (Eds.), *Research on motivation in education* (vol.3, pp. 45–71). Orlando, Fl: Academic Press.

Cunningham, C. E., Woodward, C. A., Shannon, H. S., MacIntosh, J., Lendrum, B., Rosenbloom, D., & Brown, J. (2002). Readiness for organizational change: A longitudinal study of workplace, psychological and behavioural correlates. *Journal of Occupational and Organizational Psychology, 75,* 377–392.

Demerouti, E. (2012). The spillover and crossover of resources among partners: The role of work-self and family-self facilitation. *Journal of Occupational Health Psychology, 17,* 184–195.

Demerouti, E., Bakker, A. B., Nachreiner, F., & Schaufeli, W. B. (2001). The job demands-resources model of burnout. *Journal of Applied Psychology, 86,* 499–512.

Demerouti, E., Bakker, A. B., Geurts, S. A. E., & Taris, T.W. (2009). Daily recovery from work-related effort during non-work time. In S. Sonnentag, P. L. Perrewé, & D. C. Ganster (Eds.), *Current perspectives on job-stress recovery: Research in occupational stress and well being* (vol. 7, pp. 85–123). Bingley, UK: JAI Press.

Demerouti, E., Mostert, K., & Bakker, A. B. (2010). Burnout and work engagement: A thorough investigation of the independency of both constructs. *Journal of Occupational Health Psychology, 15,* 209–222.

Demerouti, E., Bakker, A. B., & Halbesleben, J. (2014a). Daily contextual and counterproductive work behavior: The role of work engagement, exhaustion, and job crafting. *Manuscript submitted for publication.*

Demerouti, E., Bakker, A.B., & Leiter, M.P. (2014b). Burnout and job performance: The moderating role of selection optimization and compensation strategies. *Journal of Occupational Health Psychology, 19,* 96–107.

Dewett, T., & Denisi, A. S. (2007). What motivates organizational citizenship behaviors? Exploring the role of regulatory focus theory. *European Journal of Work and Organizational Psychology, 16,* 241–260.

Dubin, R. (1956). Industrial workers' worlds: a study of the "central life interests" of industrial workers. *Social Problems, 3,* 131–142.

Dubin, R,. & Champoux, J. E. (1977). Central life interests and job satisfaction. *Organizational Behavior and Human Performance, 18,* 366–377.

Edwards, J. R. & Rothbard, N. P. (2000). Mechanisms linking work and family: Clarifying the relationship between work and family constructs. *The Academy of Management Review, 25,* 178–199.

Endler, N. S., & Parker, J. D. (1994). Assessment of multidimensional coping: Task, emotion, and avoidance strategies. *Psychological Assessment, 6,* 50–60.

Folkman, S. (1984). Personal control and stress and coping processes: A theoretical analysis. *Journal of Personality and Social Psychology, 46,* 839–852.

Freudenberger, H. J. (1974). Staff burnout. *Journal of Social Issues, 30,* 159–165.

Freund, A. M., & Baltes, P. B. (1998). Selection, optimization, and compensation as strategies of life management: Correlations with subjective indicators of successful aging. *Psychology and Aging, 13,* 531–543.

Freund, A. M., & Baltes, P. B. (2000). The orchestration of selection, optimization, and compensation: An action-theoretical conceptualization of a theory of developmental regulation. In W. J. Perrig & A. Grob (Eds), *Control of human behavior, mental processes, and consciousness*. Mahwah, NJ: Lawrence Erlbaum Associates.

Freund, A. M., & Baltes, P. B. (2002). Life-management strategies of selection, optimization, and compensation: Measurement by self-report and construct validity. *Journal of Personality and Social Psychology, 82*, 642–662.

Freund, A. M., & Riediger, M. (2001). What I have and what I do: The role of resource loss and gain throughout life (Commentary). *Applied Psychology, 50*, 370–380.

Frone, M. R., Yardley, J. K. & Markel, K. S. (1997). Developing and testing an integrative model of the work-family interface. *Journal of Vocational Behavior, 50*, 145–167.

Geurts, S. A. E., & Demerouti, E. (2003). Work/non-work interface: A review of theories and findings. In M. Schabracq, J. Winnubst, & C. L. Cooper (Eds), *The Handbook of Work and Health Psychology* (2nd edn) (pp. 279–312). Chichester: Wiley.

Geurts, S. A. E., & Sonnentag, S. (2006). Recovery as an explanatory mechanism in the relation between acute stress reactions and chronic health impairment. *Scandinavian Journal of Work, Environment & Health, 32*, 482–492.

Greengross, G., & Miller, G. F. (2008). Dissing oneself versus dissing rivals: Effects of status, personality, and sex on the short-term and long-term attractiveness of self-deprecating and other-deprecating humor. *Evolutionary Psychology, 6*, 393–408

Greenhaus, J. H., & Beutell, N. J. (1985). Sources of conflict between work and family roles. *Academy of Management Review, 10*, 76–88.

Haar, J. M. (2006). The downside of coping: Work-family conflict, employee burnout and the moderating effects of coping strategies. *Journal of Management & Organization, 12*, 146–159.

Hahn, V. C., Binnewies, C., Sonnentag, S., & Mojza, E. J. (2011). Learning how to recover from job stress: Effects of a recovery training program on recovery, recovery-related self-efficacy, and well-being. *Journal of Occupational Health Psychology, 16*, 202–216.

Hahn, V. C., & Dormann, C. (2013). The role of partners and children for employees' psychological detachment from work and well-being. *Journal of Applied Psychology, 98*, 26–36.

Halbesleben, J. R., & Wheeler, A. R. (2008). The relative roles of engagement and embeddedness in predicting job performance and intention to leave. *Work & Stress, 22*, 242–256.

Hart, P. M., Wearing, A. J., & Headey, B. (1995). Police stress and well-being: Integrating personality, coping and daily work experiences. *Journal of Occupational and Organizational Psychology, 68*, 133–156.

Healy, C. M., & McKay, M. F. (2000). Nursing stress: The effects of coping strategies and job satisfaction in a sample of Australian nurses. *Journal of Advanced Nursing, 31*, 681–688.

Hobfoll, S. E. (2001). The influence of culture, community, and the nested_self in the stress process: advancing conservation of resources theory. *Applied Psychology, 50*, 337–421.

Hockey, G. R. J. (1997). Compensatory control in the regulation of human performance under stress and high workload: A cognitive-energetical framework. *Biological Psychology, 45*, 73–93.

Ilies, R., Wilson, K. S., & Wagner, D. T. (2009). The spillover of daily job satisfaction onto employees' family lives: The facilitating role of work-family integration. *Academy of Management Journal, 52*, 87–102.

Ito, J. K., & Brotheridge, C. M. (2001). An examination of the roles of career uncertainty, flexibility, and control in predicting emotional exhaustion. *Journal of Vocational Behavior, 59*, 406–424.

Jenaro, C., Flores, N., & Arias, B. (2007). Burnout and coping in human service practitioners. *Professional Psychology: Research and Practice, 38*, 80–87.

Kabanoff, B., & O'Brien, G. E. (1980). Work and leisure: A task attributes analysis. *Journal of Applied Psychology, 65*, 596–609.

Kahn, R.L., & Byosiere, P. (1992). Stress in organizations. In M. D. Dunnette & L. M. Hough (Eds), *Handbook of work and organizational psychology*, vol. 3. Palo Alto, CA: Consulting Psychologists Press.

Karanika-Murray, M., Antoniou, A. S., Michaelides, G., & Cox, T. (2009). Expanding the risk assessment methodology for work-related health: A technique for incorporating multivariate curvilinear effects. *Work & Stress, 23*, 99–119.

Karasek, R., & Theorell, T. (1990). *Healthy work: Stress, productivity and the reconstruction of working life*. New York: Basic Books.

Koeske, G. F. (1993). Coping with job stress: Which strategies work best? *Journal of Occupational and Organizational Psychology, 66*, 319–336.

Kreiner, G. E. (2006). Consequences of work-home segmentation or integration: A person-environment fit perspective. *Journal of Organizational Behavior, 27*, 485–507.

Kreiner, G. E., Hollensbe, E. C., & Sheep, M. L. (2009). Balancing borders and bridges: Negotiating the work-home interface via boundary work tactics. *Academy of Management Journal, 52*, 704–730.

Lambert, S. (1990). Processes linking work and family: A critical review and research agenda. *Human Relations, 43,* 239–257.

Latack, J.C. (1986). Coping with job stress: Measures and future directions for scale development. *Journal of Applied Psychology, 3*, 377–385.

Lazarus, R. L., & Folkman, S. (1984). *Stress, appraisal, and coping.* New York: Springer.

Lee, R. T., & Ashforth, B. E. (1993). A further examination of managerial burnout: Toward an integrated model. *Journal of Organizational Behavior, 14*, 3–20.

Lee, R. T. & Ashforth, B. E. (1996). A meta-analytic examination of the correlates of the three dimensions of job burnout. *Journal of Applied Psychology, 81*, 123–133.

Leiter, M. P. (1991). Coping patterns as predictors of burnout: The function of control and escapist coping patterns. *Journal of Organizational Behaviour, 12,* 123–144.

Leiter, M. P. (1993). Burnout as a developmental process: Consideration of models. In W. B. Schaufeli, C. Maslach, & T. Marek (Eds), *Professional burnout: Recent developments in theory and research.* Washington DC: Taylor and Francis.

Mallak, L. A. (1998). Measuring resilience in health care provider organizations. *Health Manpower Management, 24*, 148–152.

Mansfield, R., & Evans, M. G. (1975). Work and non-work in two occupational groups. *Industrial Relations, 6,* 48–54.

Martin, R. A., Puhlik-Doris, P., Larsen, G., Gray, J., & Weir, K. (2003). Individual differences in uses of humor and their relation to psychological well-being: Development of the Humor Styles Questionnaire. *Journal of Research in Personality, 37*, 48–75.

Maslach, C., & Goldberg, J. (1998). Prevention of burnout: New perspectives. *Applied Preventive Psychology, 7*, 63–74.

Maslach, C., & Jackson, S. E. (1981). *Maslach Burnout Inventory*. Palo Alto, CA: Consulting Psychology Press.

Maslach, C., Schaufeli, W. B., & Leiter, M. P. (2001). Job burnout. *Annual Review of Psychology, 52,* 397–422.

Meijman, T. F., & Mulder, G. (1998). Psychological aspects of workload. In P. J. D. Drenth & H. Thierry (Eds.), *Handbook of work and organizational psychology* (vol. 2, pp. 5–33). Hove: Psychology Press.

Meissner, M. (1971). The long arm of the job: A study of work and leisure. *Industrial Relations, 10,* 239–260

Nippert-Eng, C. (1996). Calendars and keys: The classification of 'home' and 'work'. *Sociological Forum, 11,* 563–582.

Ohly, S., Sonnentag, S., Niessen, C., & Zapf, D. (2010). Diary studies in organizational research: An introduction and some practical recommendations. *Journal of Personnel Psychology, 9,* 79–93.

Ouwehand, C., de Ridder, D. F. D., & Bensing, J. M. (2007). A review of successful aging models: Proposing proactive coping as an important additional strategy. *Clinical Psychology Review, 27,* 873–884.

Park, Y., Fritz, C., & Jex, S. M. (2011). Relationships between work-home segmentation and psychological detachment from work: The role of communication technology use at home. *Journal of Occupational Health Psychology, 16,* 457–467.

Park, Y., & Jex, S. M. (2011). Work-home boundary management using communication and information technology. *International Journal of Stress Management, 18,* 133–152.

Peeters, M. C. W., Montgomery, A. J., Bakker, A. B., & Schaufeli, W. B. (2005). Balancing work and home: How job and home demands are related to burnout. *International Journal of Stress Management, 12,* 43–61.

Peterson, U., Bergström, G., Samuelsson, M., Åsberg, M., & Nygren, Å. (2008). Reflecting peer-support groups in the prevention of stress and burnout: Randomized controlled trial. *Journal of Advanced Nursing, 63,* 506–516.

Petrou, P., Demerouti, E., Peeters, M. C. W., Schaufeli, W. B., & Hetland, J. (2012). Crafting a job on a daily basis: Contextual correlates and the link to work engagement. *Journal of Organizational Behavior, 33,* 1120–1141.

Petrou, P., Demerouti, E., & Schaufeli, W.B. (2014). Employee job crafting in changing environments: Longitudinal relationships with antecedents and outcomes. *Manuscript submitted for publication.*

Podsakoff, N. P., LePine, J. A., & LePine, M. A. (2007). Differential challenge stressor-hindrance stressor relationships with job attitudes, turnover intentions, turnover and withdrawal behavior: A meta-analysis. *Journal of Applied Psychology, 92,* 438–454.

Powell, G. N., & Greenhaus, J. H. (2010). Sex, gender, and the work-to-family interface: Exploring negative and positive interdependencies. *Academy of Management Journal, 53,* 513–534.

De Rijk, A. E., Le Blance, P. M. Le, Schaufeli, W. B., & de Jonge, J. de (1998). Active coping and need for control as moderators of the Job Demand-Control Model: Effects on burnout. *Journal of Occupational and Organizational Psychology, 71,* 1–18.

Roger, D., Jarvis, G., & Najarian, B. (1993). Detachment and coping: The construction and validation of a new scale for measuring coping strategies. *Personality and Individual Differences, 15,* 619–626.

Roth, S., & Cohen, L. J. (1986). Approach, avoidance, and coping with stress. *American Psychologist, 41,* 813–819.

Rousseau, D. M. (1978). Relationship of work to nonwork. *Journal of Applied Psychology, 63,* 513–517.

Salanova, M., & Schaufeli, W.B. (2008). A cross-national study of work engagement as a mediator between job resources and proactive behaviour. *International Journal of Human Resource Management, 19*, 116–131.

Sanz-Vergel, A. I., Demerouti, E., Moreno-Jiménez, B., & Mayo, M. (2010). Work-family balance and energy: A day-level study on recovery conditions. *Journal of Vocational Behavior, 76*, 118–130.

Schaubroek, J., & Merritt, D. E. (1997). Divergent effects of job control on coping with work stressors: The key role of self-efficacy. *Academy of Management Journal, 40*, 738–754.

Schaufeli, W. B., Leiter, M. P., & Maslach, C. (2009) Burnout: 35 years of research and practice. *Career Development International, 14*, 204 – 220.

Schmitt, A., Zacher, H., & Frese, M. (2012) The buffering effect of selection, optimization, and compensation strategy use on the relationship between problem solving demands and occupational well-being: A daily diary study. *Journal of Occupational Health Psychology, 17*, 139–149.

Singh, J., Goolsby, J. R., & Rhoads, G. K. (1994). Behavioral and psychological consequences of boundary spanning burnout for customer service representatives. *Journal of Marketing Research, 31*, 558–569.

Somech, A., & Drach-Zahavy, A. (2000). Understanding extra-role behavior in schools: The relationships between job satisfaction, sense of efficacy, and teachers' extra-role behavior, *Teaching and Teacher Education, 16*, 649–659.

Sonnentag, S. (2001). Work, recovery activities, and individual well-being: A diary study. *Journal of Occupational Health Psychology, 6*, 196–210.

Sonnentag, S., Binnewies, C., & Mojza, A.J. (2008). Did you have a nice evening?: A day-level study on recovery experiences, sleep, and affect. *Journal of Applied Psychology, 93*, 674–684.

Sonnentag, S., & Fritz, C. (2007). The recovery experience questionnaire: Development and validation of a measure for assessing recuperation and unwinding from work. *Journal of Occupational Health Psychology, 12*, 204–221.

Sonnentag, S., Kuttler, I., & Fritz, C. (2010). Job stressors, emotional exhaustion, and need for recovery: A multi-source study on the benefits of psychological detachment. *Journal of Vocational Behavior, 76*, 355–365.

Sonnentag, S., & Natter, E. (2004). Flight attendants' daily recovery from work: Is there no place like home? *International Journal of Stress Management, 11*, 366–391.

Swetz, K. M., Harrington, S. E., Matsuyama, R. K., Shanafelt, T. D., & Lyckholm, L. J. (2009). *Journal of Palliative Medicine, 12*, 773–777.

Swider, B. W., & Zimmerman, R. D. (2010). Born to burnout: A meta-analytic path model of personality, job burnout, and work outcomes. *Journal of Vocational Behavior, 76*, 487–506.

Terry, D. D. J., Callan, V. J., & Sartori, G. (1996). Employee adjustment to an organizational merger: Stress, coping and intergroup differences. *Stress Medicine, 12*, 105–122.

Thornton, P. I. (1992). The relation of coping, appraisal and burnout in mental health workers. *The Journal of Psychology, 126*, 261–271.

Tims, M., & Bakker, A.B. (2010). Job crafting: Towards a new model of individual job redesign. *South African Journal of Industrial Psychology, 36*, 1–9.

Tims, M., Bakker, A. B., & Derks, D. (2012). Development and validation of the job crafting scale. *Journal of Vocational Behavior, 80*, 173–186.

Tims, M., Bakker, A. B., & Derks, D. (2013). The impact of job crafting on job demands, job resources, and well-being. *Journal of Occupational Health Psychology, 18,* 230–240.

Van den Broeck, A., Vander Elst, T., Dikkers, J., De Lange, A., & De Witte, H. (2012). This is funny: On the beneficial role of self-enhancing and affiliative humor in job design. *Psichothema, 24,* 87–93.

Van den Heuvel, M., Demerouti, E., & Peeters, M.C.W. (2012). Succesvol job craften door middel van een groepstraining (Successful job crafting through a group training). In J. de Jonge, M. C. W. Peeters, S. Sjollema, & H. de Zeeuw (Eds), *Scherp in Werk: Vijf routes naar optimale inzetbaarheid* (pp. 7–20). Assen: Van Gorcum.

Van Eerde, W. (2000). Procrastination: Self-regulation in initiating aversive goals. *Applied Psychology: An International Review, 49,* 372–389.

Wallace, J. E., & Brinkerhoff, M. B. (1991). The measurement of burnout revisited. *Journal of Social Service Research, 14,* 85–111.

Warr, P. (1994). A conceptual framework for the study of work and mental health. *Work & Stress, 8,* 84–97.

Wilensky, H. L. (1960). Work, careers and social integration. *International Social Science Journal, 12,* 543–560.

Winningham, M. L., Nail, L. M., Burke, M. B., Brophy, L., Cimprich, L. S., Jones, S., Beck, S., et al. (1994). Fatigue and the cancer experience: The state of the knowledge. *Oncology Nursing Forum, 21,* 23–36.

Wrzesniewski, A., & Dutton, J.E. (2001). Crafting a job: Revisioning employees as active crafters of their work. *Academy of Management Review, 26,* 179–201.

Yela, J. R. (1996). Desgaste emocional, estrategias de afrontamiento y trastornos psicofisiológicos en profesionales de la enseñanza. *Boletín de Psicología, 50,* 37–52.

Zacher, H., & Frese, M. (2011). Maintaining a focus on opportunities at work: The interplay between age, job complexity, and the use of selection, optimization, and compensation strategies. *Journal of Organizational Behavior, 32,* 291–318.

Zedeck, S., & Mosier, K. L. (1990). Work in the family and employing organization. *American Psychologist, 45,* 240–251.

4 The good and bad of working relationships

Implications for burnout

Arla Day and Michael P. Leiter

The concept of burnout materialized in the 1970s (Schaufeli et al., 2009), and was defined as a multidimensional syndrome that is experienced in response to chronic job stressors (Maslach, 1993). Much has been written about burnout, and given the amount of time people spend at work each week (e.g., typical estimates across countries for full-time employees range from 40 hours/week in Canada to 42 hours/week in UK, and 43 hours/week in Australia; Organization for Economic Co-operation and Development, 2012; Statistics Canada, 2011), it is not surprising that chronic, negative working conditions can lead to feelings of exhaustion, cynicism, and inefficacy. It also is not surprising that employees form many relationships – both good and bad – with the people with whom they interact at work, including supervisors, clients, and coworkers. Ironically, these relationships constitute both potential chronic demands as well as potential resources to reduce demands. Therefore, the quality of these relationships has a huge impact on employees' level of burnout and overall health and well-being. Moreover, in an information/service economy, the quality of working relationships has vital importance for both individual career development as well as organizational productivity.

Therefore, we will review the longstanding research activity pertaining to these working relationships, with an emphasis on coworker and supervisor relationships and burnout, situating the relationships within frameworks of work demands and resources, as well as of social motivation and fit. We will also examine the somewhat elusive moderating effect of support on the relationship of work demands with burnout, and examine the potential paths through which these relationships may impact burnout, within the context of contemporary research on workplace civility and incivility.

Burnout

As discussed throughout this book, burnout is viewed as a psychological syndrome of exhaustion, cynicism and inefficacy which is experienced in response to chronic job stressors. The genesis of this construct was in the helping professions and service industry, stemming from a noted increase in stress and strain in workers dealing with high-demand customer service issues. In their discussion about the conceptualization of the burnout construct, Schaufeli et al. (2009 pp. 205–206; see also Maslach, 1976; Maslach & Jackson, 1981) noted that:

> Maslach was interested in how these workers coped with their emotional arousal using cognitive strategies such as detached concern. As a result of these interviews she learned that these workers often felt emotionally exhausted, that they developed negative perceptions and feelings about their clients or patients, and that they experienced crises in professional competence as a result of the emotional turmoil.

This research led to the emergence of the three components of emotional exhaustion, depersonalization or cynicism, and lack of personal accomplishment or professional efficacy.

Thus, the burnout literature "had its roots in care-giving and service occupations, in which the core of the job was the relationship between provider and recipient" (Maslach et al., 2001, p. 400). The initial discussions about burnout "began within the human services, because they were better able to give 'voice' to issues of emotions, values, and relationships with people – concepts that had not been widely recognized within the research literature on the workplace" (Schaufeli et al., 2009, p. 206). As such, a large number of burnout studies have been conducted in the service industry, specifically settings devoted to healthcare, social work, policing, legal or psychotherapy (Schaufeli et al., 2009).

Although Maslach originally observed this phenomenon in employees' responses to their clients, the essence of burnout was that it pertained to employees "who work with *people in some capacity*" (Maslach et al., 1996, p. 4; emphasis added). Therefore, burnout includes a variety of occupations outside of the service industry (see Schaufeli et al., 2009). Burnout also includes a variety of working relationships, including those with coworkers and supervisors, in addition to clients.

The qualities of energy, involvement, and efficacy underlie the three aspects of burnout: emotional exhaustion; depersonalization or cynicism; and personal accomplishment or professional efficacy (Maslach & Leiter, 1997). The negative end of these qualities defines burnout while the positive end defines engagement with work. These states define contrasting ends of a continuum of psychological connections with work. Exhaustion has a long-standing status as a medical or psychological syndrome (Fukuda et al., 1994). If exhaustion adequately encompassed burnout, there would be no need to define a new syndrome labeled as burnout. The emergence and persistence of the term burnout implies that it is not synonymous with exhaustion. One reason for the elevation of exhaustion as the dominant feature of burnout was the highly left-skewed distribution of depersonalization scores in the original Maslach Burnout Inventory–Human Services Scale. Because the depersonalization distribution so strongly violated assumptions of normality, it did not contribute much beyond emotional exhaustion when relating burnout to qualities of work environments or health outcomes. With the Maslach Burnout Inventory–Human Services Scale (MBI–GS; Maslach et al., 1996), the less skewed (although still somewhat skewed) cynicism distribution provided the statistical capacity for that second dimension to make distinct contributions in analyses beyond exhaustion.

Cynicism reflects the extent to which people are involved in or dedicated to their work (Maslach & Leiter, 1997). The original depersonalization construct focused on closeness to service recipients (Maslach & Leiter, 1997), whereas cynicism more broadly refers to involvement in work. Involvement is a social construct. In the most immediate sense, it references involvement in people such as service recipients, colleagues, or supervisors. Indirectly, the emotional energy, instrumental support, knowledge, and recognition employees receive from one another have the potential to increase the enjoyment and fulfillment people derive from their work.

Implicit in these definitions of burnout is the importance of the quality of relationships at work on one's level of burnout. Thus, it is not surprising that working relationships may not only increase burnout, but may also have the power to mitigate the negative consequences of stressors and negative work interactions. Given this recognition that the work relationships are important to burnout, we first examine some of the theoretical rationales pertaining to interpersonal relationships at work, in terms of Social Motivation, the Job Demands-Resources Model (Demerouti et al., 2001), Conservation of Resources (Hobfoll, 1989), and the Areas of Worklife Model (Leiter & Maslach, 1999; 2004).

The importance of social relationships to burnout becomes more apparent when considering all three aspects of burnout rather than focusing exclusively on exhaustion. As noted above, although exhaustion has been identified as the defining feature of burnout (and, by some the only feature of burnout; e.g., Shirom, 2005), the cynicism (depersonalization) and inefficacy (diminished personal accomplishment) dimensions of the syndrome justify studying burnout as a phenomenon distinct from exhaustion as a medical or psychiatric diagnosis. The involvement dimension of burnout acknowledges the possibility of connections of social relationships with burnout that go beyond the rather utilitarian perspective based on the balance between the demands and resources based on social encounters throughout the day. The involvement dimension shifts the focus to social motives.

Working relationships and burnout

The leading models of job burnout all acknowledge the importance of collegial and supervisory relationships. Each approach has a position on the nature of those relationships and the means through which they influence employees' levels of energy, involvement, and efficacy. For the most part, the predictions arising from these models regarding the associations of social relationships with burnout are consistent with one another, although it is important to contrast the specific constructs underlying these models.

Social motivation

People pursue three core social motivations within the workplace: Belonging; Nurturance (giving & receiving); and Esteem (Forbes, 2011). Each of these motives encourages constructive involvement in workgroups. We consider these three motives in the context of burnout from the perspective of their goals: that is, to belong, to participate in nurturing interactions, and to feel esteemed by colleagues. These motives have a compelling quality such that employees may evaluate their social encounters at work in terms of the extent to which the encounters help attain or thwart these goals (Forbes, 2011). Civility, as expressions of attention, appreciation, and accommodation of others (Leiter et al., 2012a) indicates that the workplace has the potential to fulfill these social motivations. That is, respectful behaviors contribute to feelings of belongingness, feelings of nurturing, as well as employees' aspirations for esteem (Leiter, 2012).

In contrast, mistreatment (which may encompass a range of behaviors from incivility through abuse and aggression) has the opposite effect: It may diminish the environments' perceived potential to fulfill those core social motives. Instead, mistreatment reduces social motivation with regard to the workgroup in that it signals that social motives are unlikely to find fulfillment in the workgroup. Ultimately, mistreatment signals that people are at risk of being excluded, abused, and denigrated. We propose that perceiving the work environment as antithetical to fulfilling core social motives encourages psychological and physical withdrawal. A risky environment is undeserving of an emotional investment, and escape seems a more reasonable course of action. This reaction can become part of a self-perpetuating process as withdrawal reduces the potential for employees to fulfill their social motives subsequently.

The general constructs underlying the continuum from burnout to engagement (energy, involvement, efficacy) have implications for social motivation, which in turn, have implications for job performance, especially team-based performance. Halbesleben and Bowler (2007, p. 93) argued that employees tended to

> target their investment of resources in response to emotional exhaustion to develop social support through social exchange; specifically, emotional exhaustion was associated with communion striving resources that were manifest in the form of organizational citizenship behaviors targeted at individuals.

We propose that the degree of civility and respect within day-to-day social encounters at work provide definitive information to employees regarding their investment of energy, involvement, and efficacy in their work.

Job demands-resources model

Demerouti et al. (2001) developed the job demands-resources model, which originally proposed that job demands can lead to exhaustion and positive work resources can lead to increased engagement. This model was later expanded such that it highlighted the dual processes of demands leading to strain, and resources increasing motivation. We can view working relationships as either a demand or a resource, depending on the quality of the relationship. Bakker and Demerouti

(2007) defined resources in terms of work-related factors that may "stimulate personal growth, learning, and development" (p. 312), which would include supervisor and coworker support. In terms of demands, mistreatment aggravates exhaustion, which in turn reduces motivation to perform as part of a group and increases motivation to find social support within the workgroup or elsewhere (Leiter, 2012). The specific sources of resources and demands (e.g., from supervisors, coworkers, and clients) may have unique effects on burnout.

Conservation of resources model

According to Hobfoll's (1989, 1998; Hobfoll & Freedy, 1993) conservation of resources model, employees are motivated to seek out and retain valuable resources. Hobfoll (1989) defined resources as "objects, personal characteristics, conditions, or energies that are valued by the individual or that serve as a means for attainment of these objects, personal characteristics, conditions, or energies" (p. 516). Positive work relationships may be viewed as such a resource and may be able to improve individual well-being and potentially reduce the negative effects of job demands/stressors. Halbesleben (2006) argued that "if social support resources are reinforcing positive images of oneself . . . an individual would be less likely to pull away from that person (thus, depersonalization would be less likely) and would improve one's perceptions of personal accomplishment" (p. 1135). Aryee et al. (2008) used the conservation of resources model to conceptualize abusive supervision as a workplace stressor, in that it threatens the subordinate's resources such as social support, and will create emotional exhaustion.

Areas of worklife model

Leiter and Maslach (1999, 2004) introduced the Areas of Worklife Model of burnout by identifying six areas of organizational life that tend to be related to the three aspects of burnout. *Manageable Workload* involves having sufficient time and resources to address work demands. Conversely, overload reflects an imbalance of work demands relative to available time and capacity. The area of *Control* involves having sufficient authority and independence to make meaningful decisions about one's work. *Reward* entails receiving sufficient recognition and compensation for work. *Community* entails participating in a positive and fulfilling workplace social climate. *Fairness* involves experiencing an appropriate level of distributive, procedural, and relational justice at work. Finally, the area of *Values* comprises the confidence that one's professional values align well with the employer's organizational values.

The model makes a direct reference to the quality of working relationships by including Community as one of the six areas of worklife. The quality of social relationships has implications for the other areas of worklife. For example, relational justice reflects the quality of social interaction of employees with decision makers and reward reflects the likelihood of leaders expressing appreciation for employees' contributions. This model points towards improving the quality of working relationships as a potential focus for interventions.

Although these four models have unique implications for how we view social interactions at work, they all share the view that social relationships at work have consequences for employees' experience of job burnout. Constructive relationships increase employees' resources directly or indirectly by providing ways of accessing information, materials, or opportunities. Although resources may be available, it requires some amount of individual initiative to put those resources to work. This ability to increase resources is related to recent work on job crafting, which explores individual strategies for improving the potential to thrive in a given work environment (Tims et al., 2013; see also Chapter 3, this volume). Mistreatment increases the demands employees experience at work. Mistreatment both absorbs energy and encourages employees to increase their psychological distance from the workplace.

Summary

The Job Demands-Resources model and the Conservation of Resources model both emphasize the utility of social relationships. The core premise is that constructive relationships with people at work serve as conduits for accessing a variety of useful assets/resources (e. g., knowledge, skills, materials, physical energy). In contrast, negative social encounters become demands or threats to one's resources. Unpleasant social encounters require employees to expend existing resources in attempts to cope, diminishing their potential for effective engagement with their work. Alternatively, the Areas of Worklife Model emphasizes the fit between employees' social motivations and the opportunities within the work environment. For example, employees who are motivated to give and receive nurturance would find fulfillment in a workgroup comprising like-minded colleagues but would have greater vulnerability to burnout in an emotionally cold or abusive social climate. From this perspective, the quality of social relationships has implications for burnout that go beyond their utility as resource channels.

Supervisor and coworker support and burnout

Based on these theoretical foundations, we examine the impact of both the quality of relationships and the source of the relationships on the components of burnout in more depth. That is, we can categorize the quality of working relationships into positive (e.g., support) and negative (e.g., aggression, bullying, incivility) research perspectives. We also can examine the "source" of relationships in terms of supervisors, coworkers, and clients or service recipients.

Research has demonstrated a link between burnout and one's relationships with coworkers and supervisors (e.g., Halbesleben, 2006; Leiter & Maslach, 1988). A lack of social support is often identified as being a key predictor of burnout (Bakker et al., 2004; Ray & Miller, 1994; Yürür & Sarikaya, 2012). Conversely, a substantial body of research has indicated that colleague and supervisor social support can reduce burnout (Collings & Murray, 1996). Additionally, a smaller body of research has suggested that it may moderate the relationship between job stressors and burnout (Um & Harrison, 1998), although some of the results are in the opposite direction as hypothesized (e.g., Jenkins & Elliott, 2004).

Direct effects of support

There is a fairly consistent literature indicating that high levels of supervisor support are associated with reduced burnout (Gibson et al., 2009; Sand & Miyazaki, 2000). For example, in his meta-analytic study of 114 studies on support and burnout, Halbesleben (2006) found that coworker and supervisor support were related negatively to exhaustion and depersonalization, and positively to personal accomplishment.

This finding seems to hold across a variety of occupations and countries. For example, teachers in Iowa who reported that they had supportive supervisors and indicated that they received positive feedback concerning their skills and abilities from others were less vulnerable to burnout (Russell et al., 1987, p. 269). In their study of correctional staff working in prisons in the US, Lambert et al. (2010) found that both coworker support and supervisor support were associated with reduced levels of depersonalization (Lambert et al., 2010). Similarly, supervisor support was associated with reduced emotional exhaustion (Lambert et al., 2010). Mental health and substance abuse staff at a prison in the US who perceived more support from the deputy wardens of special services tended to be less exhausted (Garland, 2004). In their study of midwives in Poland, Kalicińska et al. (2012) found that social support from supervisors was associated with lowered exhaustion and depersonalization, and that support from coworkers was associated with lower emotional exhaustion. Support from a supervisor was negatively related to emotional exhaustion, positively correlated with personal accomplishment, but was unrelated to depersonalization in social workers in Turkey (Yurur & Sarikaya, 2012). Finally, in their study of Dutch medical residents, Prins et al. (2007) found that residents who were dissatisfied with the level of appreciative support received from their supervisors tended to report higher levels of emotional exhaustion. Moreover, they found that the best predictor of residents' burnout was their degree of dissatisfaction with the emotional support received from supervisors.

Support as a moderator of the stressor-burnout relationship

In addition to these direct effects, support may have a moderating effect on the relationship between stressors and burnout (e.g., Etzion, 1984). According to the demands-resources model, burnout occurs when too many demands are made of a person without providing the resources necessary to accomplish the job (Bakker et al., 2005; Demerouti et al., 2001). Therefore, supervisors may serve as a buffer to stressful work environments. In support of this hypothesis, Gibson et al. (2009) found that "supervisor support acted to protect therapists from reduced personal accomplishment when faced with high levels of perceived work demands" (p.

1029). Chamberlain and Hodson (2010) argued that coworkers "can provide both emotional support and instrumental aid through provision of useful insider information about how to survive and prosper in a workplace" (p. 460), and thus they proposed that coworker support may be a method to cope with stress experienced from mistreatment. Therefore, it may be viewed as a potential moderator of the relationship between negative work relationships and burnout. Lambert et al. (2010) suggested both moderating and mediating effects as potential explanations for the negative relationship they found between support and burnout for correctional staff members. They argued that perhaps support might have buffered the negative impact of job demands and helped staff deal with their workplace issues, thus resulting in decreased burnout. However, more research is needed to examine these potential moderation relationships.

Mediators of the support-burnout relationship

Alternatively, Lambert et al. (2010) also suggested that the correctional staff members who felt more supported by their supervisor may have felt that they were more valued and respected, which consequently may have decreased the likelihood that they viewed their job as emotionally straining, leading to reduced burnout. Lambert and colleagues' subsequent research found a negative relationship between trust in supervisor and burnout in correctional staff (Lambert et al., 2012), suggesting that these perceptions may be a mediating factor in the support-burnout relationship. Similar to Lambert et al. (2010), other researchers have argued that the support-burnout relationship may be mediated by other factors. In their cross-sectional study of employees from two Spanish public organizations (i.e., a city council and a university), Blanch and Aluja (2012) found that supervisor support was associated with lower burnout for both men and women. This relationship was fully mediated by the extent to which work interfered with family, but only for women: That is, women who had high supervisor support also reported lower levels of work interference with family (WIF), and they subsequently reported lower levels of burnout. Conversely, the relationship between family support and burnout was completely mediated by WIF for men. These results suggest that the mechanism by which the quality of relationships (in terms of support) reduces burnout may be through the reduction of demands and stressors.

Support as a moderator of burnout-outcome relationships

There is a solid background of literature linking burnout to other negative physical health symptoms, such as musculoskeletal pain (Armon et al., 2010; see also Chapter 2, this volume) and cardiovascular disease (Melamed et al., 2006), negative psychological health issues (e.g., poor mental health; Tang et al., 2001), and work behavior outcomes (e.g., turnover intentions; Laschinger et al., 2009b). However, it also is possible that support may play a multi-function role, not only by reducing burnout initially and buffering the negative impact of demands on burnout, but also potentially reducing burnout's negative impact on other work outcomes, such as turnover. In their survey of 287 call center employees from seven call centers, Choi et al. (2012) concluded that 35 percent of variance in turnover intentions were explained by emotional exhaustion, depersonalization, and reduced personal accomplishment, with both exhaustion and depersonalization being most strongly related to turnover intentions. Their relevant finding in the context of supervisor support was support's impact on the burnout-turnover intentions relationship: Choi et al. (2012) found that the relationship between depersonalization and turnover intentions was moderated by supervisor support. Support may act in a similar role with other work outcomes.

Negative working relationships and burnout

There has been much written about negative working relationships in terms of violence (Hesketh et al., 2003) and bullying at work (Einarsen et al., 2011; Notelaers et al., 2006), abusive (and toxic) supervision (Tepper, 2007), and incivility (Giumetti et al., 2012), as well as their impact on individual outcomes, such as burnout (Deery et al., 2011; Hershcovis & Barling, 2010). These types of negative working relationships have deleterious effects on employees, because they threaten the resources of the individual. That is, mistreatment may decrease feelings of belongingness, nurturing, and self-esteem (Leiter, 2012).

Many of these studies highlight the proclivity to identify differences among forms of workplace mistreatment, depending on the intentions of perpetrators, the power distinctions between perpetrator and recipient, and the medium of delivery (e.g., verbal, physical, gestural). Despite these differences among the constructs, in her meta-analysis of mistreatment at work, Hershcovis (2011) found that the commonalities among diverse forms of mistreatment, such as bullying and incivility, outweigh their differences. Overall, she demonstrated that workplace mistreatment occurs more frequently in poorly managed work settings. It results in distress for perpetrators, recipients, and bystanders. One form of mistreatment does not have a consistently more powerful effect than another or have a unique association with a specific form of distress. She also noted that the many measures purporting to measure a specific form of mistreatment lack explicit reference to some of that form's distinctive qualities. For example, a widely used measure of incivility (Workplace Incivility Scale; Cortina et al., 2001) makes no reference to the defining term of "ambiguous intent." Similarly, bullying scales rarely refer to its defining and distinctive characteristic of repeated instances over a prolonged period. Subsequent research with more refined measures or designs may uncover complex patterns of distinct relationships. At present, research supports the contention that the qualities of social relationships that people maintain at work have an enduring and close association with their sense of well-being and contentment at work and beyond.

Aggression and burnout

Workplace aggression is defined as negative acts or intentionally harmful behavior committed against an organization or its members, which employees perceive to be directed against them, and which they are motivated to avoid (Hershcovis & Barling, 2010; Mitchell & Ambrose, 2012). These aggressive acts can be clustered into three categories: obstructionism, overt aggression, and expressions of hostility (LeBlanc & Barling, 2004). These types of aggression can be perpetrated by various constituents (Hershcovis & Barling, 2010) such as supervisors, coworkers, customers, and patients.

Coworker and supervisor aggression

Aggressive acts perpetrated by colleagues and supervisors have been shown to be related to decreased health (Hershcovis & Barling, 2010; LeBlanc & Barling, 2004; Schat & Kelloway, 2005). Compared to aggressive acts committed by coworkers and outsiders, aggressive acts committed by supervisors have been shown to have the most adverse effects on employees (Hershcovis & Barling, 2010). In general, supervisor aggression tends to be positively correlated with emotional exhaustion (e.g., Hershcovis & Barling, 2010). The reasons for the stronger association with supervisor mistreatment may reflect the power imbalance between employees and supervisors, supervisors' greater potential to influence employees' job or career outcomes, the symbolic quality of supervisors' behavior, or some combination of these factors. The precise mechanisms are a potentially fruitful focus of future research.

Although supervisor aggression may have the most negative effects on employees, aggression committed by coworkers also has a negative impact on individual well-being and burnout (Hershcovis & Barling, 2010; LeBlanc & Kelloway, 2002; Merecz et al., 2009). For example, Merecz et al. (2009) found that aggressive acts committed by coworkers were associated with increased depersonalization and emotional exhaustion.

Customer and patient aggression

Not surprisingly, there is a relatively large literature pertaining to customer and patient aggression and employee burnout. Although Hershcovis and Barling (2010) found that, compared to supervisor and coworker aggression, aggression by outsiders had a smaller effect on employee outcomes, there are fairly consistent findings showing that aggression is associated with increased emotional exhaustion (Grandey et al., 2004), and with some research showing that it is related to depersonalization (Ben-Zur & Yagil, 2005; Merecz et al., 2009). Moreover, in their study of British nurses, Deery et al. (2011) found that outsider aggression was more strongly related to burnout than was supervisor and coworker aggression combined. Similarly, in their study of patient aggression toward nurses, Winstanley and Whittington (2002) found that staff who reported being victimized

by patients frequently had higher levels of emotional exhaustion and depersonalization. They concluded that these results may suggest that aggression leads
to increased burnout; however, the alternative explanation (i.e., burnout may lead
to increased vulnerability to victimization) must also be considered (Winstanley &
Whittington, 2002).

Abusive supervision

Another form of mistreatment, abusive supervision, has been the topic of recent
studies. Abusive supervision is defined as "subordinates' perceptions of the extent
to which supervisors engage in the sustained display of hostile verbal and nonverbal behaviors, excluding physical contact" (Tepper, 2000, p. 178), such as
criticizing subordinates in public, rude behaviors, and coercion (Bies, 2001; Bies
& Tripp, 2005). There have been consistent findings across studies that abusive
supervision is associated with increased emotional exhaustion (e.g., Aryee et al.,
2008; Duffy et al., 2002; Tepper, 2000; Wu & Hu, 2009), although there is less
evidence for its relationship with cynicism and professional efficacy.

Other forms of mistreatment have been studied, although to a lesser extent.
For example, female correction officers who reported harassment also reported
increased burnout; however, this relationship was not significant for male correction officers (Savicki et al., 2003). Moreover, more "minor" types of mistreatment
have important implications for employee burnout levels.

Incivility

Incivility is defined as low-intensity, rude, and discourteous behaviors that violate
workplace norms for mutual interpersonal respect (Andersson & Pearson, 1999).
However, unlike some other forms of negative, deviant interpersonal behaviors,
such as aggression and bullying, a key aspect of incivility is that there is an
ambiguous intent to harm the target (Andersson & Pearson, 1999): That is, it is
not clear whether the perceived uncivil behavior was intended to be rude and/or
harm the individual.

Despite the low intensity and ambiguous intent to harm of incivility, it is an
important contributing factor to burnout for three reasons. First, incivility is a much
more frequent occurrence in the workplace than more serious forms of deviant
social behaviors, such as violence. That is, more employees engage in it and are
exposed to it, and their frequency of exposure is much higher. For example, Sliter
et al. (2010) found that 100 percent of bank tellers in their study reported
experiencing at least some degree of customer incivility during a one-month
period. Giumetti et al. (2012) found that cyber incivility was experienced by 26
percent of their sample of university staff members and by 35 percent of their
business school alumni from a southeastern university in the US.

Moreover, the frequency of reported incivility makes it an important variable
to study not only because of the numbers of employees affected, but also for

practical, methodological reasons, such that the incivility data tend to be less skewed than are aggression and violence data.

Second, uncivil behaviors tend to be reciprocated, which may create a workplace culture of incivility. Lim et al. (2008) suggested that employees tend to respond to incivility with more incivility, thus perpetuating future negative social exchanges. Similarly, Bunk and Magley (2013) found that instances of incivility were reciprocated when employees reacted emotionally to initial uncivil behaviors. Third, incivility may be an instigator of more severe workplace behaviors: Andersson and Pearson (1999) proposed an "incivility spiral," in which relatively minor uncivil behaviors may spiral into more serious behaviors and more negative interpersonal exchanges. Conversely, reciprocity of respectful and civil behaviors may promote a more respectful and civil work environment (Porath & Erez, 2009; Robinson & O'Leary-Kelly, 1998). Therefore, studying incivility in the context of burnout is valuable. There are two areas of research pertaining to incivility at work: customer incivility and supervisor/coworker incivility.

Supervisor and coworker incivility

In a longitudinal analysis, Leiter et al. (2012b) found that at a one-year interval, coworker and supervisor incivility contributed to changes in exhaustion and cynicism. In contrast, coworker civility predicted changes in professional efficacy and work engagement as measured by the Utrecht Work Engagement Scale (Schaufeli et al., 2006). Changes in instigated incivility were inversely associated with coworker civility. In a study of Romanian teachers, supervisor and coworker incivility accounted for 24 percent of the variance in cynicism and professional inefficacy (Sulea et al., 2012). Interestingly, workplace incivility does not have to be experienced face-to-face. For example, Giumetti et al. (2012) found that cyber supervisor incivility was related to increased employee burnout. Lim and Teo (2009) proposed that cyber incivility may be due to the fast-paced nature of e-mail leading people to think that they do not have the time to be courteous. Because of the lack of tone and body language in text-based messages, they have an increased chance of being interpreted as uncivil (Giumetti et al., 2012).

Customer incivility

Customer incivility has been shown to relate to an employee's level of emotional exhaustion (e.g., Kern & Grandey, 2009). Firefighters who experienced incivility from victims, or from the family and friends of the victims, reported higher levels of emotional exhaustion, even after controlling for the age and negative affectivity of the firefighters (Sliter, 2012). Van Jaarsveld et al. (2010) found that customer service employees who experienced higher customer incivility also reported higher emotional exhaustion. Dormann and Zapf (2004) identified four themes of customer-related social stressors related to aggression and incivility: disproportionate customer expectations, customer verbal aggression, disliked customers, and ambiguous customer expectations. These four stressors predicted all three components of burnout (i.e., exhaustion, personal accomplishment, and depersonalization) beyond the effects of several control variables.

Summary

The focus on workplace incivility over the previous decade has continued to be an enduring focus on social support as a direct or a moderating resource to alleviate burnout. The distinct contribution of the incivility construct is a focus on the micro level of day-to-day social encounters of employees with their coworkers, supervisors, and service recipients. In contrast, the previous focus on social support typically referred to the general social climate within a workgroup or organization. The more specific focus of incivility has the potential to identify intervention strategies based upon changing the relative frequency of specific negative social behaviors occurring within the workplace.

Interventions to improve working relationships and decrease burnout

Many researchers have argued for programs to help increase supportive work environments. For example, over 25 years ago, Russell et al. (1987) concluded that having supervisors acknowledge teachers' skills and abilities (as a form of support) would be "an important component to include in programs designed to prevent teacher burnout" (Russell et al., 1987, p. 272). More recently, Maslach et al. (2012) noted that there has always been an interest in how to deal with burnout: That is, how can we use "new knowledge gained through research [and apply it] to the design of effective interventions" (p. 296)? Despite this call for more intervention research, there has been very little validated work directed at improving work relationships and decreasing burnout.

One program that addresses incivility within work groups, CREW (i.e., Civility, Respect, and Engagement at Work; Osatuke et al., 2009) has been examined and validated in several contexts. CREW involves using organizational employees as facilitators who help groups identify civility-based workplace relationship issues, and who lead regular sessions for these workgroup members over a six-month period. Each workgroup has the autonomy and flexibility to identify their own workplace civility and relationship issues, their short- and long-term goals, and the means to achieve the goals. They have several resources available to them (e.g., a toolkit of group exercises and discussion topics to help guide their discussions and achieve their goals) and can adapt the activities and resources to meet their group needs. For example, activities may include role-playing new ways of responding civilly to colleagues and of addressing others' uncivil behaviors.

Osatuke et al. (2009) found that CREW was associated with improved civility among coworkers at the Veterans Health Administration across the US. The CREW intervention at the VHA involved having weekly meetings, facilitated by a trained practitioner, during which employees were able to discuss civility in their workplace. Based on ideas rooted in client-centered therapy, the trained facilitators allowed the organization's members to design their own remedies, while supporting their implementation, rather than simply imposing solutions. The flexibility of the CREW allowed participants to adjust their goals as change occurred (Osatuke et al., 2009).

Building on Osatuke et al.'s work, Leiter et al. (2011) studied civility and incivility in a sample of health-care workers in Canada (N=1,173 for Time 1; N=907 for Time 2). They replicated Osatuke et al.'s (2009) finding that CREW was able to improve civility compared to the control groups as well as decrease supervisor incivility. Although coworker and instigated incivility followed the same pattern as civility, this decrease did not reach statistical significance. A multivariate test indicated that a cluster comprising exhaustion, cynicism, and turnover intention improved relative to the contrast group. Examination of the univariate effects identified this interaction to be significant for exhaustion.

Moreover, Leiter et al. (2011) found that improvements in civility fully mediated the relationship between emotional exhaustion and several outcomes, such as cynicism, management trust, and organizational commitment. This mediation supports the proposition that improvements aimed at civility play a definitive role in addressing aspects of job burnout. A change in the quality of social interaction among colleagues shifts the balance of impact from social encounters towards the resource side and away from the demand side of the equation. To the extent that civility characterizes a work environment, employees experience social interactions as increasing their work-related resource base. One possible mechanism underlying these relationships is that workgroup civility increases employees' confidence that their colleagues' energy, knowledge, and emotional support are more available to them. The greater availability of these resources allows employees to improve their energetic resources resulting in lower levels of exhaustion, consistent with the construct of job crafting (Tims et al., 2013). Associated with the improvement in exhaustion is a closer involvement with the work setting, as reflected in lower levels of cynicism and turnover intentions. In this way, the mediation role of civility in the relationship of intervention with burnout is consistent with constructs within both the JD-R model and the COR model.

From the perspective of social motivation, the mediating role of civility is consistent with the proposition that the CREW intervention groups improve employees' potential to fulfill their motivation for belonging, nurturance, and esteem. In the Leiter et al. (2011) study, civility and coworker/supervisor incivility were defined and operationalized from the perspective of the recipient of these social behaviors. The CREW civility measure (Osatuke et al., 2009) explicitly refers to respect in two items, highlighting the closeness between the constructs of civility and respect. In addition, civility characterizes behavior that confirms to recipients that they belong within that social context (Cortina, 2008; Laschinger et al., 2009a). It also follows that nurturance is more readily available in civil relationships than in uncivil relationships (Zurbriggen & Capdevila, 2010). The primary distinction of the social motivation model with the resource-focused models (JD-R; COR) is that from the social motivation perspective: civil collegial relationships are an end in themselves. In contrast, the JD-R and COR models consider work-based social relationships as principally a means that facilitates the pursuit of performance objectives or personal aspirations at work. These findings provide "support for the assertion that improving working relationships plays an important role in alleviating burnout" (Maslach et al., 2012, p. 297).

Agenda for future research

We have a solid understanding of the factors leading to burnout, and more specifically, the impact of working relationships on the three components of burnout. However, more research is needed to better understand the specifics of these relationships. We have highlighted some of the current literature in Figure 4.1 as means of identifying gaps and potential avenues for future research.

Directionality of the social interactions and burnout relationship

Despite the fact that burnout is described as a "syndrome" (Maslach, 1993) or "process" (Leiter, 1993), and although longitudinal relationships with burnout and social interactions have been suggested, much of the burnout literature has used cross-sectional designs. For example, Karatepe et al. (2009) used a cross-sectional sample, and suggested that verbal abuse from customers can lead to emotional exhaustion, which can deplete available resources if it is continuous, thereby leading to increased turnover intentions and behaviors. Similarly, Winstanley and Whittington (2002, p.302) proposed that aggression can lead to increased burnout and that these

> elevated levels of burnout from all sources might increase vulnerability to victimization. Increases in emotional exhaustion lead directly to an increase in depersonalization as a coping mechanism, which subsequently manifests as a negative behavioral change toward patients, thus rendering staff more vulnerable to further aggression.

However, longitudinal research is needed to examine the direct effects of these working relationships in predicting future levels of exhaustion, cynicism, and professional efficacy.

Interestingly, there is some evidence that the relationship between working relationships and burnout could be cyclical or could spiral. That is, Blau and Andersson (2005) found that work exhaustion at Time 1 was positively related to instigated workplace incivility at Time 2. Bakker et al. (2000) found that depersonalization was longitudinally related to patient demands over a five-year interval. Although they just used a cross-sectional design, van Jaarsveld et al. (2010) found that customer incivility was associated with higher emotional exhaustion in employees, and this exhaustion was associated with higher employee instigated incivility. More longitudinal research is needed to examine this potential cyclical relationship. Finally, incorporating several methodologies typically not used in this literature (such as tracking social encounters, motives, and burnout elements through diary studies) would provide an in-depth understanding of burnout and work relationships over time.

Understanding the moderators & mediators of the working relationship-burnout link

There has been some evidence to suggest that the relationship between working relationships and burnout may be mediated by several factors, such as organizational trust (Miner-Rubino & Reed, 2010) and teacher satisfaction (Grayson & Alvarez, 2008), and may be partially mediated by wishful thinking, coping (Devereux et al., 2009), and psychological climate (Bedi et al., 2012). Future research should incorporate longitudinal designs to explore these possible mediators and to help us better understand the mechanisms for alleviating burnout.

Aside from identifying potential mediators of burnout, previous research has also discovered several workplace variables that can act as moderators of the relationship between the quality of relationships within the workplace and burnout. Supervisor support also may act as a moderator of the burnout-outcome relationship, much the same way that coworker support has been found to moderate the relationship between emotional exhaustion and job satisfaction (Um & Harrison, 1998). Furthermore, there are specific job resources, such as control and receiving feedback, that can moderate the relationship between job demands and feelings of burnout (Bakker et al., 2005).

A challenge in identifying causal directions is the ongoing nature and history of the working relationships being examined. Even when using a longitudinal design, surveys generally assess a social environment that is in equilibrium. Connections between the overall social environment and employees' experiences are more static than dynamic as reflected in large autocorrelations throughout burnout research (Maslach et al., 2001). That is, the relative levels of burnout across people and across work settings stay the same over long periods. A potential contribution of incivility research is its focus on specific social encounters. A daily diary format could identify dependencies between social events and subsequent reports of the qualities underlying the three aspects of burnout: energy, involvement, and efficacy. Parallel measures of specific acts of civility would complement the specific measures of incivility. This approach would have a potential to highlight the impact of specific events against the general background of a supportive or strained social environment.

A conceptual issue raised in the review of models is the role of social motives in the dynamics between social relationships and burnout. Although all perspectives acknowledge an important role for positive and negative social encounters, they propose differing mechanisms through which relationship quality influences burnout and vice versa. That is, the JD-R and COR perspectives emphasize supportive relationships as a means to access resources and mistreatment as occasions to experience additional demands. Alternatively, the Areas of Worklife model emphasizes compatibility between employee social motivations and the work environment, such that a mismatch defines the potential for distress. A given work environment may be pleasant for employees who respond positively to more formal social relationships, while being distressing for colleagues who prefer closer, more informal, personal working relationships. Research models that establish distinct assessments of these two qualities of social encounters could clarify these processes.

Creating an integrative framework

It is important for burnout research to take a more broad focus, incorporating both the positive (e.g., supportive supervision) and negative (e.g., toxic supervision) aspects of work relationships from a variety of sources (e.g., coworkers, supervisors, clients) in order to examine the relative importance of these relationships, as well as their additive and moderating effects: That is, what aspects of the relationships have the greatest impact on burnout? Does the source of the support (or conversely the incivility) matter when predicting burnout? Which relationships are most important in reducing or exacerbating burnout? Can the same person show both uncivil and civil behavior in the same interaction or on the same day? If yes, is civil behavior still protective if preceded by an episode of uncivil behavior, or can this instability and unpredictability in behavior actually increase burnout?

As illustrated in Figure 4.1, this line of research would help us to understand better the effects of multiple relationships. For example, are there additive effects on one's level of burnout if employees have multiple positive relationships (or conversely, multiple negative relationships)? Similarly, to what extent can positive work relationships buffer the adverse impact of the negative relationships? Sloan (2012) found that perceived coworker support moderated the relationship between perceived unfair treatment by a supervisor and job satisfaction and psychological distress. That is, workers who felt they were treated unfairly by their supervisor benefited from coworker support. It would be interesting to examine the extent to which support would buffer the relationship between negative interpersonal relationships and burnout.

Intervention research

The eventual research agenda examining working relationships and burnout should be focused on intervention research to improve relationships and reduce burnout. Although there has been some work on specific interventions (e.g., CREW to address workplace incivility; Leiter et al., 2011, 2012; Osatuke et al., 2009), it would be valuable to conduct more of these types of longitudinal burnout intervention research, incorporating other forms of mistreatment, (e.g., bullying), and using other methodological designs (e.g., diary studies; randomized control trials; nested designs). All of the above lines of research should create a solid foundation necessary for conducting these types of intervention research examining strategies and programs to reduce burnout.

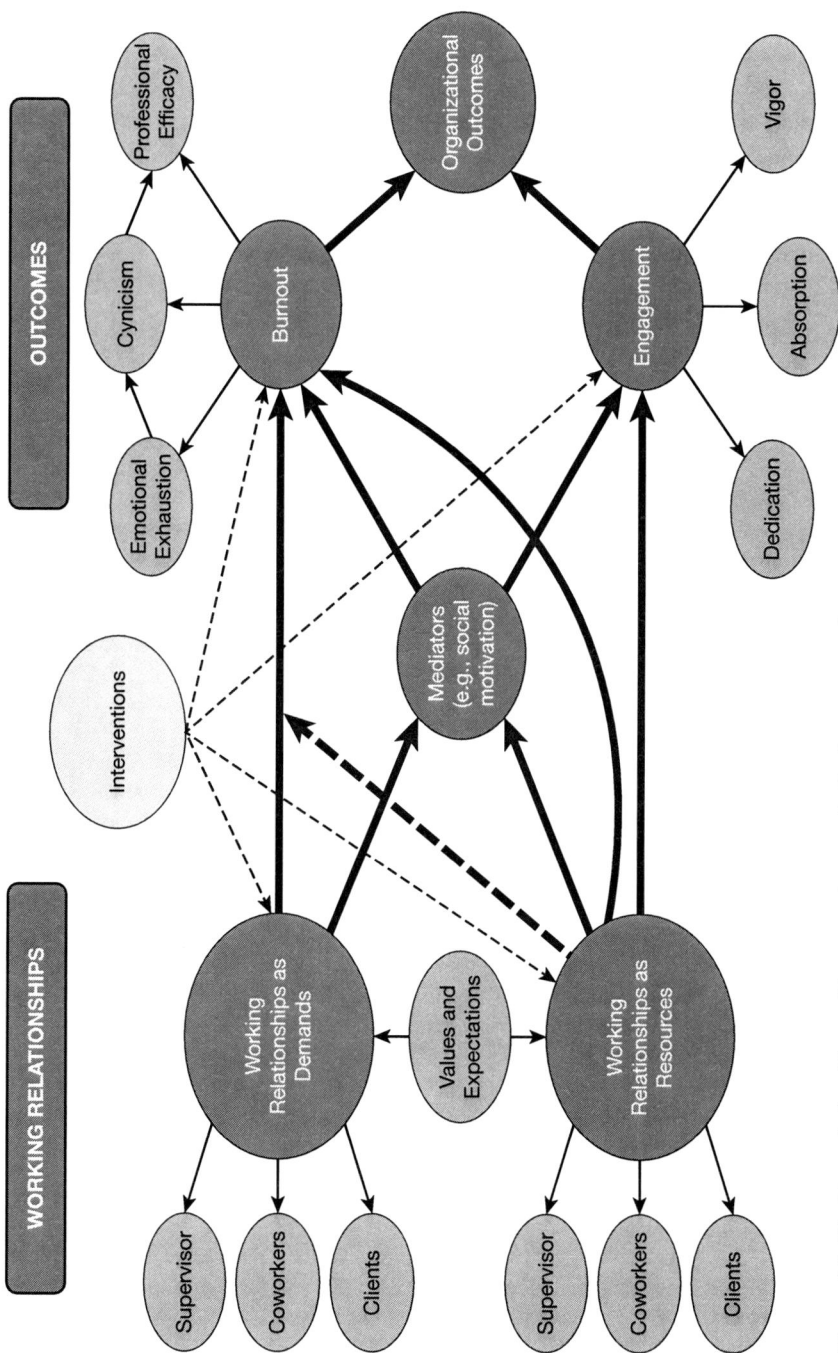

Figure 4.1 Working relationships and burnout: An agenda for future research

Concluding remarks

Given the genesis and definition of burnout in terms of a syndrome affecting employees dealing with other people in some capacity, it is not surprising that the preponderance of studies has shown both the beneficial effects of positive working relationships in reducing burnout as well as the deleterious effects of negative working relationships in increasing burnout. We incorporated several theories to help understand the mechanisms of these relationships better, identified several lines of future research to examine the subtleties of these relationships with the individual components of burnout in more detail, and developed a conceptual model to help illustrate these current and future research areas.

References

Andersson, L. M., & Pearson, C. M. (1999). Tit for tat? The spiraling effect of incivility in the workplace. *Academy of Management Review, 24*, 452–471.

Armon, G., Melamed, S., Shirom, A., & Shapira, I. (2010). Elevated burnout predicts the onset of musculoskeletal pain among apparently healthy employees. *Journal of Occupational Health Psychology, 15*, 399–408.

Aryee, S., Sun, L. Y., Chen, Z. X. G., & Debrah, Y. A. (2008). Abusive supervision and contextual performance: The mediating role of emotional exhaustion and the moderating role of work unit structure. *Management and Organization Review, 4*, 393–411.

Bakker, A. B., & Demerouti, E. (2007). The job demands-resources model: State of the art. *Journal of Managerial Psychology, 22*, 309–328.

Bakker, A. B., Schaufeli, W. B., Sixma, H. J., Bosveld, W., & Van Dierendonck, D. (2000). Patient demands, lack of reciprocity, and burnout: A five-year longitudinal study among general practitioners. *Journal of Organizational Behavior, 21*, 425–441.

Bakker, A. B., Demerouti, E., & Verbeke, W. (2004). Using the job demands-resources model to predict burnout and performance. *Human Resource Management, 43*, 83–104.

Bakker, A. B., Demerouti, E., & Euwema, M. C. (2005). Job resources may buffer the impact of job demands on burnout. *Journal of Occupational Health Psychology, 10*, 170–180.

Bedi, A., Courcy, F., Paquet, M., & Harvey, S. (2012). Interpersonal aggression and burnout: The mediating role of psychological climate. *Stress and Health*. Online version: http://onlinelibrary.wiley.com/doi/10.1002/smi.2476/full (accessed 19 December 2013).

Ben-Zur, H., & Yagil, D. (2005). The relationship between empowerment, aggressive behaviors of customers, coping, and burnout. *European Journal of Work and Organizational Psychology, 14*, 81–99.

Bies, R. J. (2001). Interactional (in)justice: The sacred and the profane. In J. Greenberg & R. Cropanzano (Eds), *Advances in organizational justice* (pp. 89–118). Stanford, CA: Stanford University Press.

Bies, R. J., & Tripp, T. M. (2005). The study of revenge in the workplace: Conceptual, ideological, and empirical issues. In S. Fox & P. E. Spector (Eds) *Counterproductive work behavior: Investigations of actors and targets (*pp. 65–81). Washington, DC: American Psychological Association.

Blanch, A., & Aluja, A. (2012). Social support (family and supervisor), work-family conflict, and burnout: Sex differences. *Human Relations, 65,* 811–833.

Blau, G., & Andersson, L. (2005). Testing a measure of instigated workplace incivility. *Journal of Occupational and Organizational Psychology, 78,* 595–614.

Bunk, J. A., & Magley, V. J. (2013). The role of appraisals and emotions in understanding experiences of workplace incivility. *Journal of Occupational Health Psychology, 18,* 87–105.

Chamberlain, L. J., & Hodson, R. (2010). Toxic work environments: What helps and what hurts. *Sociological Perspectives, 53,* 455–478.

Choi, S., Cheong, K., & Feinberg, R. A. (2012). Moderating effects of supervisor support, monetary rewards, and career paths on the relationship between job burnout and turnover intentions in the context of call centers. *Managing Service Quality, 22,* 492–516.

Collings, J. A., & Murray, P. J. (1996). Predictors of stress amongst social workers: An empirical study. *British Journal of Social Work, 26,* 375–387.

Cortina, L. M. (2008). Unseen injustice: Incivility as modern discrimination in organizations. *The Academy of Management Review, 33,* 55–75

Cortina, L. M., Magley, V. J., Williams, J. H., & Langhout, R. D. (2001). Incivility in the workplace: Incidence and impact. *Journal of Occupational Health Psychology, 6,* 64–80.

Deery, S., Walsh, J., & Guest, D. (2011). Workplace aggression: The effects of harassment on job burnout and turnover intentions. *Work, Employment & Society, 25,* 742–759.

Demerouti, E., Bakker, A. B., Nachreiner, F., & Schaufeli, W. B. (2001). The job demands-resources model of burnout. *Journal of Applied Psychology, 86,* 499–512.

Devereux, J. M., Hastings, R. P., Noone, S. J., Firth, A., & Totsika, V. (2009). Social support and coping as mediators or moderators of the impact of work stressors on burnout in intellectual disability support staff. *Research in Developmental Disabilities, 30,* 367–377.

Dormann, C., & Zapf, D. (2004). Customer-related social stressors and burnout. *Journal of Occupational Health Psychology, 9,* 61–82.

Duffy, M. K., Ganster, D., & Pagon, M. (2002). Social undermining and social support in the workplace. *Academy of Management Journal, 45,* 331–351.

Einarsen, S., Hoel, H., Zapf, D., & Cooper, C. L. (2011). The concept of bullying and harassment at work: The European tradition. In S. Einarsen, H. Hoel, D. Zapf and C. Cooper (Eds), *Bullying and harassment in the workplace. Developments in theory, research, and practice 2,* 3–39.

Etzion, D. (1984). Moderating effect of social support on the stress-burnout relationship. *Journal of Applied Psychology, 69,* 615–22.

Forbes, D. L. (2011). Toward a unified model of human motivation. *Review of General Psychology, 15,* 85–98.

Fukuda, K., Straus, S. E., Hickie, I., Sharpe, M. C., Dobbins, J. G., & Komaroff, A. (1994). The chronic fatigue syndrome: A comprehensive approach to its definition and study. *Annals of Internal Medicine, 121,* 953–959.

Garland, B. (2004). The impact of administrative support on prison treatment staff burnout: An exploratory study. *The Prison Journal, 84,* 4, 452–471.

Gibson, J. A., Grey, I. M., & Hastings, R. P. (2009). Supervisor support as a predictor of burnout and therapeutic self-efficacy in therapists working in ABA schools. *Journal of Autism and Developmental Disorders, 39,* 1024–1030.

Giumetti, G. W., McKibben, E. S., Hatfield, A. L., Schroeder, A. N., & Kowalski, R. M. (2012). Cyber incivility @ work: The new age of interpersonal deviance. *Cyberpsychology, Behavior, and Social Networking, 15,* 148–154.

Grandey, A. A., Dickter, D. N., & Sin, H. P. (2004). The customer is not always right: Customer aggression and emotion regulation of service employees. *Journal of Organizational Behavior, 25*, 397–418.

Grayson, J. L., & Alvarez, H. K. (2008). School climate factors relating to teacher burnout: A mediator model. *Teaching and Teacher Education, 24*, 1349–1363.

Halbesleben, J. R. (2006). Sources of social support and burnout: A meta-analytic test of the conservation of resources model. *Journal of Applied Psychology, 91*, 1134–1145.

Halbesleben, J. R., & Bowler, W. M. (2007). Emotional exhaustion and job performance: The mediating role of motivation. *Journal of Applied Psychology, 92*, 93–106.

Hershcovis, M. S. (2011). "Incivility, social undermining, bullying . . . oh my!": A call to reconcile constructs within workplace aggression research. *Journal of Organizational Behavior, 32*, 499–519.

Hershcovis, M. S., & Barling, J. (2010). Towards a multi-foci approach to workplace aggression: A meta-analytic review of outcomes from different perpetrators. *Journal of Organizational Behavior, 31*, 24–44.

Hesketh, K. L., Duncan, S. M., Estabrooks, C. A., Reimer, M. A., Giovannetti, P., Hyndman, K., & Acorn, S. (2003). Workplace violence in Alberta and British Columbia hospitals. *Health Policy (Amsterdam, Netherlands), 63*, 311–321.

Hobfoll, S. E. (1998). *Stress, culture and community: The psychology and philosophy of stress.* New York: Plenum.

Hobfoll, S. E. (1989). Conservation of resources. *American Psychologist, 44*, 513–524.

Hobfoll, S. E., & Freedy, J. (1993). Conservation of resources: A general stress theory applied to burnout. In W. B. Schaufeli, C. Maslach, & T. Marek (Eds.), *Professional burnout: Recent developments in theory and research* (pp. 115–129). Washington, DC: Taylor and Francis.

Jenkins, R., & Elliott, P. (2004). Stressors, burnout and social support: Nurses in acute mental health settings. *Journal of Advanced Nursing, 48*, 622–631.

Kalicińska, M., Chylińska, J., & Wilczek-Różyczka, E. (2012). Professional burnout and social support in the workplace among hospice nurses and midwives in Poland. *International Journal of Nursing Practice, 18*, 595–603.

Karatepe, O. M., Yorganci, I., & Haktanir, M. (2009). Outcomes of customer verbal aggression among hotel employees. *International Journal of Contemporary Hospitality Management, 21*, 713–733.

Kern, J. H., & Grandey, A. A. (2009). Customer incivility as a social stressor: The role of race and racial identity for service employees. *Journal of Occupational Health Psychology, 14*, 46–57.

Lambert, E., Altheimer, I., & Hogan, N. (2010). Exploring the relationship between social support and job burnout among correctional staff. *Criminal Justice and Behavior, 37*, 1217–1236.

Lambert, E. G., Hogan, N. L., Barton-Bellessa, S. M., & Jiang, S. (2012). Examining the relationship between supervisor and management trust and job burnout among correctional staff. *Criminal Justice and Behavior, 39*, 938–957.

Laschinger, H. K., Finegan, J., & Wilk, P. (2009a). New graduate burn out: The impact of professional practice environment, workplace civility, and empowerment. *Nursing, 27*, 377–384.

Laschinger, H. K., Leiter, M., Day, A., & Gilin, D. (2009b). Workplace empowerment, incivility, and burnout: Impact on staff nurse recruitment and retention outcomes. *Journal of Nursing Management, 17*, 302–311.

LeBlanc, M. M., & Barling, J. (2004). Workplace aggression. *Current Directions in Psychological Science*, *13*, 9–12.

LeBlanc, M. M., & Kelloway, E. K. (2002). Predictors and outcomes of workplace violence and aggression. *Journal of Applied Psychology*, *87*, 444–453.

Leiter, M. P. (1993). Burnout as a developmental process: Consideration of models. In W. Schaufeli, C. Maslach, & T. Marek (Eds), *Professional burnout: Recent developments in theory and research* (pp. 237–250). Washington: Taylor & Francis.

Leiter, M. P. (2012). *Analyzing and theorizing the dynamics of the workplace incivility crisis*. Amsterdam: Springer.

Leiter, M. P., & Maslach, C. (1988). The impact of interpersonal environment on burnout and organizational commitment. *Journal of Organizational Behavior*, *9*, 297–308.

Leiter, M. P., & Maslach, C. (1999). Six areas of worklife: A model of the organizational context of burnout. *Journal of Health and Human Resources Administration*, *21*, 472–489.

Leiter, M. P., & Maslach, C. (2004). Areas of worklife: A structured approach to organizational predictors of job burnout. In P. L. Perrewe & D. C. Ganster (Eds.), *Research in occupational stress and well-being* (Vol. 3, 91–134). Oxford: Elsevier.

Leiter, M. P., Laschinger, H. K., Day, A., & Gilin-Oore, D. (2011). The impact of civility interventions on employee social behavior, distress, and attitudes. *Journal of Applied Psychology, 96*, 1258–1274.

Leiter, M. P., Day, A., Gilin-Oore, D., & Laschinger, H. K. (2012a). Getting better and staying better: Assessing civility, incivility, distress and job attitudes one year after a civility intervention. *Journal of Occupational Health Psychology 17*, 425–434.

Leiter, M. P., Nicholson, R., Patterson, A., & Laschinger, H. K. S. (2012b). Incivility, burnout, and work engagement. *Ciencia & Trabajo (Science and Work)*, *14*, 22–29.

Lim, S., Cortina, L. M., & Magley, V., J. (2008). Personal and workgroup incivility. Impact on work and health outcomes. *Journal of Applied Psychology*, *93*, 95–107.

Lim, V. K., & Teo, T. S. (2009). Mind your E-manners: Impact of cyber incivility on employees' work attitude and behavior. *Information & Management*, *46*, 419–425.

Maslach, C. (1976). Burned-out. *Human Behavior, 9*, 16–22.

Maslach, C. (1993). Burnout: A multidimensional perspective. In W. B. Schaufeli, C. Maslach, & T. Marek (Eds.), *Professional burnout: Recent developments in theory and research* (19–32). Washington, DC: Taylor & Francis.

Maslach, C., & Jackson, S. E. (1981). The measurement of experienced burnout. *Journal of Occupational Behaviour*, *2*, 99–113.

Maslach, C., & Leiter, M. P. (1997). *The truth about burnout*. San Francisco: Jossey Bass.

Maslach, C., Jackson, S.E., & Leiter, M.P. (1996). *MBI: The Maslach Burnout Inventory: Manual.* Palo Alto, CA: Consulting Psychologists Press.

Maslach, C., Schaufeli, W. B., & Leiter, M. P. (2001). Job burnout. *Annual review of psychology*, *52*, 397–422.

Maslach, C., Leiter, M. P., & Jackson, S. E. (2012). Making a significant difference with burnout interventions: Research and practitioner collaboration. *Journal of Organizational Behavior, 33*, 296–300.

Melamed, S., Shirom, A., Toker, S., Berliner, S., & Shapira, I. (2006). Burnout and risk of cardiovascular disease: Evidence, possible causal paths, and promising research directions. *Psychological Bulletin*, *132*, 327–353.

Merecz, D., Drabek, M., & Moscicka, A. (2009). Aggression at the workplace – psychological consequences of abusive encounter with coworkers and clients. *International Journal of Occupational Medicine and Environmental Health*, *22*, 243–260.

Miner-Rubino, K., & Reed, W. D. (2010). Testing a moderated mediational model of workgroup incivility: The roles of organizational trust and group regard. *Journal of Applied Social Psychology, 40,* 3148–3168.

Mitchell, M. S., & Ambrose, M. L. (2012). Employees' behavioral reactions to supervisor aggression: An examination of individual and situational factors. *Journal of Applied Psychology, 97,* 1148–1170.

Notelaers, G., Einarsen, S., De Witte, H., & Vermunt, J. K. (2006). Measuring exposure to bullying at work: The validity and advantages of the latent class cluster approach. *Work & Stress, 20,* 289–302.

Organization for Economic Co-operation and Development. (2012). *LFS – Average usual weekly hours worked on the main job* (Data File). Online version: http://stats.oecd.org/Index.aspx?DatasetCode=ANHRS# (accessed 19 December 2012).

Osatuke, K., Mohr, D., Ward, C., Moore, S.C., Dyrenforth, S., & Belton, L. (2009). Civility, Respect, Engagement in the Workforce (CREW): Nationwide organization development intervention at Veterans Health Administration. *Journal of Applied Behavioral Science, 45,* 384–410.

Porath, C. L., & Erez, A. (2009). Overlooked but not untouched: How rudeness reduces onlookers' performance on routine and creative tasks. *Organizational Behavior and Human Decision Processes, 109,* 29–44.

Prins, J. T., Hoekstra-Weebers, J. E. H. M., Gazendam-Donofrio, S. M., Van De Wiel, H. B. M., Sprangers, F., Jaspers, F. C. A., & Van der Heijden, F. M. M. A. (2007). The role of social support in burnout among Dutch medical residents. *Psychology, Health & Medicine, 12,* 1–6.

Ray, E. B., & Miller, K. I. (1994). Social support, home/work stress, and burnout: Who can help? *The Journal of Applied Behavioral Science, 30,* 357–373.

Robinson, S. L., & O'Leary-Kelly, A. M. (1998). Monkey see, monkey do: The influence of work groups on the antisocial behavior of employees. *Academy of Management Journal, 41,* 658–672.

Russell, D. W., Altmaier, E., & Van Velzen, D. (1987). Job-related stress, social support, and burnout among classroom teachers. *The Journal of Applied Psychology, 72,* 269–74.

Sand, G., & Miyazaki, A. D. (2000). The impact of social support on salesperson burnout and burnout components. *Psychology & Marketing, 17,* 13–26.

Savicki, V., Cooley, E., & Gjesvold, J. (2003). Harassment as a predictor of job burnout in correctional officers. *Criminal Justice and Behavior, 30,* 602–619.

Schat, A. C., & Kelloway, E. K. (2005). Workplace aggression. *Handbook of work stress,* 189–218.

Schaufeli, W. B., Bakker, A. B., & Salanova, M. (2006). The measurement of work engagement with a short questionnaire. *Educational and Psychological Measurement, 66,* 701–716.

Schaufeli, W. B., Leiter, M. P., & Maslach, C. (2009). Burnout: 35 years of research and practice. *Career Development International, 14,* 204–220.

Shirom, A. (2005). Reflections on the study of burnout. *Work & Stress, 19,* 263–270.

Sliter, M. T. (2012). *But we're here to help! Positive buffers of the relationship between victim incivility and employee outcomes in firefighters* (Doctoral dissertation). Bowling Green State University, Ohio.

Sliter, M., Jex, S., Wolford, K., & McInnerney, J. (2010). How rude! Emotional labor as a mediator between customer incivility and employee outcomes. *Journal of Occupational Health Psychology, 15,* 468–481.

Sloan, M. M. (2012). Unfair treatment in the workplace and worker well-being: The role of coworker support in a service work environment. *Work and Occupations*, *39*, 3–34.

Statistics Canada. (2011). Table 282–0026 – Labour force survey estimates (LFS), by actual hours worked, class of worker, National Occupational Classification for Statistics (NOC-S) and sex, annual (persons unless otherwise noted). *CANSIM* (database). Online version: http://www.statcan.gc.ca/pub/71-001-x/71-001-x2012002-eng.pdf (accessed 19 December 2013).

Sulea, C., Filipescu, R., Horga, A., Orṭan, C., & Fischmann, G. (2012). Interpersonal mistreatment at work and burnout among teachers. *Cognition, Brain, Behavior: An Interdisciplinary Journal, 16,* 553–570.

Tang, C. S. K., Au, W. T., Schwarzer, R., & Schmitz, G. (2001). Mental health outcomes of job stress among Chinese teachers: Role of stress resource factors and burnout. *Journal of Organizational behavior, 22,* 887–901.

Tepper, B. J. (2000). Consequences of abusive supervision. *Academy of Management Journal, 43,* 178–190.

Tepper, B. J. (2007). Abusive supervision in work organizations: Review, synthesis, and research agenda. *Journal of Management, 33,* 261–289.

Tims, M., Bakker, A. B., & Derks, D. (2013). The impact of job crafting on job demands, job resources, and well-being. *Journal of Occupational Health Psychology, 18,* 230.

Um, M. Y., & Harrison, D. F. (1998). Role stressors, burnout, mediators, and job satisfaction: A stress-strain-outcome model and an empirical test. *Social Work Research, 22,* 100–115.

Van Jaarsveld, D. D., Walker, D. D., & Skarlicki, D. P. (2010). The role of job demands and emotional exhaustion in the relationship between customer and employee incivility. *Journal of Management, 36,* 1486–1504.

Winstanley, S., & Whittington, R. (2002). Anxiety, burnout and coping styles in general hospital staff exposed to workplace aggression: A cyclical model of burnout and vulnerability to aggression. *Work & Stress, 16,* 302–315.

Wu, T. Y., & Hu, C. (2009). Abusive supervision and employee emotional exhaustion dispositional antecedents and boundaries. *Group & Organization Management, 34,* 143–169.

Yürür, S., & Sarikaya, M. (2012). The effects of workload, role ambiguity, and social support on burnout among social workers in Turkey. *Administration in Social Work, 36,* 457–478.

Zurbriggen, E. L., & Capdevila, R. (2010). The personal and the political are feminist exploring the relationships among feminism, psychology, and political life. *Psychology of Women Quarterly, 34,* 458–459.

5 Daily burnout experiences

Critical events and measurement challenges

Despoina Xanthopoulou and
Laurenz L. Meier

Introduction

Traditionally, burnout has been defined and studied as a work-related syndrome that is characterized by high levels of exhaustion and cynicism and reduced professional efficacy (Schaufeli et al., 2009). Burnout has been mainly conceived as an enduring and static phenomenon that has detrimental effects on employee health (Shirom et al., 2005), and associates with impaired organizational behavior (e.g., poor performance and high levels of absenteeism; Schaufeli, 2006). Consequently, most empirical evidence focuses on factors that explain between-employee differences in burnout, as well as on the related outcomes (Halbesleben & Buckley, 2004; Lee & Ashforth, 1996; Maslach et al., 2001). These empirical findings have been significant for understanding the psychological processes that explain the syndrome by showing why certain employees are more prone to burnout than others.

Despite its importance, this research tradition largely neglects issues that have to do with the daily occurrence of burnout experiences, which may help explain how the syndrome manifests and evolves from one day to another over the course of an employee's life. In this chapter, we focus on daily experiences of exhaustion, cynicism, and reduced professional efficacy in an attempt to understand within-employee (linear and non-linear) changes in burnout. In the first part of the chapter, we take a critical stance toward traditional burnout approaches that neglect the state aspect of the syndrome. Following Weiss and Cropanzano's (1996) Affective Events Theory (AET) and Beal and Weiss's (2013) episodic approach to the structure of work life, we underline the importance of studying day-specific burnout experiences as a function of critical events that take place at work. Also, we discuss daily recovery from work-related demands as a decisive factor that determines whether burnout experiences will accumulate over time. In the second part of the chapter, we discuss the methodological challenges that researchers face when studying daily burnout experiences. Measurement issues, available methods, and related analytical strategies are reviewed, and new research avenues toward theory development are considered.

Defining, measuring, and understanding burnout

Job burnout is widely recognized as a three-dimensional, rather enduring syndrome of exhaustion, cynicism, and reduced professional efficacy that individuals experience in relation to their work (Maslach et al., 1996; Schaufeli et al., 1996). Exhaustion refers to a state of energy draining that takes the form of mental, emotional and physical tiredness. Cynicism concerns the development of negative attitudes toward the nature and the recipients of one's work that may be best described as dysfunctional disengagement and a gradual loss of concern. Lack of professional efficacy has to do with the tendency to feel incompetent at work and goes hand-in-hand with poor self-esteem and insufficiency. The most widely used instrument to measure the three facets of burnout is the Maslach Burnout Inventory-General Survey (Schaufeli et al., 1996) which includes items such as "I feel tired when I get up in the morning and I have to face another day on the job" (i.e., exhaustion), "I doubt the significance of my work," (i.e., cynicism), and "I have accomplished many worthwhile things in this job" (i.e., professional efficacy).

This definition and related conceptualization underline certain issues regarding the nature of the syndrome. First, burnout concerns all employees irrespective of their occupation and cannot only be found in the context of human services, as it was initially thought (Leiter & Schaufeli, 1996). Second, burnout is not context-free. Rather, it is akin to work-related experiences. Despite the fact that exhaustion may generalize to areas outside work (e.g., home), cynicism and reduced professional efficacy concern the work context only, and thus help distinguish burnout from other related psychological conditions (Schaufeli et al., 2009). This further implies that burnout is not just exhaustion. Empirical evidence supports the superiority of the three-dimensional (exhaustion, cynicism, and reduced professional efficacy) structure of burnout in comparison to alternative one-factor and two-factor models (Schaufeli et al., 2009), while the incremental validity of cynicism and professional efficacy over and above exhaustion has been also supported (Lee & Ashforth, 1990). Finally, burnout has been traditionally seen as a rather enduring state that is caused by persistent unfavorable or demanding work conditions that drain employees' energetic resources (Shirom et al., 2005). Theoretical models rest on the central assumption that a continuous imbalance between environmental demands/threats and resources leads to the accumulation of job strain that may result in burnout.

The Conservation of Resources (COR) theory (Hobfoll, 1989) provides a rich theoretical framework to understand burnout. COR theory postulates that people have a natural drive to obtain, retain, and protect those resources (i.e., objects, conditions, characteristics or energies) that they highly value. Accordingly, burnout is most likely to occur when resources are threatened by the environmental conditions, when resources are lost as a response to these threatening conditions, and when resources are invested for additional resource gain but these anticipated gains are never reached. Under conditions of resource loss, individuals try to limit the negative consequences by investing additional resources that further puts their resource reservoir at stake, and facilitates the occurrence of burnout (Shirom et al., 2005). Interestingly, COR theory suggests that burnout does not only appear when situations are threatening, but also when individuals fail to gain additional resources. Both conditions may fuel a loss spiral that may enhance feelings of exhaustion, cynicism and reduced efficacy at work, and may consequently lead to chronic health impairment (Hobfoll, 2001). Indeed, Ten Brummelhuis et al. (2011) found in their longitudinal study that baseline burnout levels related to increases in burnout through the depletion of resources and the enhancement of demands.

From a work psychological perspective, burnout is mainly seen as the outcome of the experienced imbalance between job demands and the available resources. The job demands-resources (JD-R) model (Demerouti et al., 2001) suggests that the development of burnout follows two distinct processes. According to the health impairment process, demanding aspects of the job (e.g., work pressure, cognitive and emotional demands) lead to constant overtaxing that explains the occurrence of exhaustion. According to the motivational process, a lack of environmental resources (e.g., autonomy, support, coaching, etc.) hampers goal attainment that further leads to withdrawal behaviors and cynicism. Importantly, the interaction of demands and resources predicts burnout over and above main effects. Burnout is most likely to occur when high levels of demands co-exist with low levels of resources, since employees do not have the means to deal effectively with these demands. Plenty of cross-sectional and longitudinal evidence supports the main assumptions of this model (Bakker & Demerouti, 2007).

These dominant approaches mainly perceive burnout as a dysfunctional experience that persists over extended periods of time (Shirom et al., 2005). If burnout is seen as the outcome of a continuous exposure to demanding work conditions, where resources are constantly invested but never replenished, then it is likely that as soon as a person reaches the burnout state this will last for a long period of time. Indeed, Shirom and colleagues (2005) reviewed longitudinal studies on burnout and found the diachronic correlation to range between .49 and .70, which suggests that burnout is a rather stable phenomenon. Recently, Schaufeli et al. (2011) showed that burnout has both a stable, as well as a change component. In their study among Dutch physicians, longitudinal panel data from three measurement points with a 5-year time interval were used. Results indicated that about one quarter of the variance in participants' burnout levels across a decade was accounted for by a stable component, while about three quarters was accounted for by a change component. This implies that part of the variance in burnout can be explained by individual or situational factors that are stable. However, to fully understand the phenomenon it is important to explain its change component as well. One way to do this is by investigating how burnout experiences vary over shorter periods of time (e.g., moments, days or weeks), and by looking for specific work-related events that may facilitate or inhibit daily experiences of exhaustion, cynicism, and reduced professional efficacy (Xanthopoulou et al., 2012a).

An episodic approach to study burnout

The state approach assumes that burnout experiences may vary within the same employee from one moment or day to another as a response to specific events at work. Although this approach seems contradictory to the traditional static view, we argue that both approaches are complementary in understanding the phenomenon. Take for example a burned-out teacher, who generally feels very exhausted, is disengaged from her students, cynical about the significance of her job, and who exhibits low levels of professional efficacy. The state approach suggests that this burned-out teacher may not be equally exhausted, cynical, and inefficient every day (or every moment) at work. On a day that her students perform very well at a difficult math test, or her colleagues express their appreciation towards her, she may feel less cynical and more efficacious than on days when nothing good happens at work. In a similar way, a teacher, who does not experience chronic burnout, may experience high levels of exhaustion on a day that his students misbehave in class, or high levels of cynicism on a day that he has a conflict with the school principal.

This example illustrates that experiences of exhaustion, cynicism, and professional efficacy may change substantially within the same employee from one moment or day to another as a response to the continuously changing job characteristics and work-related events. Since there is evidence suggesting that work conditions (i.e., levels of job demands and job resources) vary substantially from one workday to another (Butler et al., 2005; Xanthopoulou et al., 2009; Xanthopoulou et al., 2008), it may be argued that reactions to these conditions may vary accordingly. This micro-approach in the study of burnout is supported by Weiss and Cropanzano's (1996) AET, which proposes that specific critical events at work are the most proximal causes of employees' affective reactions to these events. For example, the occurrence of pleasant events (e.g., having a nice conversation with a client) may elicit momentary positive emotions (e.g., happiness, satisfaction), while unpleasant events (e.g., arguing with a colleague) may elicit momentary negative emotions (e.g., frustration).

Building on AET, Beal and Weiss (2013) provided a more elaborate analysis of how critical events at work explain emotional and, consequently, behavioral reactions on a daily basis. These authors proposed that life at work can be partitioned in a series of episodes, and that employee experiences and behaviors may be best examined in relation to these episodes. They distinguished between emotion episodes that concern how people *feel* with respect to a specific event at work, and performance episodes that concern what people *did* with regard to a specific event or goal at work. Events are the initiators of both types of episodes and refer to "any aspect or occurrence of one's environment that influences another element or stream of experience" (Beal & Weiss, 2013, p. 17). As such, the main characteristic of events is that they are clearly exogenous experiences that can have a potentially beneficial or harmful effect on employee momentary well-being. Beal and Weiss (2013) recognize that the extent to which an event will influence an employee is determined by its nature, with shock-like events being far more influential than routine ones.

In this context, we argue that daily experiences of exhaustion, cynicism, and professional efficacy may be examined in relation to specific events or episodes because how employees feel depends on what is happening at work on a day-to-day basis and during different instances throughout a day (Beal & Weiss, 2013). As episodic experiences, these may vary substantially within the same employee from one moment or workday to another since they depend highly on the specific critical events that take place during each day at work. A first advantage of the episodic approach in the study of burnout is that surveying individual burnout experiences the moment that they occur facilitates capturing their dynamic nature (Xanthopoulou et al., 2012a). In other words, it is possible to investigate whether and how exhaustion, cynicism, and efficacy experiences change within the same person across short periods of time as a response to specific episodes or critical work events.

Studying within-person fluctuations in burnout experiences is significant for one more reason. Despite the fact that peaks or lows in daily employee experiences are not of substantial endurance, they may be responsible for generalized levels of well-being in the long run. In other words, the accumulation of frequent and intense momentary burnout experiences may lead to chronic burnout. Although there is no empirical evidence supporting such growth effects for day-specific burnout experiences, Fredrickson et al. (2008) did show that increases in daily positive emotions produced upturns in personal resources that in turn predicted higher life satisfaction, and reduced depressive symptoms over time. These findings imply that the study of changes in daily burnout experiences may be significant because it is likely that frequent daily experiences of malfunctioning may generalize to enduring health impairments.

Next to understanding how daily burnout experiences change and evolve within the same employee, the additional advantage of this micro-approach is that it allows examining day-specific burnout experiences in relation to their proximal antecedents and outcomes. Thus, it is possible to investigate which are the shock-like critical events that are responsible for momentary increases in exhaustion or cynicism and what is the immediate result of these experiences. In this way, we can unfold the psychological processes that explain burnout at the within-person level of analysis. The critical issue at this point is whether assumptions that are based on between-person studies are applicable to day-specific burnout experiences. Cross-sectional and longitudinal studies that applied the JD-R model consistently showed that job demands are the main predictors of exhaustion, job resources are the main predictors of cynicism, while both dimensions of burnout result in negative outcomes both for employees and organizations (Bakker & Demerouti, 2007). Are these assumptions valid also at the within-person level of analysis? Scholars emphasize that assumptions that have been supported at the between-person level of analysis may be erroneous, if applied to the within-person of analysis (and vice versa; see Xanthopoulou et al., 2012a). Thus, the study of day-specific burnout experiences, the related critical events, and outcomes allows testing the homology of theoretical assumptions across levels of analysis thereby advancing burnout theory.

Daily events, burnout experiences, and outcomes

Empirical research using diary designs has clearly shown that people do not only differ from each other in terms of their burnout levels, but that they also show substantial daily variations in the burnout symptoms. Evidence from studies on daily fluctuations in work-related exhaustion (or fatigue) showed that a significant amount of the total variance (ranging from 38 percent to 79 percent) could be attributed to within-employee changes (Biron & Van Veldhoven, 2012; Gross et al., 2011; Simbula, 2010; Van Gelderen et al., 2011; Xanthopoulou et al., 2012b). Studies also showed that fatigue may vary significantly within the same person even over the course of one day (Grech et al., 2009). In a similar vein, diaries have shown that 38 percent to 50 percent in day-level professional efficacy could be attributed to within-employee variability (Xanthopoulou et al., 2008, 2009). We are not aware of any published study on daily cynicism or disengagement (Demerouti et al., 2001). However, analyses on unpublished data from the study among Greek fast-food restaurant employees (Xanthopoulou et al., 2009) indicated that 56 percent of the total variance in cynicism could be attributed to within-person changes. All in all, these results underline the importance of adopting a within-person approach over and above the between-person approach in the study of the burnout syndrome.

Which are the critical events that determine these daily fluctuations in burnout? What do these studies indicate on the drivers of burnout episodes and the proximal outcomes? Gross and colleagues (2011) conducted a diary study among employees in a Swiss government agency to investigate how specific positive and negative events at work relate to fatigue at the end of the workday. Participants were asked to fill in the diary as soon as they experienced a negative or a positive event at work, and to report on the nature (e.g., straining, pleasant) and valence of the event. Negative events that were reported had mainly to do with inter-personal conflicts (e.g., "had a tense phone call with a candidate for a position in my team") and situational constraints (e.g., "the delay of the meeting caused problems to my scheduled tasks"), while positive events concerned positive interactions with others (e.g., "a customer expressed her gratitude"), or task fulfillment (e.g., "I managed to finish a task that seemed impossible to do today"). In line with AET, results showed that negative events associated positively with fatigue, while positive events were unrelated to fatigue. Significant interaction effects suggested that positive events related negatively to fatigue only on days that employees were facing many negative events, and only for employees who experienced chronic job stressors. These findings suggest that positive events are beneficial for day-specific fatigue only in the face of adversity. Under threatening conditions, positive events help employees to conserve their resources, thus protecting them from fatigue accumulation.

Simbula (2010) found in her study among 61 Italian teachers that on days that participants were experiencing higher levels of work-family conflict than usual, their exhaustion levels were elevated. In turn, higher levels of exhaustion resulted in mental health impairments and lower job satisfaction. Biron and Van Veldhoven

(2012) performed a three-day diary study among 170 service employees. Results showed that employees, who were reporting higher levels of emotional job demands (e.g., events with difficult customers) on a daily basis, were also more exhausted than usual. Importantly, this positive relationship was stronger for those who had the tendency to fake the organizationally required emotions, while the relationship was non-existent for employees high in psychological flexibility. In a similar vein, Van Gelderen and colleagues (2011) performed a series of diary studies among police officers and found that on shifts where police officers were suppressing their anger they were more likely to experience exhaustion, while the suppression of happiness was not related to their end-of-shift exhaustion levels. Additional findings suggested that emotional dissonance explained the positive link between emotional demands and exhaustion during the shift.

In a similar context, a diary study among 50 employees in the Netherlands and Poland showed that generalized perceptions of display rules related positively to day-levels of surface acting (i.e., expressing the required emotions without changing the inner feelings) but not deep acting (i.e., the active attempt to feel the required emotions; Xanthopoulou et al., 2012b). On days that employees were using surface acting more often than usual they were ending up more exhausted, while on days they were using deep acting more they were feeling less exhausted. These results emphasize the significance of coping with emotional demands in explaining exhaustion, and suggest that deep acting is a more beneficial strategy. Regarding the outcomes of daily exhaustion, Halbesleben and Wheeler (2011) found negative relationships with in-role performance and organizational citizenship behaviors (OCB) targeted at the organization, while the relationship between exhaustion and OCBs targeted at the co-workers was positive. Furthermore, these relationships were stronger under conditions of positive inequity (i.e., when employees perceived that they contributed less or gained more than their co-workers).

Diary studies have shown that day-levels of job resources are the main determinants of professional efficacy. Flight attendants were feeling more efficacious on flights that they were working with supportive colleagues (Xanthopoulou et al., 2008). In a similar vein, on days that fast-food restaurant workers experienced higher levels of autonomy, supervisory coaching and a more positive team climate, they were more efficacious than usual (Xanthopoulou et al., 2009). Both studies showed that on days that employees were more efficacious their engagement levels were also elevated, which resulted in enhanced (self-rated) performance and financial returns, respectively. Despite the fact that studies on the drivers and outcomes of day-specific burnout experiences are limited to nonexistent, current findings generally favor the homology of the central assumptions that explain burnout across levels of analysis. In line with between-person studies, job demands and situational constraints (e.g., negative events) seem to be the strongest determinants of day-specific exhaustion, while job resources appear to be the strongest drivers of professional efficacy (Schaufeli & Bakker, 2004). However, Grech et al. (2009), who investigated within-day fluctuations in fatigue as a response to within-day changes in workload, supported a nonmonotonic relationship. Namely, both low and high workload was found to relate with the highest levels of fatigue, which implies that differential relationships may also exist when examining episodic experiences.

The role of daily recovery

Sonnentag (2005) was the first to argue that distancing mentally from one's job is not a bad thing, when it is part of the process of daily recovery from work-related demands. On days that job demands or constraints are overwhelming, switching off from work has been proven to be a good strategy to regain the lost energy. Recovery is the psychological process during which employees refill the energy resources that were used up during work in order for their functional systems to return to baseline (Sonnentag & Fritz, 2007). According to the effort-recovery model (Meijman & Mulder, 1998), effort expenditure at work as a response to environmental demands and constraints leads to acute responses (e.g., exhaustion) that can be overcome through adequate recovery. If the same functional systems remain activated after work, the process of recovery cannot take place, resulting in fatigue accumulation. Accordingly, when recovery is incomplete, reactions to daily job characteristics (e.g., enhanced exhaustion and cynicism, and reduced professional efficacy) amalgamate and may lead to chronic problems such as enduring burnout.

According to Sonnentag and Fritz (2007), when employees engage in leisure activities that facilitate relaxation, psychological detachment from work, and mastery experiences, resources are replenished and recovery is likely to occur. There is plenty of empirical evidence suggesting that employees, who manage to recover successfully during the hours after work on a daily basis, experience better well-being at bedtime (i.e., lower levels of exhaustion, higher levels of energy), and feel better at work the next day (for a review, see Demerouti & Sanz-Vergel, 2012). For example, Sonnentag and Bayer (2005) found that on days that employees failed to detach psychologically from their daily workload, they were more fatigued at night. Importantly, a previous day's psychological detachment associated negatively with next day's fatigue and negative experiences (Sonnentag et al., 2008).

Recovery theory and related research suggest that if employees fail to replenish the resources that were used up at work, they are unlikely to recover and thus daily burnout experiences may accumulate from one day to another, facilitating the occurrence of chronic burnout. In this context, daily recovery may be perceived as a critical event that determines the degree to which day-specific burnout experiences will or will not accumulate from one day to another. Namely, successful recovery prevents future chronic health impairments, while unsuccessful recovery promotes future and chronic health impairments. This proposition is depicted in Figure 5.1. As Sonnentag (2005) clarifies, the concept of psychological detachment from work in the context of recovery should not be confused with the concept of cynicism or disengagement. In the former case, detaching from work is healthy because it allows taking a break from demands in an attempt to restore

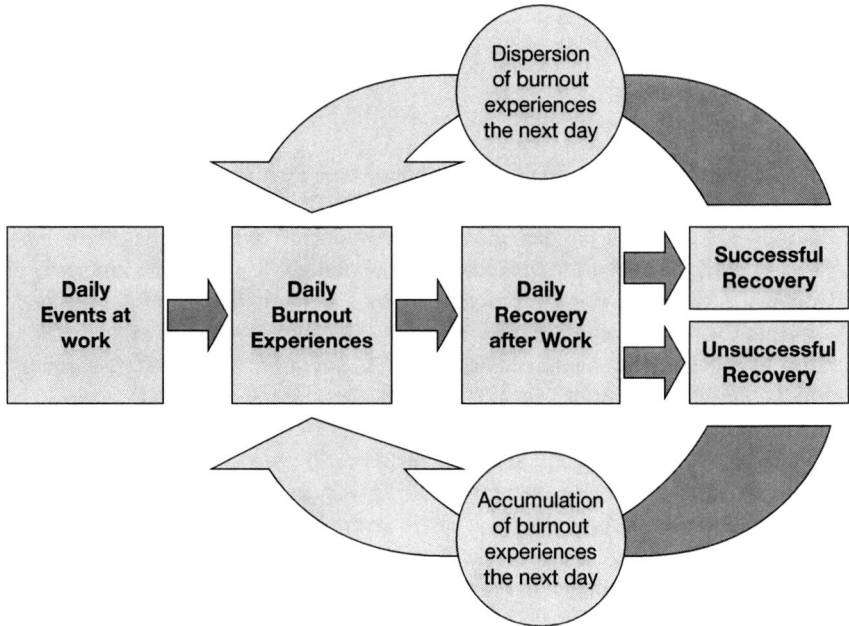

Figure 5.1 The process that explains daily burnout experiences

energy resources. In the latter case, disengagement has a negative connotation because it concerns a condition during work where resources are either not invested or are used to increase mental distance from the objects of work as a form of unsuccessful coping.

Diary methods in burnout research

The common objective of diary studies is to collect multiple measurements per person. This allows capturing within-employee changes that are of interest when investigating daily burnout experiences. Diaries differ with regard to the type of data collection protocols (Conner & Lehman, 2012). In *time-based protocols* measurements are either taken at standardized times (fixed-time based, interval-contingent; e.g., at the end of work) or at unpredictable times, when a signal is delivered (variable-time based, signal-contingent; e.g., randomly between 5 and 10 times per day). Sampling at standardized times is less burdensome for participants because it is less intrusive. However, an advantage of the variable-time based sampling is the possibility of randomly capturing experiences of participants' daily life by limiting retrospective biases. Hence, variable time-based sampling is also labeled experience sampling. In *event-based protocols* measurements are made whenever a predefined event occurs (e.g., a conflict with a client). Time-based protocols are best suited for continuous phenomena (e.g., exhaustion), whereas event-based protocols are best suited for episodic or rare events. Both protocols, however, only capture an extract of participants' daily experiences. In contrast, in *continuous sampling*, assessments are made continually without any gaps. Continuous sampling is well suited to measure physiological parameters (e.g., heart rate, bodily movements) that can be used as proxies of physical exercise (during the day) or sleep quality (during the night). Of course, it is also possible to combine different protocols within one study. For example, participants may be requested to fill in a survey whenever they experience a positive or negative event at work, and to report on their exhaustion at the end of work (e.g., Gross et al., 2011). Alternatively, participants may be asked to rate their day-specific work experiences at the end of work and then wear an actigraph to assess objective sleep quality indicators (e.g., Pereira et al., 2013).

Depending on the research question, different measurement occasions per day are required. For example, to study the trajectory of exhaustion over the course of a workday, several measurements per day are needed. In contrast, if one is interested in recovery activities during leisure time, one measurement at the end of the day is probably enough. The choice of the number of measurements per day also depends on the construct of interest. If one assumes a substantial amount of variance within one day (as in the case of exhaustion; Grech et al., 2009; Sonnenschein et al., 2007), multiple measurements are recommended to accurately capture the dynamic nature of the phenomenon. Furthermore, having several measurement occasions facilitates the temporal separation of the predictor (e.g., daily demands) and the outcome (e.g., exhaustion), which is crucial when testing the direction of a potential effect. Also, the duration of an effect can be studied in more detail. For example, it is possible to test whether day-specific or event-specific stressors have effects that not only last until the end of the day or the episode but that may spill over to the next day/episode. Additionally, the strength of these time-dependent effects may be compared (Meier et al., 2013).

Participants are often asked to report on the critical events that may influence the momentary states under study. Determining the list of potential events has the risk of preventing employees from deciding which specific event to report that may best explain their burnout experiences. In this respect, the day reconstruction method (DRM) is a good alternative for studying burnout episodes (Diener & Tay, in press). In the DRM, individuals are asked to reconstruct in chronological order all episodes of their day. Episodes are defined by start and end time, area of life (e.g., work), as well as specific interactions that occurred. After reconstructing all episodes of a particular day, participants rate how they felt regarding each episode. This method reduces the risk of missing a shock-like event, since critical events are specified by participants.

Trajectories of burnout symptoms

There is a growing literature on the trajectory of burnout over long time frames such as several months and years (Mäkikangas et al., 2012). Given that burnout is mainly considered as an enduring syndrome, such time frames are well suited and advance knowledge about long-term changes. However, it is also important to understand such a change in more detail. Is there a continuous increase of the burnout symptoms over the year, or does the trajectory follow an exponential function once a certain threshold is crossed? Moreover, are there specific circumstances in which the burnout symptoms accumulate over short periods of several episodes, days or weeks? Of course, daily data collection over an extended period of time (e.g., a year) is unrealistic. Therefore, researchers may use weekly – instead of daily – assessments of burnout (e.g., Kinnunen, 1988). Alternatively, the measurement-burst design is a very promising method for the study of burnout trajectories.

The measurement-burst design consists of repeated sequences of daily measurements, which are separated by relatively longer intervals (e.g., months); it combines features of short-term longitudinal designs (e.g., daily diaries) with those of long-term longitudinal designs (Ram & Gerstorf, 2009; Sliwinski, 2008). As such, it allows studying both a progressive change in the average level of burnout, as well as within-person, short-term fluctuations. Having several bursts of daily assessments facilitates reliably disentangling true long-term change from intra-individual (i.e., within-person) variability, which we showed is far from negligible. Moreover, measurement-burst designs allow testing whether within-person, short-term relationships (e.g., the effect of demands on exhaustion) change across time, for example, depending on the general level of burnout. In sum, measurement-burst designs are a fruitful method for studying short-term relationships between critical events and the components of burnout, as well as the interplay of the different components that may – or may not – result in the development of an enduring burnout syndrome.

Conceptualizing day-specific burnout experiences

One of the main challenges that researchers, who study day-specific burnout experiences, face is how these experiences are best conceptualized. Existing measures of burnout focus on enduring symptoms that have been experienced over a prolonged time. The MBI (Maslach et al., 1996) asks individuals about their experience during the last 12 months and hence, does not capture daily experiences and short-term changes of burnout symptoms. Therefore, for examining day-specific burnout experiences, either new instruments need to be developed or existing instruments have to be adapted. The latter practice is very common and usually involves three steps: Adapting the instruction (e.g., items refer to the actual moment), eliminating inapplicable items/wording (e.g., characteristics that are unlikely to change within short time), and shortening the measure to reduce participants' burden. Although adapting and abbreviating a scale seems a rather simple task, researchers should avoid restricting the conceptual range of the construct, and consider whether the (within-person) factor structure is similar to that of the established (between-person) measure. Special attention should be paid to the reliability of the day-level burnout that may suffer, since eliminating redundant items results in rather short scales (Shrout & Lane, 2012).

Given that the large majority of research on burnout has focused on its chronic nature, it comes as no surprise that state measures of the three burnout components are not well established. However, at least for exhaustion and (reduced) professional efficacy, day-specific measures exist and have been evaluated empirically. For example, Halbesleben and Wheeler (2011) used all eight items of the exhaustion subscale of the Oldenburg Burnout Inventory (OLBI; Demerouti et al., 2003) and adapted these to measure day-specific exhaustion (e.g., "Today, I felt tired before I went to work"). Simbula (2010) used three adapted items (i.e., "Today, I felt emotionally drained by my job/Working with people directly put too much stress on me/I felt frustrated by my job") from the emotional exhaustion subscale of the MBI that showed acceptable reliability with Cronbach's alpha ranging from .69 to .79 across the five days that the study took place. Cranford and colleagues (2006) showed that a shortened version of the fatigue subscale of the Profile of Mood States (POMS; McNair et al., 1992) has appropriate reliability to detect within-person changes. This measure consists of three adjectives (exhausted, worn out, and fatigued) for which participants indicate the extent to which they experienced each state during the last 24 hours. Of interest, van Hooff et al. (2007) showed that a single-item measure of fatigue ("How fatigued do you currently feel?") correlated highly ($r = .80$) with the fatigue-subscale of the POMS, suggesting high convergent validity. Similarly, Sonnenschein et al., (2007) measured exhaustion ("Right now, I am exhausted") and fatigue ("Right now, I am tired") each with one item.

Daily (reduced) work-related efficacy was measured in diary studies (Xanthopoulou et al., 2008, 2009) with a shortened and adapted version of the scale of Schwarzer and Jerusalem (1995). Two example items that have been used are "Today while at work, I felt I could deal efficiently with unexpected events" and "I felt I could handle every problem that came my way." These daily measures were found to be reliable with inter-item reliabilities ranging from .42 to .71 across the study occasions. In a similar vein, Holman et al. (2005) measured day-specific work goal-related expectancy with a single item ("Today, to what extent did you expect that you would be able to achieve goal X?"). Unpublished data from the study of Xanthopoulou and colleagues (2009) provide some preliminary evidence on the measurement of day-specific cynicism that was assessed with the item: "Today, I doubted the significance of my job." This item was found to correlate from .23 to .53 with a two-item daily exhaustion scale, and from -.42 to -.56 with daily engagement. These findings suggest that the adapted scales that have been used so far are quite reliable in capturing within-person changes in exhaustion, cynicism, and professional efficacy.

Statistical techniques to analyze daily burnout experiences

A shared feature of all diary studies is that the measurements are nested within individuals, which requires special attention for the data analysis. A common way to handle the independency of the data is to apply multilevel modeling. Most often, researchers use two-level models, where daily assessments (Level 1) are grouped within individuals (Level 2). Sometimes, three-level models are necessary, when one is interested in events that are nested in days that in turn, are nested in persons or when participants are nested in a higher level entity (e.g., a couple; Sanz-Vergel et al., 2012). Three-level models are also appropriate for analyzing data from measurement-burst designs, in which daily experiences are nested within bursts, which are nested within individuals (Sliwinski et al., 2009).

Multilevel modeling may also be used to examine trajectories of change over time (e.g., time nested within persons; Grech et al., 2009; Singer & Willet, 2003). However, trajectories are often studied with latent growth curve analyses based on structural equation modeling (Bollen & Curran, 2006). An extension of such latent growth modeling is called growth mixture modeling (GMM; Wang & Bodner, 2007). The aim of GMM is to identify unobserved subpopulations (classes) with similar patterns of changes. Hence, it is an interesting way to examine the number and frequency of classes of change and how these classes are related to other variables. In the context of burnout, Mäkikangas et al. (2012) studied classes of change in exhaustion and cynicism and how these relate to work engagement, while Feldt et al. (2013) investigated classes of change in effort-reward imbalance and over-commitment and how these relate to burnout. Previous research mainly focused on long-term changes and enduring levels of burnout, but the technique could also be applied to diary data. A practical limitation, however, is that GMM requires large samples, which are rather uncommon in diary research.

A statistical technique that handles small samples is time-series models, which concern a class of techniques developed to describe a substantial number of observations (usually > 50). Time series data are often characterized by auto-correlation, implying that consecutive observations are dependent on each other. For example, exhaustion at the end of work is likely to relate to exhaustion at bedtime, which in turn may associate with exhaustion the next day at work. To test such dependencies, a variety of models of different complexity exist. One of the most basic models is the first-order autoregressive model, where the autoregressive parameter reflects the correlation between y_t and its previous observation y_{t-1}. In the context of day-specific burnout experiences, using autoregressive effects of exhaustion could be an interesting way to study the inability to recover from daily demands (Kuppens et al., 2010; Suls & Martin, 2005). Successful recovery implies that one returns to its baseline, which may be considered as a (low) level of strain (e.g., exhaustion) before the onset of day-specific demands. Sleep is an important mechanism in recovery and as such people are usually able to restore their resources over night. In this case, autoregressive effects of exhaustion – measured at the end of the day and in the morning; or during workdays and days off – would be close to zero. In contrast, burned out people are assumed to take more time to return to their baseline, which would be reflected in stronger autoregressive effects. As mentioned, the first-order autoregressive model is relatively simple and many extensions exist. Among others, it is possible to investigate multiple time series in the same model and to use latent measures of the constructs (Hammaker, 2012).

Some practical recommendations

We would now like to give a practical example and discuss some issues that researchers may want to take into account when designing a diary study on within-person burnout experiences (for comprehensive presentations, see Bolger & Laurenceau, 2013; Mehl & Connor, 2012; Nezlek, 2012). Let us assume that we are interested in investigating specific tasks (i.e., episodes) across a workday for a course of a week and how these relate to momentary feelings of exhaustion. Additionally, the mediating role of daily recovery in the relationship between previous and next day's within-employee exhaustion would be examined.

To study this hypothesized process the best approach would be to use a diary design for 5 to 10 consecutive workdays by combining different protocols. First, it would be appropriate to use an event-based sampling protocol, where employees will be requested to fill in a short questionnaire as soon as they finish a specific task (e.g., meeting a client). In this way it would be possible to capture specific work-related events, as well as the concurrent feelings of exhaustion. Given that the focus is not only on how exhausted employees feel with respect to specific tasks but also how their state (e.g., exhaustion) may change over the course of the evening and the night, additional measurement occasions are required. Using a fixed-time based sampling protocol participants could be requested to evaluate their exhaustion levels before they leave work, shortly before they go to bed, and in the morning before going to work. In the latter point, participants could also report on their recovery levels. Additionally, in order to study recovery it would be possible to assess leisure activities with the day reconstruction approach by asking participants to reconstruct their evening after they came home from work (Bakker et al., 2013), and evaluate their recovery experiences with regard to the specific leisure activities.

As concerns measurement issues, one could adapt the exhaustion sub-scale of the MBI-GS in order to capture exhaustion with regard to the specific episodes at work (e.g., "During the task that I just finished, I was feeling exhausted"), as well as exhaustion right after work, at bedtime and in the morning before going to work (e.g., "Right now, I feel exhausted by my work"). As concerns recovery, it would be possible to adapt the recovery experience questionnaire (Sonnentag & Fritz, 2007) with respect to specific leisure activities (e.g., "This evening, spending time with friends helped me detach psychologically from work"). Finally, recovery in the morning, before going to work could be measured with items such as "Right now, I feel recovered" (Sonnentag, 2003).

It is clear that such a design has many advantages because it allows capturing daily experiences close to their occurrence and in relation to specific events throughout the day. Nevertheless, a significant drawback is that it is burdensome for participants. Thus, researchers need to invest some effort in keeping participants motivated until the end of the study. To this end, Oerlemans and Bakker (2013) recommend giving monetary compensation for participation or offering personalized feedback to participants. Also, they argue that using innovative ways to collect data (i.e., online surveys via smartphones) can be attractive for participants.

After finalizing data collection, the question that arises is how we analyze such data. In the present example, we measured work episodes that are nested within days, which are nested within individuals. The combination of episodes within days within individuals produces a three-level data structure and multilevel analyses are appropriate. The first step is to estimate the variance components of the predictors and outcomes. By running a multilevel model without any predictors (i.e., unconditional model), we decompose the variance across levels and test whether there are substantial differences (variance) between persons (Level 3), days (Level 2), and/or episodes (Level 1). Often, a substantial amount of the variance can be attributed to the situation (episode), as well as to the person, but less so to the day (e.g., less than 10% of the variance). In these cases, researchers may want – also depending on the research question under study – to ignore the day-level and use two-level models (i.e., episodes nested within persons).

To study the relation between work episodes and exhaustion, we can use characteristics of the episode (e.g., workload) to predict current feelings of exhaustion. In diary studies, most scholars transform the predictor variable in a way that positive values will reflect that the person had a stronger manifestation of the construct (e.g., higher workload) in the current episode relative to his or her own mean across episodes. In contrast, negative values reflect a weaker manifestation (e.g., lower workload) compared to other episodes. Importantly, this transformation [called group (or day in this case)-mean centering] removes all between-person variance in the predictor and an interpretation of the results in terms of stable differences between persons can be ruled out (Ilies et al., 2007). This, however, also implies that the mean level of the predictor (e.g., average amount of workload) is ignored. A simple way to include this potentially interesting information is to use the aggregated daily measures of the predictor as an additional between-person variable. In other words, we would predict current well-being by episode-specific deviations from the average level of the predictor (within-person effect), as well as by the average level of the predictor (as a between-person effect).

To test lagged instead of simultaneous effects (e.g., predict the outcome in the following episode/day [t_2] by a characteristic of the present episode/day [t_1]), we first have to slightly restructure the data in a way that both measurements are in the same row of the data file. Then, we regress the outcome at t_2 on the event characteristic at t_1 as well as the outcome at t_1 (i.e., autocorrelation). In our example, the time lag between one episode and the subsequent one is not equal. One way to consider unequal time lags is to use the interval between the two time points and its interactions with the outcome at t_1 and event characteristic at t_1 as additional predictors (see Beal & Weiss, 2003). Another way to test lagged effects of work episodes on well-being is to aggregate the episode data for each day to get a measure of a day instead of episode level (e.g., day-specific workload). This variable can then be used to predict exhaustion after work, at bedtime and the next morning. This same process may be applied in order to test the effect of previous day's exhaustion on next day's recovery. To test such prospective with dependent variables at multiple time points, researchers can either run separate analyses for each time point or run one (three-level) model and analyze the outcomes simultaneously (for details, see Nezlek, 2012). The latter approach further allows to directly comparing the strength of these effects (e.g., whether the effect on exhaustion at bedtime is stronger than the one on exhaustion in the morning; Meier et al., 2013).

Future challenges

Although researchers become more and more interested in understanding day-specific burnout experiences, there are still many issues that remain "terrae incognitae." Although preliminary data suggests that short-scales that have been adapted to measure daily burnout experiences are quite reliable, there is no evidence on their psychometric properties at the within-person level of analysis. Sonnentag et al. (2010) expressed doubts about the appropriateness of measuring daily experiences by simply modifying scales that have been initially developed to measure the same construct but as an enduring phenomenon. The reason is that some of the experiences captured with the main questionnaire may not be encountered on a daily or weekly basis. Infrequently occurring experiences are likely to produce low inter-item correlations, which consequently may result in different factor structures.

Inspired by this criticism, Breevaart et al. (2012) performed a multilevel factor analytic study on the day-level version of the Utrecht Work Engagement Scale and found that the three-factor structure of the engagement construct was confirmed both at the between and at the within-person level of analysis, and was superior to alternative solutions. Findings also showed that one item capturing vigor in the morning and not throughout the day functioned better at the between rather than at the within-person level of analysis. This finding suggests that one should be extremely careful when adapting items of between-person scales at the within-person level of analyses so that all items refer to the same moment in time. Evidence on the factor structure of burnout across levels of analysis is not available. Following Breevaart and colleagues (2012), scholars are encouraged to perform similar tests in order to validate the adapted day-specific burnout sub-scales.

Overall, research suggests that burnout experiences may vary from day to day, at least in a non-clinical population. However, with regard to short-term fluctuations among people with clinical burnout, very little is known. As an exception, Sonnenschein et al. (2007) compared the level, trajectory, and variability of exhaustion and fatigue of healthy and burned out people. Supporting previous research, burned out individuals reported higher levels of exhaustion and fatigue. Of particular interest, burned out people also showed a more flattened diurnal pattern of fatigue (i.e., lower within-person variance), supporting the assumption of an energy erosion and lack of recovery overnight. Future research may also want to study the dynamics of other components of burnout. Further, it would be interesting to examine whether psychological detachment is a functional way to cope with stressors particularly for those at risk of clinical burnout (Sonnentag, 2005).

Most previous research focused on the effects of stable work conditions on burnout, while relatively little is known about the short-term effects of work characteristics such as job demands and resources on the different components of burnout. This is particularly true for cynicism and reduced professional efficacy. Event-based diary studies could be used to examine critical events that trigger feelings of cynicism. Moreover, diary studies would allow testing whether burned-out individuals (e.g., measured as a between-person variable before the diary study started) react particularly strongly to day-specific demands. Because such an increased vulnerability would further undermine the already depleted resources (i.e., energy), it would point to a loss spiral (Hobfoll, 2001).

Another issue that is interesting for future research concerns reciprocal effects of the burnout components in the short run. Various types of causal relationships between the three components of burnout have been suggested (Taris et al., 2005). One prominent idea is that cynicism is used as a coping style once personal resources are depleted, where exhaustion functions as the driver of cynicism (Leiter & Maslach, 1988). Past research is limited to retrospective reports of chronic work conditions, enduring levels of burnout, and hence also rather global tendencies to cope with stressful situations. A study by Todd et al. (2004), however, indicated that there is only weak concordance between global reports and actual daily coping behavior. Moreover, Maslach et al. (2001) noted that distancing is an immediate reaction to exhaustion, which again suggests the use of shorter time frames. Therefore, researchers may want to test the proposed prospective patterns with daily assessments of the burnout components. For example, exhaustion in the morning may be assumed to trigger cynical thoughts throughout the workday. Moreover, this effect may depend on situational and personal characteristics. For example, it may be particularly strong among people with low social support by coworkers, or among those with high levels of chronic burnout.

Conclusion

In this chapter, we shifted the attention from between-employee differences in burnout to daily within-person experiences and events that are critical for the development of the syndrome. Examining within-employee changes over and above general levels in exhaustion, cynicism, and reduced professional efficacy allows answering the following questions (Sonnentag, 2005):

- Which daily critical events enhance day-specific burnout experiences irrespective of one's general burnout levels?
- Do burned-out and non-burned-out employees differ in how they deal with daily situational constraints, as well as in their within-person variations in day-specific burnout experiences?
- How do day-specific burnout experiences accumulate over time?

We, by no means, suggest that the burnout syndrome can be developed within the course of one workday or over short-periods of time (e.g., a workweek). Rather, we propose that critical events that take place at work on a daily basis fuel daily states of exhaustion, cynicism, and reduced professional efficacy that, if accumulated and not recovered, may result in an enduring burnout state (see Figure 5.1). Viewing the development of burnout as the accumulation of frequent, momentary burnout experiences, adds to our understanding of the phenomenon because it allows synthesizing micro-experiences that form a macro-reality. These micro- and macro-perspectives are complementary, and provide a more complete interpretation of the burnout experience.

Acknowledgments

Laurenz L. Meier was supported by a Swiss National Science Foundation Grant (PZ00P1-142393).

References

Bakker, A. B., & Demerouti, E. (2007). The job demands-resources model: State of the art. *Journal of Managerial Psychology, 22,* 309–328.

Bakker, A. B., Demerouti, E., Oerlemans, W., & Sonnentag, S. (2013). Workaholism and daily recovery: A day reconstruction study of leisure activities. *Journal of Organizational Behavior, 34,* 87–107.

Beal, D. J., & Weiss, H. M. (2003). Methods of ecological momentary assessment in organizational research. *Organizational Research Methods, 6,* 440–464

Beal, D. J., & Weiss, H. M. (2013). The episodic structure of life at work. In A. B. Bakker & K. Daniels (Eds), *A day in the life of a happy worker* (pp. 8–24). New York: Psychology Press.

Biron, M., & Van Veldhoven, M. (2012). Emotional labour in service work: Psychological flexibility and emotion regulation. *Human Relations, 65,* 1259–1282.

Bolger, N., & Laurenceau, J-P. (2013). *Intensive longitudinal methods: An introduction to diary and experience sampling research.* New York: Guilford.

Bollen, K. A., & Curran, P. J. (2006). *Latent curve models: A structural equation perspective.* Hoboken, NJ: Wiley & Sons.

Breevaart, K., Bakker, A. B., Demerouti, E., & Hetland, J. (2012). The measurement of state work engagement: A multilevel factor analytic study. *European Journal of Psychological Assessment, 28,* 305–312.

Butler, A. B., Grzywacz, J.G., Bass, B. L., & Linney, K. D. (2005). Extending the demands-control model: A daily diary study of job characteristics, work-family conflict and work-family facilitation. *Journal of Occupational and Organizational Psychology, 78,* 155–169.

Conner, T. S., & Lehman, B. J. (2012). Getting started: Launching a study in daily life. In M. R. Mehl & T. S. Conner (Eds), *Handbook of research methods for studying daily life* (pp. 89–107). New York: Guilford.

Cranford, J., Shrout, P., Iida, M., Rafaeli, E., Yip, T., & Bolger, N. (2006). A procedure for evaluating sensitivity to within-person change: Can mood measures in diary studies detect change reliably? *Personality and Social Psychology Bulletin, 32,* 917–929.

Demerouti, E., & Sanz-Vergel, A. I. (2012). Daily recovery and well-being: An overview. *Psicothema, 24,* 73–78.

Demerouti, E., Bakker, A. B., Nachreiner, F., & Schaufeli, W. B. (2001). The job demands-resources model of burnout. *Journal of Applied Psychology, 86*, 499–512.

Demerouti, E., Bakker, A. B., Vardakou, I., & Kantas, A. (2003). The convergent validity of two burnout instruments: A multitrait-multimethod analysis. *European Journal of Psychological Assessment, 19*, 12–23.

Diener, E., & Tay, L. (in press). Review of the Day Reconstruction Method (DRM). *Social Indicators Research.*

Feldt, T., Huhtala, M., Kinnunen, U., Hyvönen, K., Mäkikangas, A., & Sonnentag, S. (2013). Long-term patterns of effort-reward imbalance and over-commitment: Investigating occupational well-being and recovery experiences as outcomes. *Work and Stress, 27*, 64–87.

Fredrickson, B. L., Cohn, M. A., Coffey, K. A., Pek, J., & Finkel, S. M. (2008). Open hearts build lives: Positive emotions, induced through loving-kindness meditation, build consequential personal resources. *Journal of Personality and Social Psychology, 95*, 1045–1062.

Grech, M. R., Neal, A., Yeo, G., Humphreys, M., & Smith, S. (2009). An examination of the relationship between workload and fatigue within and across consecutive days of work: Is the relationship static or dynamic? *Journal of Occupational Health Psychology, 14*, 231–242.

Gross, S., Semmer, N. K., Meier, L. L., Kälin, W., Jacobshagen, N., & Tschan, F. (2011). The effect of positive events at work on after-work fatigue: They matter most in face of adversity. *Journal of Applied Psychology, 96*, 654–664.

Halbesleben, J., & Buckley, M. R. (2004). Burnout in organizational life. *Journal of Management, 30*, 859–879.

Halbesleben, J., & Wheeler, A. R. (2011). I owe you one: Coworker reciprocity as a moderator of the day-level exhaustion–performance relationship. *Journal of Organizational Behavior, 32*, 608–626.

Hammaker, E. L. (2012). Why researchers should think "within-person": A paradigmatic rationale. In M. R. Mehl & T. S. Conner (Eds), *Handbook of research methods for studying daily life* (pp. 43–61). New York: Guilford.

Hobfoll, S. E. (1989). Conservation of Resources: A new attempt at conceptualizing stress. *American Psychologist, 44*, 513–524.

Hobfoll, S.E. (2001). The influence of culture, community, and the nested-self in the stress process: Advancing conservation of resources theory. *Applied Psychology: An International Review, 50*, 337–421.

Holman, D. J., Totterdell, P., & Rogelberg, S. G. (2005). A daily diary study of goal striving: The relationship between goal distance, goal velocity, affect, expectancies and effort. In N. M. Ashkanasy, W. J. Zerbe, & C. E. J. Hartel (Eds), *Research on emotion in organizations, Volume 1: The effect of affect in organizational settings* (pp. 95–121). Oxford, UK: Elsevier Science.

Ilies, R., Schwind, K. M., & Heller, D. (2007). Employee well-being: A multilevel model linking work and nonwork domains. *European Journal of Work and Organizational Psychology, 16*, 326–341.

Kinnunen, U. (1988). Teacher stress during an autumn term in Finland: Four types of stress processes. *Work and Stress, 2*, 333–340.

Kuppens, P., Allen, N. B., & Sheeber, L. B. (2010). Emotional inertia and psychological maladjustment. *Psychological Science, 21*, 984–991.

Lee, R., & Ashforth, B. E. (1990). On the meaning of Maslach's three dimensions of burnout. *Journal of Applied Psychology, 75*, 743–747.

Lee, R., & Ashforth, B. E. (1996). A meta-analytic examination of the correlates of the three dimensions of job burnout. *Journal of Applied Psychology, 81,* 123–133.

Leiter M. P., & Maslach C. (1988). The impact of interpersonal environment on burnout and organizational commitment. *Journal of Organizational Behavior, 9,* 297–308.

Leiter, M. P., & Schaufeli, W. B. (1996). Consistency of the burnout construct across occupations. *Anxiety, Stress & Coping, 9,* 229–243.

Mäkikangas, A., Feldt, T., Kinnunen, U., & Tolvanen, A. (2012). Do low burnout and high work engagement always go hand in hand? Investigation of the energy and identification dimensions in longitudinal data. *Anxiety, Stress & Coping, 25,* 93–116.

Maslach, C., Jackson, S. E., & Leiter, M. P. (1996). *Maslach burnout inventory manual* (3rd edn). Palo Alto, CA: Consulting Psychologists Press.

Maslach, C., Schaufeli, W. B., & Leiter, M. (2001). Job burnout. *Annual Review of Psychology, 52,* 397–422.

McNair, D. M., Lorr, M., & Droppleman, L. F. (1992). *EdITS manual for the Profile of Mood States.* San Diego, CA: Educational and Industrial Testing Service.

Mehl, M. R., && Conner, T. S. (Eds) (2012). *Handbook of research methods for studying daily life.* New York: Guilford Press.

Meier, L. L., Gross, S., Spector, P. E., & Semmer, N. K. (2013). Task and relationship conflict at work: Interactive short-term effects on angry mood and somatic complaints. *Journal of Occupational Health Psychology, 18,* 144–156.

Meijman, T. F., & Mulder, G. (1998). Psychological aspects of workload. In P. D. Drenth, H. Thierry, & C. J. De Wolff (Eds), *Handbook of work and organizational psychology* (Vol. 2: Work psychology, pp. 5–33). Hove, England: Psychology Press.

Nezlek, J. B. (2012). Diary methods for social and personality psychology. In J. B. Nezlek (Ed.), *The SAGE library in social and personality psychology methods.* London: Sage Publications.

Oerlemans, W. G. M., & Bakker, A. B. (2013). Capturing the moment in the workplace: Two methods to study momentary subjective well-being. In A. B. Bakker (Ed.), *Advances in positive organizational psychology* (Vol. 1; pp: 329–346). Bigley, UK: Emerald.

Pereira, D., Meier, L. L., & Elfering, A. (2013). Short-term effects of social exclusion at work and worries on sleep. *Stress and Health, 29,* 240–252.

Ram, N., & Gerstorf, D. (2009). Time-structured and net intraindividual variability: Tools for examining the development of dynamic characteristics and processes. *Psychology and Aging, 24,* 778–791.

Sanz-Vergel, A. I., Rodriguez-Muñoz, A., Bakker, A. B., & Demerouti, E. (2012). The daily spillover and crossover of emotional labor: Faking emotions at work and at home. *Journal of Vocational Behavior, 81,* 209–217.

Schaufeli, W. B. (2006). Past performance and future perspectives of burnout research. *SA Journal of Industrial Psychology, 29,* 1–15.

Schaufeli, W. B., & Bakker, A. B. (2004). Job demands, job resources, and their relationship with burnout and engagement: A multi-sample study. *Journal of Organizational Behavior, 25,* 293–315.

Schaufeli, W. B., Leiter, M. P., Maslach, C., & Jackson, S. E. (1996). Maslach Burnout Inventory – general survey. In C. Maslach, S. E. Jackson, & M. P. Leiter (Eds), *The Maslach Burnout Inventory-Test manual* (3rd edn). Palo Alto, CA: Consulting Psychologists Press.

Schaufeli, W. B., Leiter, M. P., & Maslach, C. (2009). Burnout: 35 years of research and practice. *Career Development International, 14,* 204–220.

Schaufeli, W. B., Maassen, G. H., Bakker, A. B., & Sixma, H. J. (2011). Stability and change in burnout: A 10-year follow-up study among primary care physicians. *Journal of Occupational and Organizational Psychology*, *84*, 248–267.

Schwarzer, R., & Jerusalem, M. (1995). Generalized self-efficacy scale. In J. Weinman, S. Wright, & M. Johnston (Eds), *Measures in health psychology: A user's portfolio. Causal and control beliefs* (pp. 35–37). Windsor, UK: NFER-NELSON.

Shirom, A., Melamed, S., Toker, S., Berliner, S., & Shapira, I. (2005). Burnout and health review: Current knowledge and future research directions. In G. P. Hodgkinson & J. K. Ford (Eds), *International review of industrial and organizational psychology* (Vol. 20, pp. 269–309).

Shrout, P. E., & Lane, S. P. (2012). Psychometrics. In M. R. Mehl & T. S. Conner (Eds), *Handbook of research methods for studying daily life* (pp. 302–320). New York: Guilford.

Simbula, S. (2010). Daily fluctuations in teachers' well-being: a diary study using the Job Demands–Resources model. *Anxiety, Stress & Coping*, *23*, 563–584.

Singer, J. D., & Willett, J. B. (2003). *Applied longitudinal data analysis: Modeling change and event occurrence.* New York, NY: Oxford University Press.

Sliwinski, M. J. (2008). Measurement-burst designs for social health research. *Social and Personality Psychology Compass*, *2*, 245–261.

Sliwinski, M. J., Almeida, D. M., Smyth, J., & Stawski, R. S. (2009). Intraindividual change and variability in daily stress processes: Findings from two measurement-burst diary studies. *Psychology and Aging*, *24*, 828–840.

Sonnenschein, M., Sorbi, M. J., Doornen, L. J. P. V., Schaufeli, W. B., & Maas, C. J. M. (2007). Electronic diary evidence on energy erosion in clinical burnout. *Journal of Occupational Health Psychology*, *12*, 402–413.

Sonnentag, S. (2003). Recovery, work engagement, and proactive behavior: A new look at the interface between nonwork and work. *Journal of Applied Psychology, 88*, 518–528.

Sonnentag, S. (2005). Burnout research: Adding an off-work and day-level perspective. *Work & Stress*, *19*, 271–275.

Sonnentag, S., & Bayer, U-V. (2005). Switching off mentally: Predictors and consequences of psychological detachment from work during off-job time. *Journal of Occupational Health Psychology, 10*, 393–414.

Sonnentag, S., & Fritz, C. (2007). The recovery experience questionnaire: Development and validation of a measure for assessing recuperation and unwinding from work. *Journal of Occupational Health Psychology, 12*, 204–221.

Sonnentag, S., Binnewies, C., & Mojza, E. J. (2008). "Did you have a nice evening?" A day-level study on recovery experiences, sleep, and affect. *Journal of Applied Psychology, 93*, 674–684.

Sonnentag, S., Dormann, C., & Demerouti, E. (2010). Not all days are created equal: The concept of state work engagement. In A. B. Bakker & M. P. Leiter (Eds), *Work engagement: A handbook of essential theory and research* (pp. 25–38). New York: Psychology Press.

Suls, J., & Martin, R. (2005). The daily life of the garden-variety neurotic: Reactivity, stressor exposure, mood spillover, and maladaptive coping. *Journal of Personality*, *73*, 1485–1510.

Taris, T. W., Le Blanc, P. M., Schaufeli, W. B., & Schreurs, P. J. (2005). Are there causal relationships between the dimensions of the Maslach Burnout Inventory? A review and two longitudinal tests. *Work and Stress*, *19*, 238–255.

Ten Brummelhuis, L. L., Ter Hoeven, C.L., Bakker, A. B., & Peper, B. (2011). Breaking through the loss cycle of burnout: The role of motivation. *Journal of Occupational and Organizational Psychology, 84*, 268–287.

Todd, M., Tennen, H., Carney, M. A., Armeli, S., & Affleck, G. (2004). Do we know how to cope? Relating daily coping report to global and time-limited retrospective assessments. *Journal of Personality and Social Psychology, 86*, 310–319.

Van Gelderen, B. R., Bakker, A. B., Konijn, E. A., & Demerouti, E. (2011). Emotional labor among police service workers and criminal investigation officers. *Anxiety, Stress and Coping, 24*, 515–537.

Van Hooff, M., Geurts, S. A. E., Kompier, M. A. J., & Taris, T. W. (2007). "How fatigued do you currently feel?" Convergent and discriminant validity of a single-item fatigue measure. *Journal of Occupational Health, 49*, 224–234.

Wang, M., & Bodner, T. E. (2007). Growth mixture modeling: Identifying and predicting unobserved subpopulations with longitudinal data. *Organizational Research Methods, 10*, 635–656.

Weiss, H. M., & Cropanzano, R. (1996). Affective events theory: A theoretical discussion of affective experiences at work. In B. M. Staw & L. L. Cummings (Eds), *Research in organizational behaviour* (pp. 1– 74). Greenwich, CT: JAI Press.

Xanthopoulou, D., Bakker, A. B., Heuven, E., Demerouti, E., & Schaufeli, W. B. (2008). Working in the sky: A diary study on work engagement among flight attendants. *Journal of Occupational Health Psychology, 13*, 345–356.

Xanthopoulou, D., Bakker, A. B., Demerouti, E., & Schaufeli, W. B. (2009). Work engagement and financial returns: A diary study on the role of job and personal resources. *Journal of Occupational and Organizational Psychology, 82*, 183–200.

Xanthopoulou, D., Bakker, A. B., & Ilies, R. (2012a). Everyday working life: Explaining within-person fluctuations in employee well-being. *Human Relations, 65*, 1051–1069.

Xanthopoulou, D., Bakker, A. B., Oerlemans, W., & Koszucka, M. (2012b). *Recovering from emotional labour: A diary study on the role of deep and surface acting.* Paper presented at the European Academy of Occupational Health Psychology, Zurich, Switzerland.

6 The influence of constructive and destructive leadership behaviors on follower burnout

Kimberley Breevaart, Arnold B. Bakker,
Jørn Hetland, and Hilde Hetland

Introduction

In their position of power and as role-models, leaders play a crucial role in followers' work-related well-being. Indeed, a recent review by Skakon et al. (2010) on the relationship between leadership behavior and followers' well-being showed that leaders have a profound influence on followers' affect, job satisfaction, and job strain. Remarkably, little attention has been paid to the role of leadership behavior in followers' job burnout. This is surprising, considering the serious threats that burnout poses to employees and organizations. Burned-out individuals lack the energetic and emotional resources to perform their work, endorse a negative, cynical attitude towards work, and believe they are no longer effective at getting things done (reduced professional efficacy; Schaufeli et al., 2009). Research of the past decades has shown that burnout leads to serious health problems, increased sickness absenteeism, reduced job satisfaction and organizational commitment, as well as reduced job performance (e.g., Halbesleben & Buckley, 2004; Taris, 2006; see also Chapter 1, this volume).

Because research on the relationship between leadership behavior and follower burnout is scarce (Hetland et al., 2007; Thomas & Lankau, 2009), this chapter focuses on this underexposed topic within the leadership literature. More specifically, this chapter provides a state-of-the-art review of the existing literature on the influence of leadership behavior on follower burnout. We will argue that constructive leadership behaviors prevent follower burnout, while destructive leadership behaviors promote follower burnout. In addition, we present an agenda for future research that may serve as inspiration for further research on the relationship between various leadership behaviors and follower burnout.

Classification of leadership

Within the leadership literature, "there are almost as many definitions of leadership as there are persons who have attempted to define the concept" (Stogdill, 1974, p. 259). A classification of all these different leadership theories and research can provide structure to this overwhelming amount of literature (Yukl, 2013). For example, leadership theories can be classified according to the type of variable that describes leadership effectiveness. Some leadership theories focus mainly on characteristics of the leader (e.g., traits) to describe leadership effectiveness, while others focus on characteristics of the follower (e.g., identification with the leader), characteristics of the situation (e.g., organizational culture), or on a combination of two or three of these categories. In this chapter, we classify leadership theories and behaviors in two categories to structure our discussion of the existing literature on the relationship between leadership behavior and followers' burnout. These categories are constructive and destructive leadership.

Einarsen et al. (2007) developed a conceptual model to describe the constructiveness and destructiveness of leadership behavior. Their model consists of two dimensions; subordinate- and organization-oriented behaviors, ranging from anti-subordinate and anti-organizational to pro-subordinate and pro-organization. Subordinate-oriented behaviors refer to behaviors shown by the leader (e.g., bullying or giving praise) that influence follower motivation, well-being, or job satisfaction. Organization-oriented behaviors refer to behaviors of the leader (e.g., sabotaging goal attainment or implementing change) that influence the achievement of work goals. Constructive leaders are leaders who are both pro-subordinate and pro-organization oriented, while destructive leaders are either anti-subordinate oriented, anti-organization oriented or both.

Traditionally, leadership research focuses on the positive sides of leadership, and research has been guided by the quest to find the most effective person or method to lead (Schyns & Shilling, 2013). However, the last decade has witnessed an increased interest in the potential darker sides of leadership. Although some researchers believe that leadership should only be conceptualized as a positive construct, Schyns and Shilling (2013) show the importance of both constructive and destructive leadership behaviors. They compared results from meta-analyses on constructive leadership behaviors to the results of their own meta-analyses on destructive leadership behavior. Constructive and destructive leadership was respectively positively and negatively related to job satisfaction, commitment, well-being, and job performance, and inversely related to turnover intentions. In this chapter, we will argue and show that constructive leadership behaviors diminish follower burnout, while destructive leadership behaviors contribute to follower burnout.

Theoretical framework

Burnout is a response to the chronic experience of job demands, including role ambiguity, role conflict, and workload (Lee & Ashforth, 1996; Maslach et al., 2001). Arguably, particularly hindrance job demands play an important role in the development of burnout, because – unlike challenge job demands – hindrance job demands are highly effortful *and* they frustrate personal growth and goal achievement (Cavanaugh et al., 2000). Destructive leadership can be considered a hindrance demand, since it undermines followers' motivation and hinders goal achievement. According to the Job Demands-Resources (JD-R) model (Bakker & Demerouti, 2013; Demerouti et al., 2001), hindrance job demands initiate a health impairment process in which demands deplete employees' energy and eventually lead to burnout when these demands become chronic. Destructive leadership behaviors like interpersonal aggression or bullying are demanding and drain energy and are therefore likely to contribute to follower burnout. Furthermore, hindrance demands like role conflict or role ambiguity interfere with or inhibit goal achievement (Cavanaugh et al., 2000). Destructive leadership styles like passive-avoidant leadership have been shown to promote these hindrance demands (e.g., Skogstad et al., 2007) and may thus also be indirectly related to follower burnout.

In addition to high (hindrance) job demands, a lack of job resources contributes to burnout among employees (e.g., Lee & Ashforth, 1996; Xanthopoulou et al., 2007). Constructive leaders can be considered a valuable resource that prevents follower burnout, because these leaders stimulate followers' work-related well-being and motivation, and contribute to goal achievement. According to the JD-R model, job resources initiate a motivational process that leads to higher work engagement. Job resources can be intrinsically motivating because they stimulate personal growth and development and thereby satisfy followers' needs. Job resources can also be extrinsically motivating because they contribute to the achievement of work goals. Constructive leadership behaviors include behaviors such as offering support to employees, praising employees, and stimulating employees to think independently. These behaviors are likely to constitute and/or contribute to a resourceful work environment. Constructive leadership behaviors seem more likely to act as a resource and may therefore mainly influence followers' work attitudes (i.e., the cynicism and professional efficacy dimensions of burnout), while destructive leadership behaviors are more likely to act as a demand and may predominantly influence followers' emotional exhaustion (i.e., the core energetic dimension of burnout; see Demerouti et al., 2001).

Besides these main effects, the JD-R model also proposes interaction effects between job demands and job resources. First, job resources mainly contribute to followers' work engagement when challenging job demands are high and hindrance demands are low, because such conditions create an active and meaningful job (Bakker et al., 2007; Hakanen et al., 2005). This means that constructive leaders should not only be supportive and inspirational, but they should also set high performance expectations and delegate challenging tasks. The second interaction effect proposed by the JD-R model states that hindrance job demands in combination with low job resources predicts burnout (Bakker et al., 2005). Accordingly, destructive leadership behaviors such as bullying or displaying aggression will predominantly predict follower burnout when the work environment is not resourceful (e.g., limited autonomy and developmental opportunities). It also means that constructive leadership behaviors like supporting and praising employees may buffer the effect of job demands on follower burnout.

Constructive leadership

Although it seems likely that destructive leadership behaviors are more strongly related to follower burnout, most research on the relationship between leadership behavior and follower burnout has focused on the role of leaders in preventing follower burnout. Specifically, most research has focused on the influence of supervisory support, the leader-member exchange relationship, transformational leadership, and transactional leadership on follower burnout. We will discuss this literature in more detail below.

Supervisory support

In line with JD-R theory, research has shown that followers experience less burnout when they receive support from their leader (e.g., Bakker et al., 2005; Duxbury et al., 1984; Herman, 1983; Seltzer & Numerof, 1988). Lee and Ashforth (1996) were the first to meta-analytically examine the relationship between different sources of social support and employee burnout. Results from their meta-analysis showed that for all burnout dimensions, supervisory support was more strongly negatively related to employee burnout compared to support from coworkers. Supervisory support was mainly related to emotional exhaustion (-.37), followed by depersonalization (-.19) and professional accomplishment (.14). A more recent meta-analysis on the relationship between support from different sources and employee burnout included not only coworker and supervisor support, but also support from family and friends (Halbesleben, 2006). Similar to the results from the meta-analysis performed by Lee and Ashforth (1996), supervisory support was the most important source of support to decrease followers' burnout compared to all other kinds of support. Again, supervisory support mainly reduced followers' emotional exhaustion (-.28), followed by depersonalization (-.24) and professional accomplishment (.24).

While the aforementioned research suggests that social support has a main effect on follower burnout, other studies suggest that supervisory support interacts with job demands to prevent followers from experiencing burnout. As proposed by JD-R theory (Demerouti et al., 2001), the chronic experience of job demands initiates a health impairment process, which depletes energy and may result in burnout. However, job resources, like job autonomy, constructive feedback and social support, can buffer this effect (Bakker et al., 2005). For example, when individuals experience high workload, social support may counter possible negative health effects by distracting people from the stressors, providing a solution to handle the stressors, or reducing the importance of the stressor (Cohen, 2004). However, results regarding the buffering effect of social support on the relationship between job demands and follower burnout are inconsistent (e.g., Constable & Russell, 1986; Etzion, 1984; Fried & Tiegs, 1993).

A possible explanation for these inconsistent findings may be that the buffering effect depends on the type of support that is provided. Three types of social support are often differentiated: emotional, instrumental, and informational support (e.g., House & Kahn, 1985). Emotional support refers to expressing empathy, caring, reassurance, and trust, and providing people with the opportunity to express themselves emotionally. Instrumental support means that people receive materials that help them cope with their demands. Informational support is also about helping people to cope with their demands, by providing them with relevant information (e.g., advice). Employees may feel that instrumental and informational support actually hands them tools to deal with their job demands. Hence, instrumental and informational supervisory support may show a buffering effect on the relationship between job demands and followers' burnout. On the contrary, emotional support may moderate the relationship between job demands and burnout in a reversed manner, meaning that emotional social support may strengthen the relationship between job demands and follower burnout. Emotional support may create an inconsistency between the supervisors' actions (creation of job demands) and the subsequent emotional support. This reverse buffering effect may therefore be specific to leadership support, since leaders in their power position are held responsible for shaping the work environment, including its job demands. It could be that employees would prefer supervisors to act on the job demands themselves instead of providing support to cope with the stressors.

Leader-member exchange

Leader-member exchange (LMX) theory (Graen & Cashman, 1975; Graen & Uhl-Bien, 1995) is one of the few leadership theories that focuses on the dyadic relationship between leader and follower. LMX theory states that leaders develop unique exchange relationships with each follower and the quality of these relationships range from low to high. Low-quality LMX relationships are very formal relationships in which followers perform their work and get paid accordingly. High-quality LMX relationships, on the other hand, are based on mutual trust, respect, and obligation. Leaders in high-quality LMX relationships have high performance expectations, in exchange for the provision of additional resources. High-quality relationships are a valuable resource to followers, because these followers have a privileged way of communicating with their leader and are provided with desirable work assignments (Dulebohn et al., 2012). Accordingly, high-quality LMX relationships are often considered as a source of social support or supervisory coaching. Low-quality LMX relationships can be demanding, because followers in these relationships rarely meet with their supervisors and are often provided with undesirable, monotonous assignments (Dulebohn et al., 2012).

LMX has been included in JD-R studies as one of several job resources to examine the relationship between job resources and burnout. For example, Schaufeli and Bakker (2004) examined how job resources (i.e., LMX, support from colleagues, and performance feedback) were related to both burnout and work engagement. In four independent samples from different types of organizations, they found that a resourceful work environment contributed to employees' work engagement, while a lack of resources promoted employees' burnout. More specifically, they found that LMX was negatively related to exhaustion (-.16) and cynicism (-.14) and positively related to professional efficacy (.24). Furthermore, Xanthopoulou et al. (2007) examined the relationship between job resources (i.e., LMX, autonomy, social support, and professional development), personal resources, and burnout. Their findings suggested that a high-quality LMX relationship was a protective factor for burnout because it improved employees' resiliency beliefs (i.e., self-esteem, optimism, and self-efficacy).

Thomas and Lankau (2009) examined whether role stress can explain the relationship between LMX and emotional exhaustion. They argued that high-quality LMX relationships are associated with increased communication, which reduces uncertainty and ambiguity and therefore results in less role stress and burnout. In line with their hypothesis, Thomas and Lankau (2009) found that a high-quality LMX relationship resulted in less role stress and, consequently, less burnout. Finally, Becker et al. (2005) studied LMX as a mediator between defensive communication and burnout (i.e., exhaustion and cynicism). They showed that this type of communication resulted in lower quality LMX relationships, which increased followers' burnout.

To our knowledge, there is only one study that examined the moderating role of LMX in the relationship between job demands and follower burnout. In their study among teachers, Bakker et al. (2005) focused on the interaction between job demands and job resources in predicting follower burnout. They argued that high-quality LMX relationships help followers cope with their job demands and/or put their demands in another perspective. With regard to LMX, they found that the relationship between job demands (i.e., workload, physical demands, and work-home interference) and emotional exhaustion was less strong when followers were in a high-quality LMX relationship with their leader. High-quality LMX relationships also moderated the positive relationship between work-family conflict and cynicism.

Transformational leadership

Transformational leadership is a very popular and well-examined leadership style that has many positive implications, such as higher follower productivity, commitment, satisfaction, and work engagement (e.g., Breevaart et al., 2013b; Judge & Piccolo, 2004; Zhu et al., 2009). Transformational leadership is a multidimensional construct, consisting of four related, but distinct components (Bass, 1985; 1999). First, idealized influence means that leaders are a role model to their followers and are respected and trusted by them. Second, inspirational motivation refers to the communication of clear expectations and a positive and compelling vision of the future. These leaders inspire their followers with their vision. Third, intellectual stimulation is about encouraging followers to think independently and out of the box and to come up with new ideas. Finally, individual stimulation means that leaders acknowledge followers' unique needs and abilities and delegate tasks accordingly. Considering the status of transformational leadership within the leadership literature, it is surprising that only a few studies have examined its influence on follower burnout. Transformational leadership is likely to be a valuable resource in followers' work environments, since it includes features such as empowering employees, being supportive, and acting as a mentor.

Two studies examining the relationship between transformational leadership and follower burnout among nurses found that transformational leadership was unrelated to followers' emotional exhaustion (Kanste et al., 2007; Stordeur et al., 2001). The latter authors argued that job demands explain a substantial amount of variance in follower burnout, which makes it difficult for transformational leadership to explain additional, unique variance in follower burnout. In a similar vein, Hetland et al. (2007) found that transformational leadership and followers' emotional exhaustion were no longer related after controlling for followers' neuroticism. They reasoned that there may be certain follower characteristics that moderate the relationship between transformational leadership and follower burnout that affect how followers respond to transformational leaders. For some followers, emotionally charged interactions with leaders may be stressful and therefore contribute to rather than protect them from experiencing strain. In line with the motivational process of the JD-R model, Hetland et al. (2007) and Kanste et al. (2007) both found that transformational leadership promoted professional accomplishment and reduced cynical attitudes (depersonalization in their studies). Transformational leaders make work meaningful and challenging and show confidence in their followers, which likely explains why transformational leaders contribute to followers' feelings of professional accomplishment. Furthermore, transformational leaders increase followers' work motivation, which can explain the negative relationship between transformational leadership and depersonalization. These results may not be surprising, since transformational is a motivational leadership style that initiates a motivational process. It is therefore more strongly related to followers' motivation than to followers' levels of energy (exhaustion).

Finally, a study by Densten (2005) shows that it may be worthwhile to look at the different components of transformational leadership when studying its relationship with follower burnout. Densten (2005) examined whether visionary leadership, comprised of concept-based and image-based inspirational motivation, contributed to follower burnout. Image-based inspirational motivation refers to creating vivid ideas, visions or images among followers by using encouragement, symbols and images. Concept-based inspirational motivation is about creating a vision and expectations in order to communicate bottom-line goals that lead to a strategic focus. Concept-based inspirational motivation was negatively related to follower burnout (i.e., diminished professional accomplishment, depersonalization, and emotional exhaustion), while image-based inspirational motivation was positively related to followers' professional accomplishment and negatively related to depersonalization, but unrelated to emotional exhaustion. This study suggests that it may be important to look at the different components of transformational leadership when studying its effect on follower burnout. Inspirational motivation, being a part of transformational leadership, may be unrelated to emotional exhaustion, but other components of transformational leadership may be differently related to follower burnout. For example, individual consideration may increase followers' feelings of supervisory support, which may reduce followers' emotional exhaustion.

Destructive leadership

Although the interest in potential destructive sides of leadership is novel, a rather wide range of conceptualizations and definitions of the nature of these leadership behaviors has been given. Among the most used conceptualizations are abusive supervision (Tepper, 2000), destructive leadership (Einarsen et al., 2007), toxic leadership (Lipman-Blumen, 2005), and petty tyranny (Ashforth, 1994). Lately an overreaching concept of destructive leadership has been suggested by Krasikova et al. (2013). In their theoretical review they define destructive leadership as

> volitional behavior by a leader that can harm or intends to harm a leader's organization and/or followers by (a) encouraging followers to pursue goals that contravene the legitimate interests of the organization and/or (b) employing a leadership style that involves the use of harmful methods of influence with followers, regardless of justifications for such behavior. (pp. 23–27)

As such, destructive leadership is demanding and drains energy, thereby contributing to follower burnout. Among studies focusing on the link between destructive leadership behaviors and follower burnout, most studies have focused on abusive supervision, while much less is known about the relationship with other conceptualizations of destructive leadership.

Abusive leadership

Research has shown that interpersonal aggression results in burnout (Evers et al., 2002; Van Dierendonck & Mevissen, 2002). One of the leadership styles that is especially relevant when it comes to interpersonal aggression is abusive leadership. Abusive leaders continuously display aggressive behavior, both verbally and non-verbally, but never with physical contact (Tepper, 2000). Examples of these kinds of behaviors are blaming followers for something they did not do, breaking promises, expressing anger toward followers while the anger is caused by something or somebody else and being rude. Studies have shown that abusive leadership has detrimental effects on followers' work-related attitudes and health, including frustration, helplessness, alienation from work, and job satisfaction (e.g., Ashforth, 1997; Keashly et al., 1994).

Only a few studies have examined the relationship between abusive leadership and follower burnout. Most of these studies focused on the relationship between abusive leadership and followers' emotional exhaustion, showing that followers of abusive leaders are more emotionally exhausted (e.g., Aryee et al., 2008; Tepper, 2000). Harvey et al. (2007) examined moderators of the positive relationship between abusive leadership and followers' emotional exhaustion. Specifically, they examined the moderating effects of followers' positive affect (PA) and use of ingratiation (i.e., a social influence tactic that employees use for their personal interest such as flattery and performing favors). Harvey and colleagues argue that employees may use ingratiation to restore their feelings of freedom and control that may be threatened by abusive leaders. They also argue that employees with high levels of positive affect will use ingratiation more effectively. The results were in line with their predictions. Employees' emotional exhaustion was unaffected by abusive leaders when followers had high levels of PA and used ingratiation. However, abusive leadership was positively related to followers' emotional exhaustion for followers low in PA and who did not use ingratiation.

Wu and Hu (2009) also examined the relationship between abusive leadership and followers' emotional exhaustion and whether susceptibility to emotional contagion and coworkers' social support moderated this relationship. Abusive leaders often show behaviors accompanied by negative emotions. Employees susceptible to emotional contagion are likely to be negatively influenced by these negative emotions, which brings about an additional emotional load employees have to deal with. This additional load increases the likelihood of followers becoming emotionally exhausted. Furthermore, the authors expected social support from coworkers to buffer the effect of abusive leadership on emotional exhaustion. The cross-domain buffering hypothesis (Duffy et al., 2002) supposes that support from one domain (e.g., coworker support) may buffer the negative effects of social undermining from another domain (e.g., abusive leadership). The results confirmed that abusive leadership is positively related to followers' emotional exhaustion and this relationship is moderated in the expected direction by susceptibility to emotional contagion. However, the relationship between abusive leadership and employee emotional exhaustion was stronger for followers who received high coworker support than for followers receiving low coworker support, which was opposite to what was predicted. The authors explain this result by stating that there may be a ceiling effect; employees who receive low coworker support may already experience emotional exhaustion at such a level that any increase in abusive leadership does not lead to higher emotional exhaustion. Another possibility is that there is a reverse buffering effect because support from coworkers reminds employees of their negative work environment, which strengthens the relationship between abusive leadership and emotional exhaustion.

Instead of only focusing on emotional exhaustion, Yagil (2006) studied the effect of abusive supervisory behaviors on a composite score of follower burnout (i.e., emotional exhaustion, depersonalization, and professional efficacy). In line with the hypothesis and earlier research (Duffy et al., 2002; Tepper, 2000), it was found that abusive leadership was positively related to followers' emotional exhaustion and depersonalization. Contrary to the expectations, abusive leadership was unrelated to (a diminished sense of) professional accomplishment. As with passive-avoidant leadership, it could be that the supervisor's abusive behavior only affects followers' perception of the work environment and not the followers' self-perception, which could be a coping mechanism to deal with the leaders' behavior. It also indicates that it may be important to focus on all three subcomponents of burnout, since they may have different predictors.

Passive-avoidant leadership

One other leadership style that may be detrimental to follower burnout is passive-avoidant leadership. Being part of the full range of leadership theory (Bass, 1985), passive-avoidant leadership, also called laissez-faire leadership or non-leadership, is characterized by not taking responsibility or even being completely absent as a leader. Passive-avoidant leaders are often absent when they are needed, avoid making decisions, and avoid being involved with their followers. It has been shown that passive-avoidant leadership is very destructive in the way that it leads to more role conflict, role ambiguity, conflicts with colleagues, and bullying at work (Skogstad et al., 2007). Research has shown that the lack of clear expectations, responsibilities, and roles contribute to burnout (e.g., Maslach & Leiter, 1997; Maslach & Schaufeli, 1993), which makes it likely that passive-avoidant leadership contributes to follower burnout.

There are only a handful of studies that show the negative effects of passive-avoidant leadership on follower burnout. For example, Kanste et al. (2007) examined the relationship between passive-avoidant leadership and follower burnout among nurses. They expected and found that passive-avoidant leadership was positively related to nurses' burnout. More specifically, passive-avoidant leadership was positively related to emotional exhaustion and depersonalization and negatively related to professional accomplishment. Hetland et al. (2007) also examined the influence of passive-avoidant leadership on follower burnout. They expected passive-avoidant leadership to be positively related to follower burnout, which was partially supported by the results. When decomposing burnout into its subcomponents, passive-avoidant leadership was positively related to emotional exhaustion and cynicism. However, passive-avoidant leadership was unrelated to a diminished sense of professional accomplishment, which was unexpected. The authors explain this finding by stating that although job demands have an effect on emotional exhaustion and cynicism, this does not mean that a person feels that he or she does not make an effective contribution to the organization or has not accomplished anything valuable in his or her job. This is consistent with the suggestion of Leiter (1993) that professional efficacy is largely independent of emotional exhaustion and cynicism. Hetland et al. (2007) found that after controlling for the influence of neuroticism on burnout, passive-avoidant leadership was still moderately related to burnout. This indicates that leaders can play an important role in the development of followers' burnout, over and above other, well-known predictors of burnout.

Crossover of burnout

Up to this point, we have focused on the effect of leadership behaviors and styles on follower burnout. Yet, another way in which leaders may influence their followers' burnout is through the crossover of their own burnout. Crossover is the term used to describe the interpersonal process that occurs when job stress or psychological strain (stress reactions) experienced by one person affects the level of strain of another person (Westman, 2001). Most studies have investigated and found the crossover of psychological strains such as anxiety, distress, depression, and job burnout (Westman & Bakker, 2008). Although research has shown that burnout crosses over between colleagues and married couples (e.g., Bakker, 2009; Westman & Bakker, 2008), there is almost no research on crossover of work-related well-being between leaders and followers. It remains unclear whether leaders are mainly contagious because of their position of power (Fredrickson, 2003), or whether emotional contagion mainly takes place because of similarity among colleagues (Bakker et al., 2007). In both cases, it is important to control for the experience of common stressors due to the shared social environment, because common stressors may explain both leaders' and followers' level of burnout. That is, common stressors may cause a spurious crossover effect when they are not controlled for (Westman, 2001).

There are several reasons why burnout may cross over from the leader to his or her followers. A first reason is that individuals who closely collaborate and are dependent on each other often take the perspective of each other, and therefore their experiences may converge. Thus, if a leader endorses a cynical attitude towards work, then it is likely that followers will attend to this and take over the cynical attitude. Second, individuals who frequently interact are inclined to mimic and synchronize each other's facial expressions, postures, and movements. As a consequence, they may converge emotionally (Hatfield et al., 1994). Thus, leaders may also act as role models, whose symptoms are imitated through a process of "emotional contagion."

Although there are no studies that directly examined the crossover of leaders' burnout on followers' burnout, there is some indirect evidence that leader and follower burnout are related. For example, Price and Weiss (2000) showed that when coaches were emotionally exhausted, they provided less training and social support. In turn, this contributed to followers' anxiety and burnout. Glasø and Einarsen (2006) found that leaders and followers often experience similar emotions when they interact. However, while positive emotions are experienced equally strong by both leaders and followers, negative emotions are often more strongly experienced by followers compared to leaders. Furthermore, in their experiment, Sy et al. (2005) showed that the mood and affective tone of work of group members were positively affected by the leaders' mood. Specifically, individual group members experienced more positive and less negative mood and the group had a more positive and less negative affective tone when leaders were in a positive mood, compared to when leaders were in a negative mood. Finally, Bono and Ilies (2006) examined the relationship between charismatic leadership and positive emotions in four different studies. First, they found that charismatic leaders express more positive emotions. Next, they found that leaders' positive emotional expressions directly affected followers' mood.

Agenda for future research

We have summarized the existing literature on the relationship between leadership behavior and follower burnout and focused on specific constructive and destructive leadership behaviors and/or styles. We must say that there may be many other constructive (e.g., servant leadership, empowering leadership) and destructive (e.g., tyrannical leadership, narcissistic leadership) leadership behaviors and styles that we did not include in our review, because their relationship with follower burnout has not yet been examined. Our agenda for future research will point out that the burnout literature can benefit from several other approaches to examine the influence of leadership behavior on follower burnout. This will hopefully serve as an inspiration for researchers to examine the relationship between different kinds of leadership behaviors and follower burnout in more depth.

Indirect effects

After reading this chapter, it becomes evident that most research on leadership behavior and follower burnout has focused on the direct relationship, sometimes taking into account the well-known direct effect of job demands on follower burnout. However, limited research attention has been addressed to the question of *how* leaders influence follower burnout. What are the mechanisms underlying this relationship? This would be interesting considering that leaders are not always able to explain additional variance over other well-known predictors of burnout, such as job demands or personality. Maybe leadership behaviors are more distal predictors of follower burnout, while job demands are more proximal predictors of follower burnout.

One promising direction for future research is to examine leaders' influence on the work environment to explain how leaders affect follower burnout. For example, research has shown that transformational leaders contribute to a favorable work environment (e.g., Piccolo & Colquitt, 2006) and that transformational leaders initiate a motivational process, whereby followers become more engaged because of the positive influence of transformational leaders on followers' work environment (Breevaart et al., 2013a; Breevaart et al., 2013b). Destructive leadership behavior, such as passive-avoidant leadership, may be related to follower burnout, because it contributes to role conflict and role ambiguity (Skogstad et al., 2007). Following the health impairment process and the motivational process of JD-R theory (Bakker & Demerouti, 2014; Demerouti et al., 2001), it seems likely that leadership behaviors influencing followers' job demands affect followers' burnout more strongly compared to leadership behaviors influencing followers' job resources. According to Schaufeli et al. (2009), research on burnout and work engagement (the positive antithesis of burnout) can complement each other. In line with the emergence of positive organizational psychology, we argue that it is not only important to prevent burnout, but also to stimulate work engagement. In this regard, leaders can play an important role by creating a positive, resourceful work environment (i.e., low hindering job demands, high challenging job demands, and job resources) to both stimulate follower work engagement and reduce follower burnout.

Moderator effects

We further argue that more research is needed on the moderating effects of leadership on the relationship between job demands and follower burnout. Stordeur et al. (2001) suggest that job demands explain a large amount of variance in follower burnout, which makes it very difficult for leaders to have any effect on follower burnout. Since job demands are well-known predictors of burnout, future research could more specifically study how leadership interacts with job demands in order to predict follower burnout. In line with the interaction effects proposed by the JD-R model, it is likely that supportive behaviors by the leader alleviate the detrimental effects of job demands on follower burnout or that aggressive behavior by the leader enhances the negative effects of hindrance job demands on follower burnout. For example, it seems likely that transformational leaders are able to provide followers with the tools to handle their job demands and therefore alleviate the detrimental effects of job demands on follower burnout. Transformational leaders challenge their followers to come up with new ideas or solutions to their problems, allowing followers to cope with their problems in a way that suits them best. As referred to earlier, it seems important that leaders provide their followers with this specific kind of support that helps them to actually cope with the stressors.

Furthermore, the literature on the influence of leaders on follower burnout can benefit from more research on contingencies of leadership behavior. Such an approach would allow us to say something about the circumstances under which leaders are more or less able to influence their followers' burnout. This is in line with the suggestion by Hetland et al. (2007) that individual characteristics may sometimes explain why we do not find a direct relationship between leadership behavior and follower burnout. For example, the relationship between passive-avoidant leadership and follower burnout could be moderated by followers' need for leadership. Followers low in need for leadership act independently of their leader and also show little response to interventions by their leader, while followers high in their need for leadership rely heavily upon their leader to facilitate the paths toward individual, group, and/or organizational goals (De Vries, 1997). Since passive-avoidant leaders do not take their responsibilities and can therefore not be relied on, it seems likely that followers with a high need for leadership are negatively affected by this leadership style. In other words, the relationship between passive-avoidant leadership and follower burnout will be stronger for followers with a high need for leadership. Being a relatively new concept, there is not much research on followers' need for leadership. One exception is a study by Breevaart et al. (2013a), which shows that need for leadership moderates the relationship between transformational leadership and followers' fulfillment of their basic psychological needs (i.e., need for autonomy, competence, and relatedness). They showed that the fulfillment of followers' basic needs was unaffected by their leaders' transformational leadership behavior for followers low (vs high) in their need for leadership. Followers high in need for leadership have their needs for autonomy, competence, and relatedness more fulfilled when their leader shows more transformational leadership behavior.

Finally, burnout is often considered as an outcome variable. However, we believe that burnout as a trait-like phenomenon is an individual characteristic that may determine how individuals react to certain leadership behaviors. Burned-out employees have developed a negative and uncaring attitude toward their work, which makes it likely that they are less responsive to their leaders' leadership style when this style is focused on creating positive work attitudes, like transformational leadership. For example, transformational leaders provide meaning to followers' work (Seibert et al., 2011) and stimulate followers to transcend their self-interests in favor of the interests of the group (Avolio & Yammarino, 2002), which makes it likely that followers become more involved and engaged in their work (e.g., Breevaart et al., 2013b; Tims et al., 2011). Burned-out employees are exhausted and have distanced themselves from their work, which makes it likely that they are less susceptible to transformational leaders' efforts to give meaning to the work. Future research could test these propositions and shed some more light on the moderating role of follower burnout.

Multilevel approach

Complementary to the trait approach to burnout described above is the state approach to burnout. Burnout as a state is considered as a variable that fluctuates within individuals over a short-term period of time. In other words, although someone may not be emotionally exhausted and/or cynical about work in general, he or she may be highly emotionally exhausted on a specific day because of what happened on that day. For example, followers may show more signs of burnout on a day when their leader shows more interpersonal aggression toward the follower. Diary studies could provide more insight into daily variations in symptoms of burnout and the antecedents and consequences of these variations. Furthermore, daily burnout scores are less prone to bias, because employees only have to think back over a couple of hours instead of over weeks or months. Although the state approach has gained interest in the work engagement literature (e.g., Breevaart et al., 2013b; Xanthopoulou et al., 2007), it has not received much attention within the burnout literature. Van Gelderen et al. (2011) are among the few to examine emotional exhaustion on a daily basis. In three different diary studies, they found that employees were more emotionally exhausted on days that they needed to perform more emotional labor.

Another interesting approach to the relationship between leadership behaviors and follower burnout is that of individual and group level effects (see also Chapter 7, this volume). For example, destructive leaders create a negative work environment, which is shared by all followers, and may therefore contribute to follower burnout at the team level. Alternatively, leadership may be shared within a team, either by the team members or by multiple designated leaders, which gives rise to various interesting research questions. For example, how does shared leadership among team members affect team well-being and performance? In what way do teams benefit from self-management? Is it possible that leaders who use constructive leadership behaviors compensate for destructive behaviors shown by other leaders or do destructive leaders undermine the positive effects of constructive leadership? These individual or group level effects may be dependent on leaders' span of control. It may be increasingly difficult to be considerate of each follower's needs as the span of control grows, whereas leaders may be more reluctant to show destructive leadership behavior when their span of control is small.

One construct or separate factors?

In line with JD-R theory, constructive leadership behaviors may predominantly influence followers' professional efficacy, while destructive leadership behavior mainly influences followers' emotional exhaustion and cynicism. Accordingly, it is important to split burnout into its three sub-dimensions when studying the relationship between leadership behavior and follower burnout. Some of the studies in the area address burnout as a composite measure (e.g., Yagil, 2006), while others split burnout into three sub-dimensions (e.g., Kanste et al., 2007), or even address just one or two of these (e.g., Wu & Hu, 2009). Accordingly, the conclusions of these studies are not always pointing in the same direction. This is not surprising, as many of these studies are not based on identical premises to begin with. The fact that some findings contradict each other in this research area can be partly explained by measurement issues.

In fact, future research expanding the use of both a single measure *and* subcomponents can give valuable information about the relationship between leadership and burnout in general. Beyond this, important findings related to leadership and its links specifically to employee exhaustion, cynicism, and professional efficacy, respectively, can be unraveled in research actively using these sub-dimensions. Interestingly, as stated earlier in the chapter, the fact that constructive and destructive forms of leadership are often inversely linked to the three sub-components provides support for the two paths – the motivational and the health impairment process – suggested by JD-R theory.

Research challenges

Examining the effect of leadership behavior on follower or team level burnout comes with several challenges. For example, ensuring participants' anonymity is difficult, because it is necessary to match leaders and followers. In dyad research, where dyads consist of one leader and one follower, this problem can be solved by asking dyads to create their own unique code that both use when filling out the questionnaire. For example, this code could exist of both the leader's and the follower's initials and date of birth. In this way, the researcher is able to connect data from each dyad without infringing confidentiality. Another approach is needed when leaders participate with several of their followers or when a team has multiple leaders. Although it may be difficult to ensure complete anonymity in these specific cases, providing leaders and followers with unique login codes to gain access to online questionnaires can maintain confidentiality. The researcher, providing each individual with a unique code, can then identify participants by number.

Conclusion

This chapter shows the important, but scarcely examined role of leaders in the prevention or promotion of follower burnout. The existing literature suggests that constructive leadership (e.g., supervisory support, guidance, and inspiration) diminish follower burnout, while destructive leadership (e.g., aggression and avoiding responsibility) promotes follower burnout. In line with JD-R theory, constructive leadership not only diminishes follower burnout, it also promotes follower work engagement. Accordingly, organizations benefit from investing in leadership training that is aimed at reducing destructive behaviors and enhancing constructive behaviors. More research on the relationship between leadership behaviors and follower functioning is needed to unravel its underlying mechanisms and possible boundary conditions.

References

Aryee, S., Sun, L. Y., Chen, Z. X. G., & Debrah, Y. A. (2008). Abusive supervision and contextual performance: The mediating role of emotional exhaustion and the moderating role of work unit structure. *Management and Organization Review, 4,* 393–411.

Ashforth, B. (1994). Petty tyranny in organizations. *Human Relations, 47,* 755–778.

Ashforth, B. E. (1997). Petty tyranny in organizations: A preliminary examination of antecedents and consequences. *Canadian Journal of Administrative Sciences, 14,* 126–140.

Avolio, B. J., & Yammarino, F. J. (2002). *Transformational and charismatic leadership: The road ahead.* Elsevier Science, Oxford.

Bakker, A. B. (2009). The crossover of burnout and its relation to partner health. *Stress & Health, 25,* 343–353.

Bakker, A. B., & Demerouti, E. (2014). Job demands – resources theory. In C. Cooper & P. Chen (Eds.), *Wellbeing: A complete reference guide* (pp. 37–64). Chichester, UK: Wiley-Blackwell.

Bakker, A. B., Demerouti, E., & Euwema, M. C. (2005). Job resources buffer the impact of job demands on burnout. *Journal of Occupational Health Psychology, 10,* 170–180.

Bakker, A. B., Hakanen, J. J., Demerouti, E., & Xanthopoulou, D. (2007a). Job resources boost work engagement, particularly when job demands are high. *Journal of Educational Psychology, 99 ,* 274–284.

Bakker, A. B., Westman, M., & Schaufeli, W. B. (2007b). Crossover of burnout: An experimental design. *European Journal of Work and Organizational Psychology, 16,* 220–239.

Bass, B. M. (1985). *Leadership performance beyond expectations.* New York: Academic Press.

Bass, B. M. (1999). Two decades of research and development in transformational leadership. *European Journal of Work and Organizational Psychology, 8,* 9–32.

Becker, J. A. H., Halbesleben, J. R. B., & O'Hair, H. D. (2005). Defensive communication and burnout in the workplace: The mediating role of leader-member exchange. *Communication Research Reports, 22,* 143–150.

Bono, J. E., & Ilies, R. (2006). Charisma, positive emotions and mood contagion. *Leadership Quarterly, 17,* 317–334.

Breevaart, K., Bakker, A. B., Demerouti, E., Sleebos, D. M., & Maduro, V. (2013a). *Exploring the path from transformational leaders to followers' job performance.* Manuscript submitted for publication.

Breevaart, K., Bakker, A. B., Hetland, J., & Demerouti, E. (2013b). *The daily influence of transactional and transformational leaders on followers' work engagement.* Manuscript submitted for publication.

Cavanaugh, M. A., Boswell, W. R., Roehling, M. V., & Boudreau, J. W. (2000). An empirical examination of self-reported work stress among U.S. managers. *Journal of Applied Psychology, 85,* 65–74.

Cohen, S. (2004). Social relationships and health. *American Psychologist, 59,* 676–684.

Constable, J. F., & Russell, D. W. (1986). The effects of social support and the work environment upon burnout among nurses. *Journal of Human Stress, 12,* 20–26.

Demerouti, E., Bakker, A. B., Nachreiner, F., & Schaufeli, W. (2001). The Job Demands-Resources model of burnout. *Journal of Applied Psychology, 86,* 499–512.

Densten, I. L. (2005). The relationship between visioning behaviours of leaders and follower burnout. *British Journal of Management, 16,* 105–118.

De Vries, R. E. (1997). *Need for leadership: a solution to empirical problems in situational theories of leadership.* (Unpublished dissertation). Tilburg University, Netherlands.

Duffy, M. K., Ganster, D. C., & Pagon, M. (2002). Social undermining in the workplace. *Academy of Management Journal, 45,* 331–351.

Dulebohn, J. H., Bommer, W. H., Liden, R. C., Brouer, R. L., & Ferris, G. R. (2012). A meta-analysis of antecedents and consequences of leader-member exchange: Integrating the past with an eye toward the future. *Journal of Management, 38,* 1715–1759.

Duxbury, M. L., Armstrong, G. D., Drew, D. J., & Henly, S. J. (1984). Head nurses leadership style with staff nurse burnout and job satisfaction in neonatal intensive care units. *Nursing Research, 33,* 97–101.

Einarsen, S., Aasland, M. S., & Skogstad, A. (2007). Destructive leadership behaviour: A definition and conceptual model. *The Leadership Quarterly, 18,* 207–216.

Etzion, D. (1984). Moderating effect of social support on the stress-burnout relationship. *Journal of Applied Psychology, 69,* 615–622.

Evers, W., Tomic, W., & Brouwers, A. (2002). Aggressive behavior and burnout among staff of homes for elderly. *International Journal of Mental Health Nursing, 11,* 2–9.

Fredrickson, B. L. (2003). The value of positive emotions: The emerging science of positive psychology is coming to understand why it's good to feel good. *American Psychologist, 91,* 330–335.

Fried, Y., & Tiegs, R. B. (1993). The main effect model versus the buffering model of shop steward social support: A study of rank-and-file auto workers in the U.S.A. *Journal of Organizational Behavior, 14,* 481–493.

Glasø, L., & Einarsen, S. (2006). Experienced affects in leader-subordinate relationships. *Scandinavian Journal of Management, 22,* 49–73.

Graen, G., & Cashman, J. (1975). A role-making model of leadership in formal organization: A development approach. In J. G. Hunt & L. L. Larson (Eds), *Leadership frontiers* (pp. 143–165). Kent, OH: Kent State University Press.

Graen, G. B., & Uhl-Bien, M. (1995). Relationship-based approach to leadership: Development of leader-member exchange (LMX) theory of leadership over 25 years: Applying a multi-level multi-domain perspective. *The Leadership Quarterly, 6,* 219–247.

Hakanen, J. J., Bakker, A. B., & Demerouti, E. (2005). How dentists cope with their job demands and stay engaged: The moderating role of job resources. *European Journal of Oral Sciences, 113,* 479–487.

Halbesleben, J. R. B. (2006). Sources of social support and burnout: A meta-analytic test of the conservation of resources model. *Journal of Applied Psychology, 91,* 1134–1145.

Halbesleben, J. R. B., & Buckley, M. R. (2004). Burnout in organizational life. *Journal of Management, 30,* 859–879.

Harvey, P., Stoner, J., Hochwarter, W., & Kacmar, C. (2007). Coping with abusive leadership: The neutralizing effects of ingratiation and positive affect on negative employee outcomes. *The Leadership Quarterly, 18,* 264–280.

Hatfield, E., Cacioppo, J. T., & Rapson, R. L. (1994). *Emotional contagion.* New York: Cambridge University Press.

Herman, S. (1983). The relationship between leader consideration and teacher burnout. *Graduate Research in Urban Education and Related Disciplines, 15,* 52–74.

Hetland, H., Sandal, G. M., & Johnson, T. B. (2007). Burnout in the information technology sector: Does leadership matter? *European Journal of Work and Organizational Psychology, 16,* 58–75.

House, J. S., & Kahn, R. L. (1985). Measures and concepts of social support. In S. Cohen & L.S. Syme (Eds), *Social support and health* (pp. 83–108). New York: Academic.

Judge, T. A., & Piccolo, R. F. (2004). Transformational and transactional leadership: A meta-analytic test of their relative validity. *Journal of Applied Psychology, 89,* 755–768.

Kanste, O., Kyngäs, H., & Nikkilä, J. (2007). The relationship between multidimensional leadership and burnout among nursing staff. *Journal of Nursing Management, 15,* 731–739.

Keashly, L., Trott, V., & MacLean, L. M. (1994). Abusive behavior in the workplace: A preliminary investigation. *Violence and Victims, 9,* 341–357.

Krasikova, D. V., Green, S. G., & LeBreton, J. M. (2013). Destructive leadership: A theoretical review, integration, and future research agenda. *Journal of Management, 39,* 1308–1338.

Lee, R. T., & Ashforth, B. E. (1996). A meta-analytic examination of the correlates of the three dimensions of job burnout. *Journal of Applied Psychology, 81,* 123–133.

Leiter, M. P. (1993). Burnout as a developmental process: Consideration of models. In W.B. Schaufeli (Ed.), *Professional burnout: Recent developments in theory and research* (pp. 237–250). Philadelphia: Taylor & Francis.

Lipman-Blumen, J. (2005). Toxic leadership: When grand illusions masquerade as noble visions. *Leader to Leader, 36,* 29–36.

Maslach, C., & Leiter, M. P. (1997). The truth about burnout. San Francisco: Jossey Bass.

Maslach, C., & Schaufeli, W. B. (1993). Historical and conceptual development of burnout. In W.B. Schaufeli, C. Maslach, & T. Marek (Eds.), *Professional Burnout: Recent Developments in Theory and Research* (pp. 1–16). Washington DC: Taylor and Francis.

Maslach, C., Schaufeli, W. B., & Leiter, M. P. (2001). Job burnout. *Annual Review Psychology, 52,* 397–422.

Piccolo, R. F., & Colquitt, J. A. (2006). Transformational leadership and job behaviors: The mediating role of core job characteristics. *Academy of Management Journal, 49,* 327–340.

Price, M. S., & Weiss, M. R. (2000). Relationships among coach burnout, coach behaviors, and athletes' psychological responses. *Sport Psychologist, 14,* 391–409.

Schaufeli, W. B., & Bakker, A. B. (2004). Job demands, job resources, and their relationship with burnout and engagement: A multi-sample study. *Journal of Organizational Behavior, 25,* 293–315.

Schaufeli, W. B., Leiter, M. P., & Maslach, C. (2009). Burnout: 35 years of research and practice. *Career Development International, 14,* 204–220.

Schyns, B., & Shilling, J. (2013). How bad are the effects of bad leaders? A meta-analysis of destructive leadership and its outcomes. *The Leadership Quarterly, 24,* 138–158.

Seibert, S. E., Wang, G., & Courtright, S. H. (2011). Antecedents and consequences of psychological and team empowerment in organizations: A meta-analytic review. *Journal of Applied Psychology, 96,* 981–1003.

Seltzer, J., & Numerof, R. E. (1988). Supervisory leadership and subordinate burnout. *Academy of Management Journal, 31,* 439–446.

Skakon, J., Nielsen, K., Borg, V., & Guzman, J. (2010). Are leaders' well-being, behaviours and style associated with the affective well-being of their employees? A systematic review of three decades of research. *Work & Stress, 24,* 107–139.

Skogstad, A., Einarsen, S., Torsheim, T., Aasland, M. S., & Hetland, H. (2007). The destructiveness of laissez-faire leadership behavior. *Journal of Occupational Health Psychology, 12,* 80–92.

Stogdill, R. M. (1974). *Handbook of Leadership: A Survey of Theory and Practice.* New York, NY, US: Free Press.

Stordeur, S., D'hoore, W., & Vandenberghe, C. (2001). Leadership, organizational stress, and emotional exhaustion among hospital nursing staff. *Journal of Advanced Nursing, 35,* 533–542.

Sy, T., Cote, S., & Saavedra, R. (2005). The contagious leader: Impact of the leader's mood on the mood of group members, group affective tone, and group processes. *Journal of Applied Psychology, 90,* 295–305.

Taris, T. W. (2006). Is there a relationship between burnout and objective performance? A critical review of 16 studies. *Work & Stress, 20,* 316–334.

Tepper, B. J. (2000). Consequences of abusive supervision. *Academy of Management Journal, 43,* 178–190.

Thomas, C. H., & Lankau, M. J. (2009). Preventing burnout: The effects of LMX and mentoring on socialization, role stress, and burnout. *Human Resource Management, 48,* 417–432.

Tims, M., Bakker, A. B., & Xanthopoulou, D. (2011). Do transformational leaders enhance their followers' daily work engagement? *The Leadership Quarterly, 22,* 121–131.

Van Dierendonck, D., & Mevissen, N. (2002). Aggressive behavior of passengers, conflict management behavior, and burnout among trolley car drivers. *International Journal of Stress Management, 9,* 345–355.

Van Gelderen, B. R., Konijn, E. A., & Bakker, A. B. (2011). Emotional labor among trainee police officers: The interpersonal role of positive emotions. *The Journal of Positive Psychology, 6,* 163–172.

Westman, M. (2001). Stress and strain crossover. *Human Relations, 54,* 557–591.

Westman, M., & Bakker, A. B. (2008). Crossover of burnout among health care professionals. In J. Halbesleben (Ed.), *Handbook of stress and burnout in health care* (pp. 111–125). New York: Nova Science Publishers.

Wu, T. Y., & Hu, C. (2009). Abusive supervision and employee emotional exhaustion. *Group & Organization Management, 34,* 143–169.

Xanthopoulou, D., Bakker, A. B., Demerouti, E., & Schaufeli, W. B. (2007). The role of personal resources in the job demands-resources model. *International Journal of Stress Management, 14,* 121–141.

Yagil, D. (2006). The relationship of abusive and supportive workplace supervision to employee burnout and upward influence tactics. *Journal of Emotional Abuse, 6,* 49–65.

Yukl, G. (2013). *Leadership in organizations.* Pearson Education Limited, Harlow.

Zhu, W., Avolio, B. J., & Walumbwa, F. O. (2009). Moderating role of follower characteristics with transformational leadership and follower work engagement. *Group & Organization Management, 34,* 590–619.

7 Multilevel models of burnout

Separating group level and
individual level effects in
burnout research

Jonathon R. B. Halbesleben and
Matthew R. Leon

For nearly two decades, there has been a growing trend toward a multilevel perspective of individual behavior in organizations (Klein et al., 1994; Kozlowski & Klein, 2000). More recently, there has been an increasing emphasis on multilevel explanations within the stress literature, both from psychological and public health researchers (Bliese & Jex, 2002). Burnout research has followed a similar pattern to many organizational behavior constructs. Throughout the years, burnout has fairly consistently been defined as an individual phenomenon (Halbesleben & Buckley, 2004; Maslach et al., 2001). However, throughout that same time, there have been suggestions that burnout has a collective or shared element to it (Edelwich & Brodsky, 1980; Gonzalez-Morales et al., 2012). For example, Gonzalez-Morales et al. (2012) defined collective burnout in terms of the shared experience of burnout among coworkers in the same work environment. They argued that the contextual antecedents and experiences of burnout (e.g., Bakker & Schaufeli, 2000; Bakker et al., 2009) suggest that burnout can be conceptualized as an individual phenomenon or a socially constructed experience.

In this chapter, we review studies from the previous decade of burnout research to understand how researchers have conceptualized burnout at multiple levels and the implications of those conceptualizations for the ways we study burnout and, with any luck, reduce it in organizations. We begin that review by examining the ways in which demands and resources at the group and organizational levels have impacted individual burnout. Then, we will review the notion of collective burnout. We will follow that with a review of the theoretical mechanisms explaining burnout at multiple levels, including an extension of conservation of resources theory (Hobfoll, 1988, 1989, 2001) to understand how resources might move through multiple levels and impact burnout at those levels. We conclude with implications for research, including analysis considerations for researchers hoping to test multilevel burnout models.

A brief review of multilevel studies of burnout

There have been several studies that have examined multilevel effects of burnout. Below, we review those studies. We organize them around the job demands-resources (JD-R) model of burnout (Demerouti et al., 2001), which proposes that burnout is the result of high demands and low levels of resources (Bakker & Demerouti, 2007). There can be team- or organizational-level demands that lead to burnout and there can be team- or organizational-level resources that help reduce burnout. We address both possibilities before getting into the theoretical mechanisms that might help explain how those demands and resources work across levels.

Team/organizational demands leading to burnout

Several authors have proposed that demands at the team or organizational levels can impact the experience of individual burnout. Kroon et al. (2009) examined the manner in which organizational-level high performance work practices (HPWPs) impacted individual employee burnout. They argued that although HPWPs had widely been seen in a positive light with respect to employee well-being, they could very well have a negative impact because they often required employees to work harder (Appelbaum et al., 2000; Godard, 2001; Legge, 1995). In a study of nearly 400 employees from 86 organizations, they found support for the idea that HPWPs are associated with higher demands and burnout among employees.

In some cases, effects of variables frequently seen as individual demands have been explored at the group level. For example, average work hours in a unit were associated with burnout above and beyond individuals' work hours (Park & Lake, 2005).

One issue faced in this line of research is how one sorts out the impact of organizational-level demands and an individual's response to those demands. For example, Halbesleben et al. (2013) found that organization-wide furlough policies dramatically increased levels of emotional exhaustion immediately following the implementation of furloughs. Thus, this policy seems to have increased burnout. However, they also found individual differences between employees in their response to the furloughs based on what the employees did during their time away from work. Those employees who engaged in recovery experiences (e.g., spent time relaxing or participating in a hobby) saw less of an increase in exhaustion following the furlough. Fortunately, multilevel modeling approaches allow researchers to sort out the impact of organization- or team-level demands on individuals both by exploring the group-level effects and the individual-level effects.

Team/organizational resources relieving burnout

Just as team-level demands can impact burnout, team- and organizational-level resources can help to reduce burnout. In this section, we review a small sample of studies that have addressed group-level resources as a means to reduce individual burnout. Justice has been widely associated with burnout, with the idea that an unfair environment would be more demanding and a fair climate could be a resource for employees (Brotheridge, 2003; Cropanzano et al., 2005). Moliner et al. (2005) considered the role that work-unit justice climate plays on work-unit level burnout. They argued that because many employees have shared justice experiences (e.g., similar treatment or decisions from the same supervisor), exploring these processes at the work-unit level was necessary. They found support for the impact of justice on burnout at the work-unit level, particularly for interpersonal justice. In this case, the examination of burnout at the work-unit level offered a unique insight into psychological processes – whereas procedural and distributive justice are typically quite important at the individual level, perhaps due to more individuality in interpretation of what is to be gained or lost in a decision, at the group level interpersonal treatment was the critical factor.

High-quality team interactions have been the subject of study as well. Sonnentag et al. (1994) found that openness to criticism was inversely associated with some aspects of individual burnout. Further, they found that competition in a team negatively moderated the relationship between individual stress and burnout, such that stress was less likely to lead to burnout in high competition. They noted that competition does not seem like it would reduce the negative impact of stress, but in their context and the way they measured competition, it may have been seen as more collegial competition. They had measured competition as part of a measure of group interactions that was generally positively focused. In this context, it may have been the case that competition actually brought out positive interactions with coworkers that might have otherwise been isolated, thus enhancing their resources.

The multilevel processes through which resources can reduce burnout among employees have translated to practice. Much of the work on burnout interventions have occurred at the individual level, emphasizing how providing individuals with resources such as support or stress management skills can positively impact their burnout experiences (cf., Bono et al., 2013; Chen et al., 2009). However, there has been an increasing emphasis on interventions that target work groups with the goal of reducing burnout at the individual level (Halbesleben et al., 2006; Le Blanc et al., 2007). These approaches fit with ideas that we will return to momentarily – that resources at one level can operate at other levels of analysis. For example, developing a stronger collective feeling of social support and participation in decision-making at the group level can impact the individual burnout experiences of all employees working in that department (Le Blanc et al., 2007).

Of course, some studies acknowledge that there may be complex effects as a result of higher-level phenomena such that the same phenomenon could be both a resource and a demand. Kroon et al.'s (2009) original model treated HPWPs as something that could lead to higher demands but also higher perceived justice; thus, they believed there could be some counteracting effects of HPWPs on burnout (though, as noted above, they only found the demands path to be significant).

In line with the JD-R model, the literature suggests that group- and organization-level demands can increase burnout while group- and organization-level resources can reduce burnout. The studies we have reviewed focused on *individual* burnout as the outcome variable. In the next section, we discuss the idea that burnout may also be considered as a group-level phenomenon.

The notion of collective burnout

As noted at the start of the chapter, while burnout has traditionally been viewed as an individual experience, there has been greater attention in the literature placed on whether burnout may be a shared experience among members of a group or organization. The notion of collective burnout has taken two perspectives. The first is a shared-event approach – where an outside event yields a similar response for multiple individuals (Totterdell, 2000; Westman, 2002). Similar demands or resources in a work environment could lead to similar levels of burnout among those working in that environment (Bakker et al., 2003; Demerouti et al., 2000, 2001). For example, the shared experience of time demands during the tax season may lead to similar burnout among tax accountants. This approach helps to account for situations when human contact may not be possible or likely (Gonzalez-Morales et al., 2012).

The shared event approach can work through other mechanisms as well. Gonzalez-Morales et al. (2012) proposed a social information processing theory process (Salancik & Pfeffer, 1978) that suggests that perceptions of others' burnout symptoms could impact employees' own ratings of burnout. They argue that this happens because others' burnout highlights the negative components of the environment. If employees perceive high levels of burnout among others, Gonzalez-Morales et al. (2012) suggested that employees would adjust their ratings of individual burnout to match what they observe. Note that this mechanism does rely on communication (either verbal or nonverbal) to send cues regarding collective burnout; however, it does not necessarily require close human contact, consistent with the broad notions of the shared event approach to collective burnout.

The second approach to collective burnout is built on the processes of emotional contagion, or the idea that emotional states can be transmitted from one employee to another (cf., Bakker et al., 2003; Bakker et al., 2005; Bakker et al., 2006; Westman, 2002). This is a more direct approach, where the emotions of one employee impact another employee's emotions (Totterdell, 2000). The directness of the emotional influence may vary across contexts. Bakker et al. (2006) suggested that the transmission of mood from one employee to another can be either nonconscious or conscious. Nonconscious processing occurs automatically, for example, the automatic matching of facial expressions leading to an emotional response consistent with that expression (Hatfield et al., 1994). On the other hand, conscious responses involve perception of others' emotions and reaction in kind (e.g., Bakker & Schaufeli, 2000). Bakker et al. (2006) proposed that the exhaustion component of burnout is more subject to nonconscious processing whereas the disengagement/cynicism and reduced personal efficacy elements of burnout are more subject to conscious processing.

A variant on the emotional contagion approach involves workload compensation and the increased demands faced by coworkers of those who are burned out (Bakker et al., 2009). Employees who experience burnout tend to have lower performance (Halbesleben & Bowler, 2007; Halbesleben & Wheeler, 2008, 2011;

Wright & Bonnett, 1997; Wright & Cropanzano, 1998), take shortcuts that could lead to injuries to themselves or others (Halbesleben, 2010), and tend to be more often absent from work, because of increased health problems (Kahill, 1988; Melamed et al., 1999; Melamed et al., 2006; Schaufeli et al., 2009). The reduced performance of burned-out workers may put greater pressure on their coworkers, which could then lead to greater burnout among those coworkers (Bakker et al., 2003; Gonzalez-Morales et al., 2012). In this sense, burnout is passed from one employee to the next through increases in job demands caused by lack of performance of one of the employees.

The notion of collective burnout will continue to be an important avenue for future research in burnout. While there have now been a series of studies to examine the collective burnout construct, much more work is needed to separate out the effects of individual and collective burnout and the mechanisms by which collective burnout is created. One of the difficulties in this type of research is incorporation of the element of time (George & Jones, 2000; Mitchell & James, 2001) in understanding the development of collective burnout. For example, Gonzalez-Morales et al. (2012) argued that collective burnout develops from individual-level burnout, but then individual-level burnout is increased in situations where collective burnout is high. This raises some interesting questions regarding the development of collective burnout, for example, if a shared event leads directly to a collective perception or if emotional contagion leads one employee's burnout to impact others. The nature of individual and collective burnout also suggests the possibility that more advanced longitudinal modeling (cf., Halbesleben & Wheeler, in press) might be necessary to capture the reciprocal effects of the individual and the collective as well as the accumulation effects that appear over time.

There also remain some research opportunities in understanding the more fine-grained details of how collective burnout is created. It is clear from the long line of research concerning emotional contagion that burnout can be transmitted directly from one person to another (Bakker et al., 2003a; Bakker et al., 2005; Bakker et al., 2006; Westman, 2002). Moreover, research evidence from the shared events approach suggests that direct contact with a burned-out individual is not necessary for collective burnout to emerge. In the next section of the chapter, we expand on the processes outlined above to understand how an expansion of a current theory of strain in the workplace, conservation of resources theory, can inform our understanding of how burnout, both individual and collective, can emerge through a multilevel process.

A broader view of COR through multiple levels of resources

While the job demands-resources model of burnout has seen a lot of deserved attention in the burnout literature over the past decade, another commonly cited theory is the Conservation of Resources (COR) theory (Hobfoll, 1988, 1998, 2001). The main tenet of COR theory is that we are motivated to protect the resources we currently have and are similarly motivated to increase our resources

(Hobfoll, 1988; Hobfoll & Shirom, 1993, 2001). Resources are broadly defined as things that we value – they could be material objects, conditions, or states (Hobfoll, 1998). COR theory is used to explain burnout by stating that burnout (or other strains) is the result of a threat to our resources, a loss of resources, or an investment of resources that does not yield expected returns (Hobfoll & Freedy, 1993).

COR theory is very similar to the JD-R model in that it suggests that burnout results from fewer resources (Halbesleben & Buckley, 2004). Moreover, many of the processes outlined in the theories are very similar (Bakker & Demerouti, 2007; see especially page 315). The key differences relate to the treatment of demands. Whereas the JD-R model explicitly includes demands in the model (Demerouti et al., 2001), COR theory emphasizes resources and suggests that demands are essentially processes that reduce resources rather than being a unique source of stress. Despite this key difference, the ideas behind the JD-R model and COR theory are largely the same with regard to the effect of low resources and high demands.

Another area of difference is in the processes by which resources and demands impact burnout. Whereas the JD-R model proposes two mechanisms, an emotional path (demands → exhaustion) and a motivational path (resources → disengagement) to burnout (Bakker et al., 2003b; Bakker et al., 2003a; Demerouti et al., 2001; Hakanen et al., 2006), both of the COR paths are motivation focused.

COR theory proposes two primary processes related to resources: one of conservation and one of acquisition. The conservation process is a process whereby individuals are motivated to conserve what resources they have because resource loss is seen as being significantly more problematic than equivalent gain (Hobfoll, 1988). As a result, when individuals experience stress, they are more likely to engage in coping efforts to stem future resource losses (Shirom, 2003). The second process is related to resource acquisition. In part to protect against resource losses, COR proposes that we engage in behaviors meant to acquire new resources (Hobfoll, 2001). Those behaviors typically require investment of our current resources with the understanding that such an investment will lead to greater resources in the future. For example, we spend time, energy, and money on education in order to (hopefully) improve our prospects for employment in the future. The investment of time, energy, and money then hopefully leads to more pay, status, and activities that enrich our well-being. The idea that we gain resources in groups (e.g., higher pay typically comes with higher status) is called a resource caravan (Hobfoll, 2001, 2011). As noted, the resource acquisition process is related to the resource conservation process. In our example, we often assume that more education will protect us from future resource losses since it will give greater job security.

Tims et al. (2013) specifically explored this process in their recent work on job crafting. In line with the arguments above, job crafting represents an investment of resources with the intention of reducing current and future demands as well as increasing future resources (Tims & Bakker, 2010; Tims et al., 2012). Tims et al. (2013) found, in a sample of employees from a Dutch plastics factory, that those employees that invested in increasing resources did indeed increase resources when assessed two months later. They also found that employees crafting challenging job demands (in other words, specifically seeking out and engaging in new projects that would not produce overload) led to decreases in burnout and increases in well-being (see also Crawford et al., 2010 and Petrou et al., 2012 for similar effects). These findings support the idea that employees can invest their current resources to protect and acquire resources in the future and that such an approach might be beneficial, particularly during times of change within the organization (Van den Heuvel et al., 2010).

COR theory has been interpreted largely as a psychological theory applied at the individual level. However, Hobfoll's writings were fairly clear in his view that resources held meaning within a larger community and societal context. In this final section, we propose an expansion to COR theory that involves an integration of COR with other resource theories and looking at the resource concept at multiple levels, both in terms of traditional levels of analysis (societal, organizational, group, individual), but also examining how individuals change over time. In this section, we propose an extension to COR theory that suggests that conservation and acquisition occur at multiple levels. We suggest that by understanding this multilevel process, it will become more clear how resources play a role at multiple levels of analysis and how that can help us to understand burnout at those multiple levels. We outline this framework in Figure 7.1.

The basic premise of our multilevel framework is that the conservation and acquisition processes of resources can work across levels and in both directions. Just as a resource developed at the team level can impact individual behavior, individual resource investment can lead to positive team-level outcomes. At the top of the framework are societal resources (or macro resources; ten Brummelhuis & Bakker, 2012). Such resources can make their way down to the individual through institutional structures in society. Joplin et al. (2003) looked at country-level influences, both in terms of the effects of resources and demands, on work-family conflict. Their work is intriguing because they examined macro resources and their impact on individual experiences through an emphasis on change in country-level variables.

Macro resources work through organizations. Alvaro et al. (2010) examined the organizational resources necessary for knowledge transfer, including organizational culture, human resources, economic resources, and condition resources (the latter were defined as opportunities or fortuitous timing that facilitated knowledge transfer). Each of these was more specifically conceptualized to provide greater guidance to managers about changes that could impact knowledge transfer (e.g., culture was further defined in terms of policies, training, access to information, leadership, flexibility, buy-in, and history). Their study is important in that it helps to provide a multilevel structure to resources; for example, whereas the application of research evidence is an individual behavior in most cases, it is impacted by resources at a higher level, such as access to the evidence base that is intended for application (see also Bacharach et al., 2008; Vandenberghe et al., 2007).

Resources exist at the group level as well. The relationships that develop within a group can give rise to resources that would not have been seen in the individuals

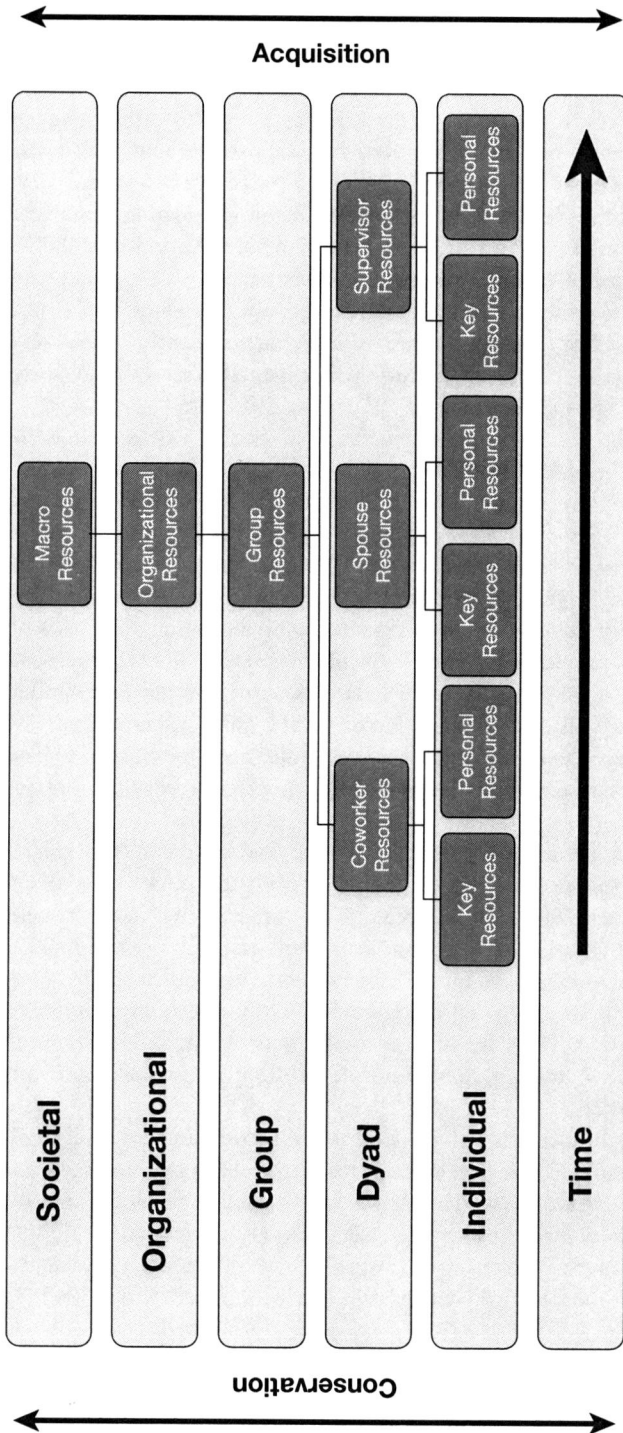

Figure 7.1 A multilevel conservation of resources model

alone (Oh et al., 2006). These additional resources can translate to higher levels of performance both for the team and organization (Collins & Clark, 2003; Kozlowski & Ilgen, 2006). The notion of group-level resources and burnout was noted in the study by Gonzalez-Morales et al. (2012); they suggested that collective burnout could be the result of a shared perception that resources are not available in the environment. Similarly, one can conceive of a shared perception of threat or loss of resources at the group level that might lead to heightened group-level burnout effects while still demonstrating some variation at the individual level. For example, as noted above, Halbesleben et al. (2013) found that government furloughs generally led to shifts toward greater emotional exhaustion in employees, but that those shifts showed individual variability based on recovery experiences during the furlough (those who engaged in recovery experiences saw smaller increases in exhaustion).

At the dyadic level, resources can cross over between spouses to reduce strain (ten Brummelhuis & Bakker, 2012; Westman, 2002, 2006; Westman & Etzion, 1995). Additionally, resources can be exchanged between leaders and employees as well as between coworkers (Halbesleben & Wheeler, in press; Wilson et al., 2010). What could be particularly interesting as researchers develop models of these group- and dyadic-level resource pools is the notion of resource caravans. This creates a unique situation of resource caravans among caravans of people. That is, while individual resources typically occur together (e.g., self-esteem and self-efficacy; Judge et al., 1997), we also know that people with similar characteristics are attracted to each other (Byrne, 1961). Thus, resources may be attracted to other resources to create larger pools of group resources that can be conserved and invested. This could then translate to greater resources at the individual level as well.

Greater instrumental support seems like a clear candidate for such a process. Instrumental support involves providing tangible assistance or advice to others (Beehr & Glazer, 2001; Semmer et al., 2008). A group with more resources such as knowledge about the work process and self-efficacy may be more naturally likely to come together and more inclined to provide advice and tangible support to employees than groups with non-compatible interests or resources (Stroebe & Stroebe, 1996). Thus, the unique combination of individual resources, when brought together in a group setting, yields more individual resources for the individuals involved.

Finally, our framework includes time as the bottom level of analysis. There are several time-related issues regarding resources that have not been adequately addressed in the literature. The first is the impact of resource timing over the lifespan and how that impacts their usefulness (Kooij & Van de Voorde, 2011). The nature of motivation changes as we age (Inceoglu et al., 2012) suggesting that the value of resources also changes over our lifespan (Hobfoll, 2001; Treadway et al., 2005).

Another related issue concerns the timing of resources over the course of one's career. For example, Lopina et al. (2012) noted that resource timing was important in reducing turnover of employees in "dirty work" occupations (in their case, animal shelter employees responsible for euthanasia), particularly when they had access to that job information prior to being hired (see also Phillips, 1998, for a meta-analysis of similar effects in the context of recruitment studies). The notion of providing resources at critical times within one's career and life may be a fruitful avenue of research (Alvaro et al., 2010). The timing of family-friendly resources may be a popular avenue to explore. Family-friendly resources such as childcare yield positive outcomes for employees (Payne et al., 2012). However, those resources are of little value before or after one has children that would utilize such care. Examining the timing of these resources might hold practical value for organizations as well, as they seek to maximize their return on such human resource investments.

Resource conservation and acquisition at multiple levels

Our framework suggests that while there are different meanings for resources at different levels, the processes of conservation and acquisition remain the same. We suggest that those COR processes help complement other theories of resources to understand resource dynamics at multiple levels. For example, for organizational level resources, another avenue for exploring the resource concept could examine how COR fits resource-based-view (RBV) theories of the firm that highlight how organizations utilize the notion of resources. COR original tenets may help provide additional insights on such "micro-organizational processes" (Barney et al., 2001, p. 635) that are often overlooked when considering the *how* of resource investment and development from an organizational perspective. For instance, at a firm level, COR theory can offer interesting perspectives in relating aggressive firm investment behaviors to a motivational drive for resource conservation.

Researchers may also consider whether COR-based processes can be extended to the level of the firm (i.e. entrepreneurial/risk taking versus conservative/risk avoidant; Covin, 1991). Future research could also explore how COR fits RBV theories that highlight how organizations utilize their human capital resources (Wright et al., 2001). RBV approaches have highlighted the strategic importance of access to, and control of such core human capital competencies as knowledge, skill, and ability sharing (Fossas-Olalla, 1999; Litz, 1996; Wright et al., 1994). The COR corollaries may also be useful in understanding firm-level activities. Since investment is more successful when there is some level of resources in place, is there a minimal level of resource possession from which a COR-motivated strategy is to be expected? COR theory could usefully complement and extend the RBV approach on the issue of cooperative dynamics in the perspective of sharing strategic organizational knowledge. Indeed, studies have stressed difficulties in implementing knowledge sharing practices due to fears of perceived deprivation, including power, self-worth, and value (Alvaro et al., 2010; Ardichvili, 2008; Chen et al., 2009).

Similar suggestions can be extended to the other levels of analysis. For example, at the dyadic level, initial research proposing an integration of COR theory with boundary theory (Ashforth et al., 2000) has offered a mechanism by which resources cross work-family boundaries so that they can be invested either at work or home (Halbesleben et al., 2010; Halbesleben et al., 2012). More work is needed to better understand how resources move across levels and the implications of that movement for resource investment.

Implications for research designs and analysis

Throughout this chapter, we have suggested multiple avenues for future research; in this section we discuss research design issues that are important for those seeking to study burnout at multiple levels. When choosing to study multilevel effects in the context of burnout, one must make some critical decisions in the design and analysis phases to ensure that the research questions can be appropriately answered. For example, one must clearly decide whether the effects being considered are most appropriately individual-level in nature, group-level in nature, or some combination of the two. For example, just because one is working in a group context does not mean that the individual effects can or should be attributed to that context (Bliese & Jex, 2002; Diez-Roux, 1998). One must be careful in highlighting the group context when the study is entirely individually focused (Elloy et al., 2001). To examine issues at the group level, there must be variation at that level. If that variation is not examined, then the emphasis should remain at the individual level.

At the group level of analysis, researchers must also consider the expected nature of the group level effects. Some variables vary only between groups (no within-group variation) while other variables vary both between and within groups (Susser, 1994). The latter, termed contextual variables (Susser, 1994), offer opportunities to examine more complex effects because of the added within-group variation.

A key design issue concerns the appropriate sample size for multilevel studies. To examine variability at multiple levels, there must be adequate variation at those levels – and that requires adequate numbers of measurement at those levels. We will focus on two-level models and discuss the implications of different sample sizes at the lower level (e.g., the individual) and the higher level (e.g., the group/team/department). These ideas can generally be extrapolated to models with more levels.

A common consideration is the number of members of each group that are needed to represent the group. One issue is making sure that there is adequate power at all levels of the model to detect significant effects (Scherbaum & Ferreter, 2009). Sample size in the context of statistical power quickly becomes a rather complicated issue, since calculating power at multiple levels concerns more than just sample size at each level, but also the estimation procedure, covariates included in the model (Reise & Duan, 2003), the parameter one is interested in, and the level of dependence in the data (typically indicated by an ICC(1) value, which we will discuss a bit later in the chapter; Scherbaum & Ferreter, 2009). As a result, there is wide variability in what is recommended for the number of individuals needed in each group. Kreft and De Leeuw (1998) suggested 30 groups of at least 30 members (see also Busing, 1993; van der Leeden & Busing, 1994). Hox (1998) suggested 50 groups with at least 20 members each. Some studies have suggested as few as 10 members per group, given the number of groups is high (Bryk & Raudenbush, 1992; Clarke & Wheaton, 2007). As it turns out, the number of groups is actually more important in terms of statistical power and maximizing sample size than the number of individuals in those groups (Bassiri, 1988; Hofmann, 1997; Snijders, 2005). As a result, it is difficult to provide specific recommendations at the individual level, though the use of widely available power calculators might help to justify a researcher's use of a group size (see Scherbaum & Ferreter, 2009 for a good reference on this issue and sources of power calculators).

Considering the number of groups, Snijders and Bosker (1999) suggest that multilevel modeling could be useful with even as few as 10 groups. Maas and Hox (2005), based on a simulation study, reported that studies of less than 30 groups could lead to biased estimates of the group-level standard errors (see Browne & Draper, 2000, for similar findings). However, they reported that small numbers of groups did not meaningfully bias parameter estimates or lower-level variance estimates. More groups will also tend to lead to higher levels of the statistics researchers typically use to justify aggregation (Cohen et al., 2001; these statistics are discussed in more detail in the next section). In the end, the number of groups may be dictated by more practical concerns. For example, one may be limited by the number of departments or groups within an organization and the size of those groups or departments. Thus, while it may be unclear what the ideal number of groups is, one must be in a position to justify the number of groups utilized in the study, particularly if it is below 30.

Measuring variables

Contextual variables are frequently calculated by taking an average (e.g., mean) score of the construct at the group or organizational level (cf., Chen & Bliese, 2002). For example, one could simply take the mean of individual burnout scores to come up with a collective burnout score (e.g., Moliner et al., 2005). A similar approach was employed by Bakker et al. (2006), who first calculated individual burnout scores and mapped them on to a high-medium-low taxonomy and then took the percentage of employees in a unit that scored high. The aggregation approach is occasionally employed for the predictors of burnout as well. For example, Sonnentag et al. (1994) examined how team variables impacted individual burnout through a mean-aggregation of the scores for the team-level predictor variables.

When making the decision to aggregate scores in this way, researchers need to consider whether aggregation is justified by the data. Typically, this is done by examining several statistics. First is an interclass correlation, which can come in several forms (Shrout & Fleiss, 1979). ICC(1) is an indicator of the amount of variance in individual scores that can be explained at the group level (Bliese, 2000;

Castro, 2002). While perhaps not directly used to test whether aggregation is justified, ICC(1) provides some indication if there is adequate variation in multiple levels to justify examination of a multilevel model (or alternatively, a high ICC(1) might suggest that examination through multilevel modeling is essential to address dependence within the data (Bliese & Hanges, 2004)). LeBreton and Senter (2008) suggest that ICC(1) values as low as .05 might suggest meaningful variation at the group level and warrant investigation through multilevel modeling.

ICC(2), on the other hand, provides one with estimates of the reliability of group means (Bliese, 1998; Hofmann, 2002). Put another way, ICC(2), as an index of interrater reliability, provides an assessment of how consistent raters are when multiple people rate something (e.g., multiple people fill out a scale on the same topic; LeBreton et al., 2003). Guidelines regarding acceptable levels of ICC(2) to justify aggregation are not well understood and often misapplied (Lance et al., 2006); however, LeBreton and Senter (2008) suggest levels around .70 and higher could be used as evidence that aggregation is warranted.

Another common option for justifying aggregation is to assess the level of agreement among raters, in effect determining whether one person's rating of a construct is interchangeable with another person's (LeBreton & Senter, 2008). The various r_{wg} indices are one option for this assessment (James et al., 1984). An r_{wg} value can be calculated for each group to determine the level of agreement on a construct within that group and then fitted to a distribution to determine an overall r_{wg} value for the sample (Biemann et al., 2012; Castro, 2002). Generally, researchers use an overall cutoff value of .70 to justify aggregation based on r_{wg} values (Lance et al., 2006; LeBreton & Senter, 2008). This value can be strongly influenced, however, by which distribution the researcher chose; most researchers appear to choose a distribution that is not necessarily expected of the data but offers higher r_{wg} values (LeBreton & Senter, 2008). Because an r_{wg} is calculated for each group and then aggregated, low r_{wg} values could result from several groups that show less agreement. Researchers might be tempted to remove those groups from the analysis in order to bump their overall r_{wg} value higher. However, caution needs to be exercised, as group differences could be tied to some systematic explanation that could even be tied to one's model (LeBreton & Senter, 2008). It is worth noting that while ICC(2) and r_{wg} are the two most commonly employed measures of interrater agreement in organizational research, other indicators of agreement exist and may be valuable for a researcher to consider (see LeBreton & Senter, 2008 for a review)

Alternatively, one can examine how consensus of experience impacts an outcome as well (Bliese & Halverson, 1998). For example, Moliner et al. (2005) calculated a "burnout strength" variable using an average deviation index to give them a measure of agreement regarding burnout scores among work-unit members. They found that level of agreement in interpersonal justice was a significant predictor in level of agreement in burnout, offering support for the idea that shared interpretation of work events leads to shared outcomes (Ostroff & Bowen, 2000). These types of models can be quite interesting and are worth exploring for burnout researchers. The average deviation index is one potential predictor in such models.

Moreover, since an r_{wg} can be calculated for each group, this could serve as the input into a multilevel model where the predictor is agreement within the group (Chan, 1998; Roberson et al., 2007; see González-Romá et al., 2002; Lindell & Brandt, 2000; and Schneider et al., 2002 for examples).

These approaches highlight an additional area of consideration for researchers – whether the group-level construct represents something meaningfully different from the individual-level construct (Bliese & Jex, 2002). Kozlowski and Klein (2000), for example, differentiated between situations where the group-level construct is rather similar to the individual level construct (called composition processes) and situations where there is little theoretical similarity between the individual and group level processes (called compilation processes). The mean aggregation approach is more closely aligned with composition processes – the mean level of burnout in a group shares similar meaning to the individual experience of burnout. However, the consensus of experience approach (e.g., Moliner et al., 2005) is a bit different. The level of agreement or consistency within a group is different from the actual mean level on that variable. In other words – we can have groups with the same mean level of burnout but drastically different levels of consistency in their responses to burnout measures.

Similarly, when measuring collective burnout, one must decide whether to aggregate the perceived individual experience (e.g., take the mean of an item like "I feel used up at the end of the workday" for the group) or apply a referent shift model (Chan, 1998; Van Mierlo, Vermunt, & Rutte, 2009) whereby the items are rephrased to represent a different referent group. Gonzalez-Morales et al. (2012) utilized this approach, where the item above would have been reworded to be "The teachers of my school feel used up at the end of the workday;" they termed the response to these items collective exhaustion or cynicism, depending on the scale that was rephrased. They found correlations of .45 between individual exhaustion and individual reports of collective exhaustion and .47 between individual cynicism and individual reports of collective cynicism. This suggests some overlap between one's individually perceived burnout and his or her perception of the group's burnout, but not so much overlap so as to suggest they are the same. As such, the referent-shift approach may be worth considering, particularly for studies where one hopes to measure both individual experiences and perceptions of the group (Arthur et al., 2007; Van Mierlo et al., 2009).

Fitting multilevel models

The most frequently applied approach to multilevel modeling in the literature has been random coefficient modeling (sometimes call hierarchical linear modeling – HLM – for the program that is often used to fit such models; Bryk & Raudenbush, 1992; Hofmann, 1997; Zhang et al., 2009). Due to advances in statistical analysis software, researchers are increasingly utilizing multilevel structural equation models to test more complicated (e.g., mediation) multilevel models (Preacher et al., 2010; Preacher et al., 2011). While the specific code and approach to fitting these models is beyond the scope of the article, we encourage readers to examine the many good sources that explain how to run such models and the theory behind them (e.g., Bryk & Raudenbush, 1992; Klein & Kozlowski, 2000; Luke, 2004). Moreover, we suggest authors review several seminal works that outline key analytic decisions beyond the aggregation decisions discussed above (Hofmann, 1997; Hofmann & Gavin, 1998; Ohly et al., 2010).

Multilevel models are flexible in that they can be extended to understand more levels of analysis (e.g., individuals nested in departments nested in organizations; see for example van Veldhoven et al., 2002). One of those levels could include multiple measurements of the same person, such that time is another level of analysis (cf., Halbesleben et al., 2013). In addition to random coefficient modeling, there are several other innovative variants of structural equation modeling that can be used to test different types of models where repeated observations of the same person are the source of dependence in the data (e.g., McArdle, 2009).

Regarding the modeling of specific effects in a model, one can examine both direct effects models, where a higher-level effect directly impacts a lower-level variable and cross-level moderating effects, where the higher-level variable impacts the relationship between two lower-level variables (Bliese & Jex, 2002; Kozlowski & Klein, 2000). In the latter, one is interested in how a higher-level variable explains variation in the slopes among individuals. These models are useful because they can help a researcher identify the variability in the lower level effect that is attributable to that lower level and the variability that is attributable to a higher level. For example, in their study of high-performance work practices and burnout, Kroon et al. (2009) found that 11 percent of the variance in burnout was at the organization level of analysis, whereas the remaining variance was at the individual level.

While their model incorporated both moderating and mediating effects, Chowdhury and Endres (2010) provide a good example of a cross-level moderator. They found that department-level safety climate served as a moderator of the relationship between client variability and strain such that in departments with a high safety climate, there was less of a relationship between client variability and strain. Such models offer an opportunity to examine how the work context impacts the relationships between what would typically be considered individual-level effects. Alternatively, they offer researchers an opportunity to examine how characteristics of the individual impact variation in burnout within that individual (cf., Kammeyer-Mueller, Simon, & Judge, in press).

Conclusion

Our goal with this chapter was to provide some background on how burnout has been considered at multiple levels and the implications of multilevel models of burnout for our understanding of the experience of burnout. Similar to Bliese and Jex (2002), we do not intend to suggest that individual-level models of burnout are not valuable; nor are we suggesting that a multilevel perspective is relevant for all studies of burnout. We hope, however, that this chapter will encourage researchers to think carefully about multilevel modeling as an opportunity to expand our understanding of the burnout phenomenon.

References

Alvaro, C., Lyons, R. F., Warner, G., Hobfoll, S. E., Martens, P. J., Labonte, R., & Brown, E. R. (2010). Conservation of resources theory and research use in health systems. *Implementation Science, 5*, 79–98.

Appelbaum, E., Bailey, T., Berg, P., & Kalleberg, A. (2000). *Manufacturing advantage: Why high-performance work systems pay off.* Ithaca, NY: Cornell University Press.

Ardichvili, A. (2008). Learning and knowledge sharing in virtual communities of practice: Motivators, barriers, and enablers. *Advances in Developing Human Resources, 10*, 541–554.

Arthur, W., Bell, S. T., & Edwards, B. D. (2007). A longitudinal examination of the comparative criterion-related validity of additive and referent-shift consensus operationalizations of team efficacy. *Organizational Research Methods, 10*, 35–58.

Ashforth, B. E., Kreiner, G. E., & Fugate, M. (2000). All in a day's work: Boundaries and micro-role transitions. *Academy of Management Review, 25*, 472–491.

Bacharach, S. B., Bamberger, P., & Doveh, E. (2008). Firefighters, critical incidents, and drinking to cope: The adequacy of unit-level performance resources as a source of vulnerability and protection. *Journal of Applied Psychology, 93*, 155–169.

Bakker, A. B., & Demerouti, E. (2007). The job demands-resources model: State of the art. *Journal of Managerial Psychology, 22*, 309–328.

Bakker, A. B., & Schaufeli, W. B. (2000). Burnout contagion processes among teachers. *Journal of Applied Social Psychology, 30*, 2289–2308.

Bakker, A. B., Demerouti, E., & Schaufeli, W. B. (2003a). The socially induced burnout model. In S. P. Shohov (Ed.), *Advances in psychology research* (Vol. 25, pp. 13–30). New York: Nova Science Publishers.

Bakker, A. B., Demerouti, E., De Boer, E., & Schaufeli, W. B. (2003b). Job demands and job resources as predictors of absence duration and frequency. *Journal of Vocational Behavior, 62*, 341–356.

Bakker, A. B., Le Blanc, P. M., & Schaufeli, W. B. (2005). Burnout contagion among nurses who work at intensive units. *Journal of Advanced Nursing, 51*, 276–287.

Bakker, A. B., van Emmerik, H., & Euwema, M. C. (2006). Crossover of burnout and engagement in work teams. *Work and Occupations, 33*, 464–489.

Bakker, A. B., Westman, M., & van Emmerik, I. H. (2009). Advancements in crossover theory. *Journal of Managerial Psychology, 24*, 206–219.

Barney, J., Wright, M., & Ketchen, D.J. (2001). The resource-based view of the firm: Ten years after 1991. *Journal of Management, 27*, 625–641.

Bassiri, D. (1988). *Large and small sample properties of maximum likelihood estimates for the hierarchical linear model.* Unpublished doctoral dissertation, Michigan State University, East Lansing, Michigan.

Beehr, T. A., & Glazer, S. (2001). A cultural perspective of social support in relation to occupational stress. *Research in occupational stress and well-being, 1*, 97–142.

Biemann, T., Cole, M. S., & Voelpel, S. (2012). Within-group agreement: On the use (and misuse) of rWG and rWG (J) in leadership research and some best practice guidelines. *The Leadership Quarterly, 23*, 66–80.

Bliese, P. D. (1998). Group size, ICC values, and group-level correlations: A simulation. *Organizational Research Methods, 1*, 355–373.

Bliese, P. D. (2000). Within-group agreement, non-independence, and reliability: Implications for data aggregation and analysis. In K. J. Klein and S. W. J. Kozlowski (Eds), *Multilevel theory, research, and methods in organizations* (pp. 349–381). San Francisco: Jossey-Bass.

Bliese, P. D., & Halverson, R. R. (1998). Group consensus and psychological well-being: A large field study. *Journal of Applied Social Psychology, 28,* 563–580.

Bliese, P. D., & Hanges, P. J. (2004). Being both too liberal and too conservative: The perils of treating grouped data as though they were independent. *Organizational Research Methods, 7,* 400–417.

Bliese, P. D., & Jex, S. M. (2002). Incorporating a multilevel perspective into occupational stress research: Theoretical, methodological, and practical implications. *Journal of Occupational Health Psychology, 7,* 265–276.

Bono, J. E., Glomb, T. M., Shen, W., Kim, E., & Koch, A. J. (2013). Building positive resources: Effects of positive events and positive reflection on work-stress and health. *Academy of Management Journal, 56,* 1601–1627.

Brotheridge, C. M. (2003). The role of fairness in mediating the effects of voice and justification on stress and other outcomes in a climate of organizational change. *International Journal of Stress Management, 10,* 253–268.

Browne, W. J., & Draper, D. (2000). Implementation and performance issues in the Bayesian and likelihood fitting of multilevel models. *Computational Statistics, 15,* 391–420.

Bryk, A. S., & Raudenbush, S.W. (1992). *Hierarchical linear models: Applications and data analysis methods.* Newbury Park, CA: Sage.

Busing, F. (1993). *Distribution characteristics of variance estimates in two-level models.* Unpublished manuscript, Leiden University, the Netherlands.

Byrne, D. (1961). Interpersonal attraction and attitude similarity. *The Journal of Abnormal and Social Psychology, 62,* 713.

Castro, S. L. (2002). Data analytic methods for the analysis of multilevel questions: A comparison of intraclass correlation coefficients, rwg (j), hierarchical linear modeling, within- and between-analysis, and random group resampling. *The Leadership Quarterly, 13,* 69–93.

Chan, D. (1998). Functional relations among constructs in the same content domain at different levels of analysis: A typology of composition models. *Journal of Applied Psychology, 83,* 234.

Chen, G., & Bliese, P. D. (2002). The role of different levels of leadership in predicting self- and collective efficacy: Evidence for discontinuity. *Journal of Applied Psychology, 87,* 549.

Chen, S. Westman, M., & Eden, D. (2009). Impact of enhanced resources on anticipatory stress and adjustment to new information technology: A field-experimental test of conservation of resources theory. *Journal of Occupational Health Psychology, 14,* 219–230.

Chowdhury, S. K., & Endres, M. L. (2010). The impact of client variability on nurses' occupational strain and injury: Cross-level moderation by safety climate. *Academy of Management Journal, 53,* 182–198.

Clarke, P., & Wheaton, B. (2007). Addressing data sparseness in contextual population research using cluster analysis to create synthetic neighborhoods. *Sociological Methods & Research, 35,* 311–351.

Cohen, A., Doveh, E., & Eick, U. (2001). Statistical properties of the rWG (J) index of agreement. *Psychological Methods, 6,* 297–310.

Collins, C. J., & Clark, K. D. (2003). Strategic human resource practices, top management team social networks, and firm performance: The role of human resource practices in creating organizational competitive advantage. *Academy of Management Journal, 46,* 740–751.

Covin, J. G. (1991). Entrepreneurial versus conservative firms: A comparison of strategies and performance. *Journal of Management Studies, 28,* 439–462.

Crawford, E. R., LePine, J. A., & Rich, B. L. (2010). Linking job demands and resources to employee engagement and burnout: a theoretical extension and meta-analytic test. *The Journal of Applied Psychology, 95,* 834–848.

Cropanzano, R., Goldman, B., & Benson, L. (2005). Organizational justice. In J. Barling, K. Kelloway, & M. Frone (Eds), *Handbook of work stress.* Beverly Hills, CA: Sage.

Demerouti, E., Bakker, A. B., Nachreiner, F., & Schaufeli, W. B. (2000). A model of burnout and life satisfaction among nurses. *Journal of Advanced Nursing, 32,* 454–464.

Demerouti, E., Bakker, A. B., Nachreiner, F., & Schaufeli, W. B. (2001). The job demands-resources model of burnout. *Journal of Applied Psychology, 86,* 499–512.

Diez-Roux, A. V. (1998). Bringing context back into epidemiology: Variables and fallacies of multilevel analyses. *American Journal of Public Health, 88,* 216–222.

Edelwich, J., & Brodsky, A. (1980). *Burnout: Stages of disillusion in the helping professions.* New York: Human Sciences Press.

Elloy, D. F., Terpening, W., & Kohls, J. (2001). A causal model of burnout among self-managed work team members. *The Journal of Psychology, 135,* 321–334.

Fossas-Olalla, M. (1999). The resource-based theory of human resources. *International Advances in Economic Research, 5,* 84–92.

George, J. M., & Jones, G. R. (2000). The role of time in theory and theory building. *Journal of Management, 26,* 657–684.

Godard, J. (2001). Higher performance and the transformation of work? The implications of alternative work practices for the experience and outcomes of work. *Industrial and Labor Relations Review, 54,* 776–805.

Gonzalez-Morales, M. G., Peiro, J. M., Rodriguez, I., & Bliese, P. D. (2012). Perceived collective burnout: A multilevel explanation of burnout. *Anxiety, Stress, & Coping, 25,* 43–61.

González-Romá, V., Peiró, J. M., & Tordera, N. (2002). An examination of the antecedents and moderator influences of climate strength. *Journal of Applied Psychology, 87* 465–473.

Hakanen, J. J., Bakker, A. B., & Schaufeli, W. B. (2006). Burnout and work engagement among teachers. *Journal of School Psychology, 43,* 495–513.

Halbesleben, J. R. B. (2010). The role of exhaustion and workarounds in predicting occupational injuries: A cross-lagged panel study of health care professionals. *Journal of Occupational Health Psychology, 15,* 1–16.

Halbesleben, J. R. B., & Bowler, W. M. (2007). Emotional exhaustion and job performance: The mediating role of motivation. *Journal of Applied Psychology, 92,* 93–106.

Halbesleben, J. R. B., & Buckley, M. R. (2004). Burnout in organizational life. *Journal of Management, 30,* 859–879

Halbesleben, J. R., & Wheeler, A. R. (2008). The relative roles of engagement and embeddedness in predicting job performance and intention to leave. *Work & Stress, 22,* 242–256.

Halbesleben, J. R. B., & Wheeler, A. R. (2011). I owe you one: Coworker reciprocity as a moderator of the day-level exhaustion-performance relationship. *Journal of Organizational Behavior, 32,* 608–626.

Halbesleben, J. R. B., & Wheeler, A. R. (in press). Reciprocal helping behavior as a source of personal resources: A day-level study of coworker pairs. *Journal of Management*.

Halbesleben, J. R. B., Osburn, H. K., & Mumford, M. D. (2006). Action research as a burnout intervention: Reducing burnout in the Federal Fire Service. *Journal of Applied Behavioral Science, 42*, 244–266.

Halbesleben, J. R. B., Zellars, K., Carlson, D. C., Perrewe, P. L., & Rotondo, D. (2010). Moderating effect of work-linked couple relationships and work-family integration on the spouse instrumental support-emotional exhaustion relationship. *Journal of Occupational Health Psychology, 15,* 371–387.

Halbesleben, J. R. B., Wheeler, A. R., & Rossi, A. M. (2012). The costs and benefits of working with one's spouse: A two-sample examination of spousal support, work-family conflict, and emotional exhaustion in work-linked relationships. *Journal of Organizational Behavior, 33,* 597–615.

Halbesleben, J. R. B., Wheeler, A. R., & Paustian-Underdahl, S. C. (2013). The impact of furloughs on emotional exhaustion, performance, and recovery experiences. *Journal of Applied Psychology, 98*, 492–503.

Hatfield, E, Cacippo, J. T., & Rapson, R. L. (1994). *Emotional contagion.* New York: Cambridge University Press.

Hobfoll, S. E. (1988). *The ecology of stress.* New York: Hemisphere.

Hobfoll, S. E. (1989). Conservation of resources: A new attempt at conceptualizing stress. *American Psychologist, 44*, 513–524.

Hobfoll, S. E. (1998). *Stress, culture, and community.* New York: Plenum.

Hobfoll, S. E. (2001). The influence of culture, community, and the nested self in the stress process: Advancing conservation of resources theory. *Applied Psychology: An International Review, 50*, 337–370.

Hobfoll, S. E. (2011). Conservation of resources caravans in engaged settings. *Journal of Occupational and Organizational Psychology, 84*, 116–122.

Hobfoll, S. E., & Freedy, J. (1993). Conservation of resources: A general stress theory applied to burnout. In W. B. Schaufeli, C. Maslach, & T. Marek (Eds.), *Professional burnout: Recent developments in theory and research.* Washington, DC: Taylor & Francis.

Hobfoll, S. E., & Shirom, A. (1993). Stress and burnout in the workplace: Conservation of resources. In: T. Golombiewski (Ed.), *Handbook of Organizational Behavior* (pp. 41–61). New York: Marcel Dekker.

Hobfoll, S. E., & Shirom, A. (2001). Conservation of resources theory: Applications to stress and management in the workplace. In: R. T. Golembiewski (Ed.), *Handbook of Organization Behavior* (pp. 57–81). New York: Dekker.

Hofmann, D. A. (1997). An overview of the logic and rationale of hierarchical linear models. *Journal of Management, 23*, 723–744.

Hofmann, D. A. (2002). Issues in multilevel research: Theory development, measurement, and analysis. In S. G. Rogelberg (Ed.), *Handbook of research methods in industrial and organizational psychology* (pp. 247–274). Malden, MA: Blackwell.

Hofmann, D. A., & Gavin, M. B. (1998). Centering decisions in hierarchical linear models: Implications for research in organizations. *Journal of Management, 24*, 623–641.

Hox, J. (1998). Multilevel modeling: When and why. In I. Balderjahn, R. Mather, & M. Schader (Eds), *Classification, data analysis, and data highways* (pp. 147–154). New York: Springer.

Inceoglu, I., Segers, J., & Bartram, D. (2012). Age-related differences in work motivation. *Journal of Occupational and Organizational Psychology, 85*, 300–329.

James, L. R., Demaree, R. G., & Wolf, G. (1984). Estimating within-group interrater reliability with and without response bias. *Journal of Applied Psychology, 69*, 85.

Joplin, J. R., Shaffer, M. A., Francesco, A. M., & Lau, T. (2003). The macro-environment and work-family conflict development of a cross cultural comparative framework. *International Journal of Cross Cultural Management, 3*, 305–328.

Judge, T. A., Locke, E. A., & Durham, C. C. (1997). The dispositional causes of job satisfaction: A core evaluations approach. *Research in Organizational Behavior, 19*, 151–188.

Kahill, S. (1988). Symptoms of professional burnout: A review of the empirical evidence. *Canadian Psychology, 29*, 284–297.

Kammeyer-Mueller, J. D., Simon, L. S., & Judge, T. A. (in press). A head start or a step behind? Understanding how dispositional and motivational resources influence emotional exhaustion. *Journal of Management.*

Klein, K. J., Danserau, F., & Hall, R. J. (1994). Levels issues in theory development, data collection, and analysis. *Academy of Management Review, 19*, 195–229.

Klein, K. L., & Kozlowski, S. W. J. (2000). *Multilevel theory, research, and methods in organizations.* San Francisco: Jossey-Bass.

Kooij, D., & Van de Voorde, K. (2011). How changes in subjective general health predict future time perspective, and development and generativity motives over the lifespan. *Journal of Occupational and Organizational Psychology, 84*, 228–247.

Kozlowski, S. W. J., & Ilgen, D. R. (2006). Enhancing the effectiveness of work groups and teams. *Psychological Science in the Public Interest, 7*, 77–124.

Kozlowski, S. W. J., & Klein, K. J. (2000). A multilevel approach to theory and research in organizations: Contextual, temporal, and emergent processes. In K. J. Klein and S. W. J. Kozlowski, (eds), *Multilevel theory, research, and methods in organizations* (pp. 3–90). San Francisco: Jossey-Bass.

Kreft, I. G., & De Leeuw, J. (1998). *Introducing multilevel modeling.* Newbury Park, CA: Sage.

Kroon, B., van de Voorde, K., & van Veldhoven, M. (2009). Cross-level effects of high-performance work practices on burnout: Two counteracting mediating mechanisms compared. *Personnel Review, 38*, 509–525.

Lance, C. E., Butts, M. M., & Michels, L. C. (2006). The sources of four commonly reported cutoff criteria: What did they really say? *Organizational Research Methods, 9*, 202–220.

Le Blanc, P. M., Hox, J. J., Schaufeli, W. B., Taris, T. W,. & Peeters, M. C. W. (2007). Take Care! The evaluation of a team-based burnout intervention program for oncology care providers. *Journal of Applied Psychology, 92*, 213–227.

LeBreton, J. M., Burgess, J. R., Kaiser, R. B., Atchley, E. K., & James, L. R. (2003). The restriction of variance hypothesis and interrater reliability and agreement: Are ratings from multiple sources really dissimilar? *Organizational Research Methods, 6*, 80–128.

LeBreton, J. M., & Senter, J. L. (2008). Answers to 20 questions about interrater reliability and interrater agreement. *Organizational Research Methods, 11*, 815–852.

Legge, K. (1995). *Human resource management: Rhetorics and realities.* London: Macmillan.

Lindell, M. K., & Brandt, C. J. (2000). Climate quality and climate consensus as mediators of the relationship between organizational antecedents and outcomes. *Journal of Applied Psychology, 85*, 331.

Litz, R. A. (1996). A resource-based-view of the socially responsible firm: Stakeholder interdependence, ethical awareness, and issue responsiveness as strategic assets. *Journal of Business Ethics, 15*, 1355–1363.

Lopina, E. C., Rogelberg, S. G., & Howell, B. (2012). Turnover in dirty work: A focus on pre-entry individual characteristics. *Journal of Occupational and Organizational Psychology, 85*, 396–406.

Luke, D. A. (2004). *Multilevel modeling: Quantitative applications in the social sciences.* Thousand Oaks, CA: Sage.

Maas, C. J., & Hox, J. J. (2005). Sufficient sample sizes for multilevel modeling. *Methodology: European Journal of Research Methods for the Behavioral and Social Sciences, 1*, 86–92.

Maslach, D., Schaufeli, W. B., & Leiter, M.P. (2001). Job burnout. *Annual Review of Psychology, 52*, 397–422.

McArdle, J. J. (2009). Latent variable modeling of differences and changes with longitudinal data. *Annual Review of Psychology, 60*, 477–605.

Melamed, S., Ugarten, U., Shirom, A., Kahana, L., Lerman, Y., & Froom, P. (1999). Chronic burnout, somatic arousal and elevated cortisol levels. *Journal of Psychosomatic Research, 46*, 591–598.

Melamed, S., Shirom, A., Toker, S., Berliner, S., & Shapira, I. (2006). Burnout and risk of cardiovascular disease: Evidence, possible causal paths, and promising research directions. *Psychological Bulletin, 132*, 327–353.

Mitchell, T. R., & James, J. R. (2001). Building better theory: Time and the specification of when things happen. *Academy of Management Review, 26*, 530–547.

Moliner, C., Martinez-Tur, V., Peiro, J. M., Ramos, J., & Cropanzano, R. (2005). Relationships between organizational level justice and burnout at the work-unit level. *International Journal of Stress Management*, 12, 99–116.

Oh, H., Labianca, G., & Chung, M-H. (2006). A multilevel model of group social capital. *Academy of Management Review, 31*, 569–582.

Ohly, S., Sonnentag, S., Niessen, C., & Zapf, D. (2010). Diary studies in organizational research. *Journal of Personnel Psychology, 9*, 79–93.

Ostroff, C., & Bowen, D. E. (2000). Moving HR to a higher level: HR practices and organizational effectiveness. In K. J. Klein, & S. W. Kozlowski (Eds), *Multilevel theory, research, and methods in organizations: Foundations, extensions, and new directions* (pp. 211–266). San Francisco, CA, US: Jossey-Bass.

Park, S., & Lake, E. T. (2005). Multilevel modeling of a clustered continuous outcome: Nurses' work hours and burnout. *Nursing Research, 54*, 406–413.

Payne, S. C., Cook, A. L., & Diaz, I. (2012). Understanding childcare satisfaction and its effect on workplace outcomes: The convenience factor and the mediating role of work-family conflict. *Journal of Occupational and Organizational Psychology, 85*, 225–244.

Petrou, P., Demerouti, E., Peeters, M. C., Schaufeli, W. B., & Hetland, J. (2012). Crafting a job on a daily basis: Contextual correlates and the link to work engagement. *Journal of Organizational Behavior, 33*, 1120–1141.

Phillips, J. M. (1998). Effects of realistic job previews on multiple organizational outcomes: A meta-analysis. *Academy of Management Journal, 41*, 673–690.

Preacher, K. J., Zyphur, M. J., & Zhang, Z. (2010). A general multilevel SEM framework for assessing multilevel mediation. *Psychological Methods, 15*, 209–233.

Preacher, K. J., Zhang, Z., & Zyphur, M. J. (2011). Alternative methods for assessing mediation in multilevel data: The advantages of multilevel SEM. *Structural Equation Modeling, 18*, 161–182.

Reise, S. P. & Duan, N. (2003). *Multi-level modeling.* Mahwah, NJ: Lawrence Erlbaum.

Roberson, Q. M., Sturman, M. C., & Simons, T. L. (2007). Does the measure of dispersion matter in multilevel research? A comparison of the relative performance of dispersion indexes. *Organizational Research Methods, 10*, 564–588.

Salancik, G. R., & Pfeffer, J. (1978). A social information processing approach to job attitudes and task design. *Administrative Science Quarterly*, 224–253.

Schaufeli, W. B., Bakker, A. B., & Van Rhenen, W. (2009). How changes in job demands and resources predict burnout, work engagement, and sickness absenteeism. *Journal of Organizational Behavior, 30*, 893–917.

Scherbaum, C. A., & Ferreter, J. M. (2009). Estimating statistical power and required sample sizes for organizational research using multilevel modeling. *Organizational Research Methods, 12*, 347–367.

Schneider, B., Salvaggio, A. N., & Subirats, M. (2002). Climate strength: A new direction for climate research. *Journal of Applied Psychology, 87*, 220–229.

Semmer, N. K., Elfering, A., Jacobshagen, N., Perrot, T., Beehr, T. A., & Boos, N. (2008). The emotional meaning of instrumental social support. *International Journal of Stress Management, 15*, 235–251.

Shirom, A. (2003). Feeling vigorous at work? The construct of vigor and the study of positive affect in organizations. *Research in Occupational Stress and Well-being, 3*, 135–164.

Shrout, P. E., & Fleiss, J. L. (1979). Intraclass correlations: uses in assessing rater reliability. *Psychological Bulletin, 86*, 420–428.

Snijders, T. A. (2005). Power and sample size in multilevel linear models. In B. S. Everitt & D. C. Howell (Eds), *Encyclopedia of statistics in behavioral science* (Vol. 3, pp. 1570–1573). Chichester, UK: Wiley.

Snijders, T., & Bosker, R. (1999). *Multilevel modeling: An introduction to basic and advanced multilevel modeling.* Thousand Oaks, CA: Sage.

Sonnentag, S., Brodbeck, F. C., Heinbokel, T., & Stolte, W. (1994). Stressor-burnout relationship in software development teams. *Journal of Occupational and Organizational Psychology, 67*, 327–341.

Stroebe, W., & Stroebe, M. (1996). The social psychology of social support. In E. T. Higgins and A. W. Kruglanski (Eds), *Social psychology: Handbook of basic principles* (pp. 597–621). New York: Guilford Press.

Susser, M. (1994). The logical in ecological: I. The logic of analysis. *American Journal of Public Health, 85*, 825–829.

ten Brummelhuis, L., & Bakker, A. (2012). A resource perspective on the work-home resource model. *American Psychologist, 67*, 545–556.

Tims, M., & Bakker, A. B. (2010). Job crafting: Towards a new model of individual job redesign. *South African Journal of Industrial Psychology, 36*, 1–9.

Tims, M., Bakker, A. B., & Derks, D. (2012). Development and validation of the job crafting scale. *Journal of Vocational Behavior, 80*, 173–186.

Tims, M., Bakker, A. B., & Derks, D. (2013). The impact of job crafting on job demands, job resources, and well-being. *Journal of Occupational Health Psychology, 18*, 230–240.

Totterdell, P. (2000). Catching moods and hitting runs: Mood linkage and subjective performance in professional sports teams. *Journal of Applied Psychology, 85*, 848–859.

Treadway, D. C., Ferris, G. R., Hochwarter, W. A., Perrewe, P., Witt, L. A., & Goodman, J. M. (2005). The role of age in the perceptions of politics – job performance relationship: A three-study constructive replication. *Journal of Applied Psychology, 90*, 872–881.

Vandenberghe, C., Bentein, K., Michon, R., Chebat, J., Tremblay, M., & Fils, J. (2007). An examination of the role of perceived support and employee commitment in employee-customer encounters. *Journal of Applied Psychology, 92*, 1177–1187.

Van den Heuvel, M., Demerouti, E., Bakker, A. B., & Schaufeli, W. B. (2010). Personal resources and work engagement in the face of change. In J. Houdmont, & S. Leka (Eds), *Contemporary occupational health psychology* (Vol. 1, pp. 124–150). Chichester: John Wiley & Sons Ltd.

Van der Leeden, R., & Busing, F. (1994). *First iteration versus IGLS RIGLS estimates in two-level models: A Monte Carlo study with ML3.* Unpublished manuscript, Leiden University, the Netherlands.

Van Mierlo, H., Vermunt, J. K., & Rutte, C. G. (2009). Composing group-level constructs from individual-level survey data. *Organizational Research Methods, 12*, 368–392.

van Veldhoven, M. V., de Jonge, J., Broersen, S., Kompier, M., & Meijman, T. (2002). Specific relationships between psychosocial job conditions and job-related stress: A three-level analytic approach. *Work & Stress, 16*, 207–228.

Westman, M. (2002). Crossover of stress and strain in the family and in the workplace. In P. L. Perrewe & D. C. Ganster (Eds), *Research in occupational stress and well-being* (Vol. 2, pp. 141–181). Greenwich, CT: JAI.

Westman, M. (2006), Crossover of stress and strain in the work-family context. In F. Jones, R. J. Burke, and M. Westman (Eds), *Work-life balance: A psychological perspective.* Hove: Psychology Press.

Westman, M., & Etzion, D. (1995), Crossover of stress, strain and resources from one spouse to another. *Journal of Organizational Behavior, 16,* 169–81.

Wilson, K. S., Sin, H. P., & Conlon, D. E. (2010). What about the leader in leader-member exchange? The impact of resource exchanges and substitutability on the leader. *Academy of Management Review, 35*, 358–372.

Wright, P. M., Dunford, B. B., & Snell, S. A. (2001). Human resources and the resource based view of the firm. *Journal of Management, 27*, 701–721.

Wright, P. M., McMahan, G. C., & McWilliams, A. (1994). Human resources and sustained competitive advantage: A resource-based perspective. *International Journal of Human Resource Management, 5*, 301–326.

Wright, T. A., & Bonnett, D. G. (1997). The contribution of burnout to work performance. *Journal of Organizational Behavior, 18*, 491–499.

Wright, T. A., & Cropanzano, R. (1998). Emotional exhaustion as a predictor of job performance and voluntary turnover. *Journal of Applied Psychology, 83*, 486–493.

Zhang, Z., Zyphur, M. J., & Preacher, K. J. (2009). Testing multilevel mediation using hierarchical linear models problems and solutions. *Organizational Research Methods, 12*, 695–719.

8   Interventions to prevent and alleviate burnout

Michael P. Leiter and Christina Maslach

Burnout is a syndrome that develops in response to problematic relationships between employees and their workplaces. A poor alignment of organizational structures and processes with employees' inclinations and aspirations creates tensions that deplete energy, reduce involvement, and discourage employees' sense of efficacy (Brotheridge & Grandey, 2002; Maslach & Leiter, 1997). These relationships are also described in terms of imbalance or mismatch or incongruity — for example, the imbalance between demands and resources (Bakker & Demerouti, 2007), or the job-person mismatch in six areas of the workplace: workload, control, reward, community, fairness, and values (Leiter & Maslach, 2004). When these problematic relationships last a long time, and become a more chronic condition, then the detrimental impact of burnout on well-being and performance becomes even more significant – and leads to increasing calls for effective solutions to this problem.

The enduring nature of employees' relationship with their workplaces is reflected in the relative stability of burnout, evident in longitudinal surveys spanning intervals of years (Maslach et al., 2001; Schaufeli et al., 2011). Burnout's stability argues against hopes of the syndrome generating a self-healing process that will naturally replace exhaustion with vigor, cynicism with dedication, and inefficacy with efficacy. Although this shift may happen occasionally through happenstance or exceptional resiliency, such improvements are the exception rather than the rule. These considerations lead to the conclusion that preventing or alleviating burnout requires a concerted, planned, deliberate intervention.

Ever since burnout was identified, in the 1970s, as both a personal and organizational problem, there have been repeated calls for answers on how to deal with it. There has never been a shortage of ideas for what to do about burnout, which has led to a large array of workshops, self-help books, and pamphlets, as well as therapeutic and coaching programs. Many of these options have been adapted from other work done on stress, coping, and health. The most popular proposals have focused on changing work patterns (e.g., working less, taking more breaks, avoiding overtime work, balancing work with the rest of one's life); developing coping skills (e.g., cognitive restructuring, conflict resolution, time management); obtaining social support (both from colleagues and family); utilizing relaxation strategies; promoting good health and fitness; and developing a better self-understanding (via various self-analytic techniques, counseling, or therapy). However, there have been relatively few assessments of the effectiveness of any of these ideas. There have been no clear definitions of burnout or of what kind of "problem" is being fixed, no clear criteria for what would be successful outcomes, and no solid evaluation research methods (see Maslach & Goldberg, 1998 for a more extensive review).

In contrast to the variety of interventions proposed by practitioners, most burnout researchers did not begin with a focus on intervention. Rather, their goal was to understand and define what this phenomenon was, and to identify its sources and consequences. Various theoretical models have been proposed, but so far, there have not been many efforts to actually use this theorizing in the development of specific burnout interventions. However, given the growing concern about burnout from government agencies and organizations in both the public and private sectors, there is a new interest in using and applying research to address the question of "what to do about burnout."

There are several ways to think about burnout interventions. Addressing burnout includes both alleviating burnout when it arises and preventing it before it occurs. In the most severe situations, alleviation interventions focus on efforts to facilitate employees' return to work after they have gone on disability leave. Alleviation interventions may also occur with individuals or workgroups experiencing levels of burnout that, although elevated, are not sufficiently severe to prevent them from working. Prevention strategies tend to focus on employees who are generally in good shape, and help them to not become at risk of burnout.

Another approach has applied a public health framework to occupational health risks within the workplace (Quick, 1992). The elimination or modification of worksite stressors is considered to be primary prevention, because the intent is to reduce the incidence of new cases of stress. Interventions designed to help individuals manage or cope with these worksite stressors are designated as secondary prevention, because their intent is to reduce the prevalence of stress. Interventions that treat individuals who are already suffering from exposure to these worksite stressors are designated as tertiary prevention, because their intent is to reduce the residual deficits following the stress experience. However, another way of framing these approaches is to note that primary prevention strategies focus on the situation, while both secondary and tertiary prevention strategies focus on the individual (by either changing or treating). This distinction between person-centered vs. situation-centered interventions is probably a better way to characterize much of the research on burnout interventions.

Recent research on burnout intervention

What have been the most recent research articles to focus on interventions for burnout? To address that question, we have compiled a review based on the following criteria. Articles were identified with the words "burnout," and "intervention" on the PsycINFO or Google Scholar search engine since the year 2000, in order to capture articles that were not available for Maslach et al. (2001).

The studies elicited were then examined to determine that they reported the actual results of an intervention. Unless another measure is specifically noted, the studies used one of the versions of the Maslach Burnout Inventory (MBI; Maslach, Jackson et al., 1996), which provides scores on exhaustion, cynicism, and efficacy. We summarize this review in Table 8.1.

Literature reviews of interventions

A review of research on medical resident burnout found that only 9 of the 160 articles on the topic focused on interventions. "Interventions included workshops, a resident assistance program, a self-care intervention, support groups, didactic sessions, or stress-management/coping training either alone or in various combinations" (McCray et al., 2008, p. 626). Procedural shortfalls in all of the reviewed studies limited the potential validity and generalizability of these findings. Another review came to a similar conclusion about burnout studies in a broad range of human service professions: Intervention studies were rare, their samples were generally small, and their research designs were flawed (Buljac-Samardzic et al., 2010). In addition, some cases of intervention resulted in no changes in burnout, but this maintenance of the status quo in the face of adverse events was a more positive outcome in comparison to control groups who got worse over time (e.g., Innstrand et al., 2004; LeBlanc et al., 2007).

A comprehensive literature review of 63 stress-oriented interventions (Van den Bossche & Houtman, 2003) used a 2X2 framework (Kompier & Kristensen, 2001) of Focus (work environment v. individual or group) by Prevention (primary v. secondary/tertiary). Only three of these studies reported changes in burnout. Individual interventions generally sought to increase employees' resiliency to endure the pressures of worklife. These programs included relaxation (e.g., van der Hek & Plomp, 1997) or meditation (e.g., Murphy, 1996). Other programs utilized cognitive behavioral therapy (CBT) or stress inoculation therapy (SIT). The review identified one individually oriented study that reported decreases in exhaustion (Lindquist & Cooper, 1999), and one that reported improvements in all three aspects of burnout (Ewers et al., 2002). Another study found a decrease in exhaustion associated with participation in a workshop teaching cognitive strategies to address inequity perceptions in conjunction with relaxation techniques (Van Dierendonck et al., 1998). However, no studies were found in Van den Bossche and Houtman's review (2003) that addressed burnout through interventions focusing on the individual/organizational interface or organizational interventions. The authors recognized valuable contributions in the existing literature, but found the amount of intervention research, its scope, and experimental rigor to be inadequate to the task of developing, implementing, and evaluating methods for addressing stress and burnout.

Table 8.1 Intervention summary

Study	N	Control Group	Occupation	Approach	Improvement
Van Dierendonck et al. (1998)	84	Yes	Staff working with mentally disabled persons	Cognitive strategies to address inequity perceptions in conjunction with relaxation techniques	Yes, Exhaustion
Ossebaard (2000)	42	Yes	Employees at an addiction care center in The Netherlands	Biofeedback: Synchro-Energizer standard program	No Improvement
Westman & Etzion (2001)	87	No	Employees working in a food company	Vacation	Only short term effects on exhaustion
Ewers et al. (2002)	20	Yes	Forensic health nurses	Individual – Psychosocial Intervention Training (PSI)	Yes, all three
Innstrand et al. (2004)	112	Yes	Staff working with persons with intellectual disabilities	Variety of intervention strategies such as group discussions, exercise programmes, educational seminars, and organizational interventions	Yes, Exhaustion
Salmela-Aro et al. (2004)	64	Yes	Employees with severe burnout symptoms	(1) Psychodrama group and (2) Analysis of work issues from a psychoanalytic perspective	Yes, all three
Cohen & Gagin (2005)	25	No	Social workers	Skills development workshop	Yes, increased personal accomplishment and decreased depersonalization
Cohen-Katz et al. (2005)	11	Yes	Healthcare professionals	Eight-week mindfulness meditation program (MBSR)	Yes, Exhaustion and Personal Accomplishment
Galantino et al. (2005)	84	No	Healthcare professionals	Eight-week mindfulness meditation program (MBSR)	Yes, Exhaustion

Study	N	Controlled	Population	Intervention	Improvement
Shapiro et al. (2005)	18	Yes	Healthcare professionals	Eight-week mindfulness meditation program (MBSR)	Yes, all three
Van Weert et al. (2005)	60	Yes	Psychogeriatric care providers – CNAs (certified nursing assistants)	Snoezelen – multisensory stimulation (MSS)	Yes, Exhaustion
Halbesleben et al. (2006)	95	No	Firefighters	Group problem-solving exercises	Yes, Exhaustion & Cynicism
Mommersteeg et al. (2006)	74	No	Psychotherapy patients with burnout diagnoses	Cognitive behavioral treatment	Yes, all three
Hätinen et al. (2007)	52	Yes	White-collar workers diagnosed with job-related psychological health problems	Both traditional and participatory interventions	Yes, Exhaustion & Cynicism, in Participatory Interventions only
LeBlanc et.al. (2007)	260	Yes	Care providers in 29 oncology wards at 18 general hospitals	"Take Care" intervention program; 6 monthly sessions of 3 hr each, educational (group discussions) and action components (problem-solving teams)	No Improvement
Butow et al. (2008)	30	Yes	Oncologists from six hospitals in Australia	CST – Communication Skills Training	No Improvement
de Vente et al. (2008)	82	Yes	Recruited from two occupational health services, practitioners, and ads; must have symptoms of neurasthenia, impaired daily functioning, etc.	CBT-based Stress Management Training (SMT)	No Improvement
Duijts et al. (2008)	76	Yes	Employees from three companies in educational and healthcare sectors	Preventative coaching program	Yes, Exhaustion

Table 8.1 Continued

Study	N	Control Group	Occupation	Approach	Improvement
Elo et al. (2008)	652	No	Finnish public service employees	Program focusing on understanding the psycho-social work environment	No Improvement
Long et al. (2008)	12	No	Staff at developmental disabilities ward	Increased staff support and education	Yes, Exhaustion
Visser et al. (2008)	52	Yes	Health care providers working with dementia patients	Peer Support Program and Education Program	No Improvement
Stenlund et al. (2009)	136	No	Employees on sick leave caused by burnout	Cognitive Behavioural Rehabilitation (CBR); relaxation & discussions; with Physical Activity Training (Qigong)	Yes, general burnout levels decreased
Bresó et al. (2011)	23	Yes	University students	Four-month individual cognitive behavioral intervention	Yes, Exhaustion & Cynicism
Leiter et al. (2011)	262	Yes	Health care providers mostly hospital nurses taken from 8 units	CREW	Yes, Exhaustion and Cynicism
Goodman & Schorling (2012)	93	No	Healthcare professionals	Mindfulness	Yes, all three
Lagerveld et al. (2012)	168	No	Sick leave due to psychological problems	CBT	Yes, Exhaustion & Return to Work
Leiter et al. (2012)	262	Yes	Health care providers mostly hospital nurses taken from 8 units	CREW	Yes, Exhaustion and Cynicism; Sustained at 1-year follow-up
Vuori et al. (2012)	369	Yes	Organizations from both private and public sectors of work life	Career development Workshop; in-company training program	No Improvement

Cognitive behavioral therapy

Individual interventions to address burnout often focus on strengthening both physical and psychological resiliency. Cognitive behavioral therapy (CBT) has been included in the intervention strategy of several studies. One study found decreases in burnout, as measured by the single-factor exhaustion-oriented Melamed Burnout Scale (Melamed et al., 1992), following participation in an individually oriented intervention that combined CBT with physical activity training (Stenlund et al., 2009). Another CBT study found reductions in exhaustion and in the time required for participants to recover sufficiently to return to work, for 168 employees on disability leave (Lagerveld et al., 2012). A study that contrasted 10 forensic nurses with a control group found that a coping skills intervention produced improvements in all three dimensions of burnout at the end of the six-month training. There were no corresponding changes in the control group (Ewers et al., 2002).

However, several other studies have not found any positive effects of CBT interventions. For example, de Vente et al. (2008), finding no reduction in burnout, concluded: "this study adds to the evidence that CBT-based interventions as currently practiced are not successful in treating patients with clinical levels of work-related stress" (p. 214). Butow et al. (2008) also failed to find an impact on burnout for their communication skills intervention, although it did increase participants' confidence in their communication abilities. Vuori et al. (2012) found no change in exhaustion in response to their career development workshops despite its beneficial effects on depression and intention to retire early. Ossebaard (2000) found no enduring impact of biofeedback training on exhaustion. Visser et al. (2008) found no effect on burnout for a peer support program for 52 health care providers working with dementia patients. Elo et al. (2008) found no change in exhaustion in an otherwise successful program focusing on understanding the psycho-social work environment for 625 Finnish public service employees.

Mindfulness

Another approach to addressing burnout, especially within health care, has been mindfulness (Kabat-Zinn et al., 1985). Mindfulness is defined as a "non-elaborative awareness of present-moment experience" (Chambers et al., 2009, p. 561) that involves intentional, nonjudgmental, present-focused attention (Thomas & Otis, 2010). The potential of mindfulness to address burnout may lie in its use as a relaxation technique, which could reduce exhaustion, or improve emotion-focused coping with distressing events at work and help people feel a greater sense of efficacy and confidence. Also, its use of a non-judgmental psychological detachment might help prevent the development of cynicism. Future research is needed to identify what the actual mechanisms might be.

In one study, 84 health care providers who participated in an eight-week mindfulness meditation program showed a reduction in exhaustion, but not the other two aspects of burnout; however, the study did not have a control group

(Galantino et al., 2005). Similarly, a reduction in exhaustion was found for 11 health care providers participating in an 8-week mindfulness course (Cohen-Katz et al., 2005). Another study contrasted 18 intervention participants with a control group to find improvements in all three aspects of burnout (Shapiro et al., 2005). More recently, a study found improvement in burnout among 93 health care providers who met for eight 2.5-hour weekly sessions plus a day-long retreat focusing on mindfulness meditation (Goodman & Schorling, 2012).

Workplace interventions

Interventions that have focused directly on the employees' workplace seem to have a more consistent impact on burnout. For example, a program for nurses, which targeted workplace equity issues using guided imagery and group discussions, had a positive impact on both exhaustion and efficacy (van Dierendonck et al., 2001). A program based on discussions of worklife quality among psychogeriatric care providers also found improvement in exhaustion, although not efficacy (Van Weert et al., 2005). A reduction in exhaustion, relative to control groups, was found for a program that provided workplace coaching sessions to 76 participants over a six-month period (Duijts et al., 2008). Improvement in all three burnout dimensions was found for 10 nurses participating in a program teaching a method of managing extreme behavior in a developmental disabilities ward (Long et al., 2008). A skills development workshop resulted in improvements on all three dimensions of burnout for 25 social workers (Cohen & Gagin, 2005). A study that assessed employees' burnout scores before, immediately after, and four weeks after returning from vacation, found that burnout (as measured by the one-dimensional Burnout Measure; Pines et al., 1981) decreased from baseline immediately after vacation but returned to baseline at the four-week follow-up (Westman & Etzion, 2001).

Long-term interventions

Some studies have found success for prolonged intervention methods. For example, Salmela-Aro et al. (2004) found reductions in burnout for nurses participating in one of two 16-week intervention groups: (1) a psychodrama group based on work-related themes, and (2) an analysis of work issues from a psycho-analytic perspective. There were 32 nurses in each intervention group and 34 nurses in a control group. When assessed with the Bergen Burnout Indicator (Matthiesen, 1992), a uni-dimensional measure of exhaustion, both intervention groups showed decreased exhaustion, in contrast to the control group. Bresó et al. (2011) found increases in work engagement along with decreases in exhaustion and cynicism among 23 students who completed a four-month individual cognitive behavioral intervention, in contrast to a control group that did not improve. Psychotherapy patients with burnout diagnoses (n=74) in a Dutch clinic were found to have improved on all three aspects of burnout after 8.5 months of treatment, with these gains remaining constant six months later (Mommersteeg et al., 2006). However, the latter study did not use a control group.

Organizational interventions

Progress has occurred in exploring organizational interventions in recent years. Halbesleben et al. (2006) reported an innovative approach to applying action research as a means to reduce burnout. This descriptive study drew upon a group problem-solving exercise to address problems that managers and employees identified in their work as firefighters. They found reductions in exhaustion and cynicism over the intervention period. In another study, the active involvement of participants (20 white-collar workers) in designing their individual rehabilitation treatment plan led to a stronger impact on exhaustion and cynicism than was found in a control group using traditionally structured therapy sessions (Hätinen et al., 2007). Another organizational intervention was a small-scale (n=20) study of nurses that found a decrease in exhaustion when implementing an individualized patient care model within a Swedish hospital (Berg et al., 2008). Le Blanc and Schaufeli (2008) argue that by encouraging participants' active involvement in the planning, design, and implementation of interventions, an action research approach increases the potential for success. The sense of agency, as well as the access to local knowledge resulting from such collaborations, is fundamental to the impact and long-term sustainability of interventions.

Current issues in burnout intervention research

Several themes emerge from this review of research on burnout interventions. First, there continues to be a relative paucity of actual evaluative research on this issue, a trend that has not changed much in the past 15 years (see Maslach & Goldberg, 1998). Considering that there have been hundreds of published articles about burnout every year, the number of studies focusing on any kind of intervention is relatively small. The relative lack of research on burnout interventions has not been due to a lack of interest in such work. Rather, there are a number of constraints that have made such research both difficult to do, and difficult to get published. In general, applied research is often viewed as less worthy or important than basic research, and thus is less likely to appear in the more prestigious research journals. Consequently, this becomes a major disincentive for researchers who are concerned about their career path and about the more or less successful choices that they can make. Even though there is now more attention being paid to "translational research" and to the practical implications of basic research for various social issues, there is still more to be done if we want to have more support for empirical tests of potential solutions to burnout.

Some of the more recent studies reviewed in this chapter utilize more rigorous methodologies than in the past, which is an encouraging sign. But the review also points to various methodological shortcomings (such as a lack of a control/comparison group, or small sample sizes). In some cases, these problems result from the difficulties involved in getting permission to carry out some type of intervention research within an organization. There are often organizational concerns about privacy and confidentiality, or about the public sharing of the findings. This kind of research often takes a longer time commitment and requires more effort and management by the researcher, in order to both implement the intervention and do follow-up assessments. The researcher may have less control over how the research is carried out, and may have to make compromises in order to get the study done at all.

Person-centered vs. situation-centered interventions

One major theme in the literature review is the contrast between interventions that focus on the individual and those that focus on a group or team or organizational unit. Clearly, much more attention has been given, for many years, to individual approaches (and there are many). However, there is not a lot of strong, consistent evidence that supports the effectiveness of these individual strategies. Even though there have been fewer attempts to implement and evaluate intervention strategies at the level of the work context (the job, the organizational unit, or the organization as a whole), the current evidence suggests that these sorts of strategies are more likely to have a positive impact.

It is interesting to note that the preference for individual interventions does not parallel the research on burnout, which has consistently found more evidence for the impact of social and organizational factors, than for personal ones. Why should there be such a focus on what to do with the individual, either in terms of treatment or prevention? One answer has been that individual strategies tend to be less costly for the organization, at least immediately, than interventions that target organizational change. However, there is not a lot of evidence to test this assumption, in terms of all the costs that are involved (such as absenteeism and poor job performance), as well as whether cheaper individual interventions are as effective as group or organizational ones.

A better answer may lie in the fact that burnout has been defined and described in terms of the individual experience (exhaustion, cynicism, inefficacy). This individualistic concept is not unique to burnout – indeed, it is characteristic of definitions of various forms of mental illness and stress – but the fact that a person's psychological and physical experience is the starting point may frame the question of "what do we do about burnout?" into the form of "what do we do about the person?" This person-centered framing dovetails with the philosophy of North America's individualistic society, which not only sees people as responsible for their own outcomes, but which celebrates the triumph of the individual over any obstacle. From this point of view, stressors are to be overcome, not eliminated. It is believed that a person's ability and character can be assessed by how well he or she deals with stress, and this assumption is reflected in the value placed on "stress interviews" or "stress tests" as necessary challenges to separate out the better employees from the weaker ones.

There are other implications of this person-centered framework. First, it is often presumed that the source of burnout lies more within the individual employee than the work setting. Even when lip service is paid to the presence of a stressful work environment, it is not uncommon to target the individual's personal qualities as the more important factor (e.g., "it may be a tough job, but his real problem is that he is such a workaholic" or "that she has anger management issues," etc.). Second, regardless of the source of burnout, it is often presumed that it is the responsibility of the person, not the organization, to do something about the problem. Again, even when lip service is paid to a stressful work environment, the focus will more often be on the failure of the person to deal with that reality (e.g., "if you can't take the heat, you should stay out of the kitchen"). Employees who complain about the workplace stressors are often viewed as weak and whiny, and as people who are behaving in inappropriate ways and abdicating all responsibility for taking care of themselves.

This is not to say that individual interventions are not useful – they certainly can be. But they are not the *only* way to think about the burnout experience, given that the person is behaving within, and responding to, a larger environmental context. In other words, the individual experience should not constrain our thinking to simply the individual form of interventions. Moreover, the widespread tendency to frame the philosophical issue in an "either-or" form – is it the person *or* is it the organization – prevents a "both-and" approach that may be more realistic. In other words, *both* the person *and* the organization have a role to play in improving the workplace and people's performance within it.

Employee participation in the design and implementation of the intervention

Another key theme that has emerged from the literature review is the importance of getting direct input and feedback from employees at all levels within an organization. The people who work there can point to key issues and perspectives that might not be as apparent to researchers. Employees may be able to better identify the kind of interventions that will yield more meaningful benefits to them, or will be easier to implement, or will be better supported by the other workers. The priorities for the employees – in terms of what are the more important problems, and what would be the most meaningful improvements in the workplace – are not necessarily the same ones identified by the researchers (which are more likely to be based on their review of the literature, and/or their personal research preferences). Getting a "reality check" on the extent to which research hypotheses are in accord with employee experience, is probably a critical step on the path to formulating an effective intervention for burnout.

A related theme is the importance of worker collaboration, and ownership of the intervention. No matter how brilliant the plan for reducing or alleviating burnout, it will not be successful if it is not adopted and put into practice. Prior consultation with employees at all levels, including front-line and managerial, is essential for any intervention to succeed. First, such consultation may yield modifications of the intervention, which will increase the likelihood of it being effective. Second, if people are on board with the proposed intervention, are willing to put in the necessary time and effort to make the changes and to maintain them, and are committed to achieving the eventual outcome, then the intervention will have a much greater chance of success.

The importance of employees' active participation in interventions is reflected in the Self Determination Theory (SDT) of Deci and Ryan (1991) that proposes autonomy, competence, and relatedness as core motivations. An active role in a workplace intervention fulfills employees' autonomy motivation in that they experience themselves as deciding on their participation rather than feeling manipulated by authority figures. An active role also confirms a sense of efficacy through its implication that employees have the capacity to contribute to improving their experience at work rather than being entirely dependent on others. Working together with colleagues on a shared intervention confirms relatedness by identifying burnout as a shared workplace concern rather than an individual affliction. Aligning interventions with employees' core motives increases their chances of success.

Implementation and evaluation of burnout interventions

A primary goal of research on burnout is identifying interventions that make a difference in preventing or alleviating the syndrome. This goal requires an understanding not only of the dynamics of burnout, but of the basic principles of how individuals, workgroups, or organizations change. Effective interventions must build upon core qualities of a model of change.

Given that burnout is a response to chronic job stressors, it seems highly unlikely that a short-term, one-shot intervention will make a meaningful difference. The prior literature review seems to support this point, in that long-term interventions were usually more effective, but additional research with follow-up assessments is needed to confirm this proposition. Obviously, a longer framework means that people have more time to learn new skills and behaviors, and more time to practice these until they become familiar and second-nature for everyone. Moreover, there are more opportunities for reciprocal practice and feedback between colleagues, which will both improve and sustain the changes over time.

Models of change processes

But there is much more to successful change than simply practice, because the change process is complex and involves a number of distinct phases. The successful management of these different stages of change requires a lot of time, which is another reason why long-term interventions are likely to be more effective in reaching their change goal than short-term interventions. Several models of change have proposed a basic three-stage process. The first stage focuses on overcoming people's natural resistance to change and on preparing them to move. The second stage involves the actual transition to a different position or situation. The third stage solidifies and maintains the new change. These three stages have been described as "unfreezing, transition, and (re)freezing" by Lewin (1951). A more modern version of the Lewinian model talks about the three stages in terms of "disconfirmation, cognitive restructuring, and refreezing" (Schein, 2004).

Another model by Bridges (2003) describes the three stages as "a) Ending. Losing, Letting Go; b) Neutral Zone; and c) New Beginning."

Kotter (1996) proposed an elaborated, multi-stage model of organizational change. This is an eight-step model that is framed in terms of how leaders can manage change successfully within their organizations. The first step is to establish a sense of urgency about accomplishing a particular change, because people must understand why the change is needed and must be convinced that it is important to take immediate action. The second step involves the creation of a powerful coalition to lead the change effort, and the support to help this group work as a team. The third step is the development of a vision for change, and of strategies for achieving that vision, so that it will help direct the change effort. The fourth step is communication of the vision, in a clear and effective way, so that everyone will understand and buy in to it. The fifth step focuses on empowering broad-based action, by removing obstacles to change and by encouraging innovation and risk-taking. The sixth step is to generate short-term wins, by planning for immediate and visible achievements, and by rewarding those who accomplish them. The seventh step builds on the initial changes by never letting up on the implementation of the vision and by reinvigorating the change process. Finally, the eighth step incorporates the changes into the organizational culture, by connecting the new behaviors to organizational success and future progress.

All of these change models underscore the necessity of a long-term process to achieve some new organizational goals. Clearly, there are parallels and shared themes between all of these models. However, it has been argued that the Kotter model is a better framework for actual change implementation, because it goes beyond descriptions of processes by delineating specific action steps that can be clearly applied throughout the organization (Stragalas, 2010).

A new change model for burnout interventions

Our earlier review of published intervention studies reflected a variety of approaches, evaluation frameworks, and basic assumptions about the methods for addressing burnout. Admittedly, the current state of the research does not identify the definitive intervention format for burnout, but it does point towards qualities that characterize the most informative research on the issue. These qualities are compatible with Kotter's (1996) perspectives on the design and implementation of change initiatives (also see Lowe, 2008; NIOSH, 2008; and Peersman et al., 1998).

- **Urgency**: Successful change initiatives have a sense of addressing issues of critical importance to participants. They have a goal that describes the pre-ferred end state and how it differs from the current state. Reducing burnout presents serious challenges due to its stability over long periods.
- **Targeted and Strategic**: Successful change initiatives focus on the key leverage points for effecting change. A large body of research identifying the primary antecedents of job burnout provides direction for focusing

interventions. Successful change initiatives identify strategies that encompass a variety of specific tactics, any or all of which have a potential to make a difference. A clear focus on an identified target has been recognized as a success factor for organizational interventions that are subject to "mission-creep" (a term that refers to the expansion of project objectives beyond the original goal, or mission, of the program design; Dejoy et al., 2010).

- **Collaborative**: Employee participation throughout the intervention process improves chances of success. People do not take kindly to being told what to do. Successful change initiatives begin with, and maintain throughout, a dialogue characterized by close listening, continuous learning, and ongoing adaptation of implementation. This point was emphasized by Halbesleben et al. (2006) and also by Dejoy et al. (2010).
- **Sustained**. Addressing burnout requires an ongoing commitment. Burnout is an enduring condition closely linked with the structure of the work environment. Long-term success requires sustained efforts to maintain gains. Without such effort, the original baseline conditions may become re-established. The interventions reviewed earlier generally lasted for many months of individual or group sessions (e.g., Mommersteeg et al., 2006; Salmela-Aro et al., 2004).
- **Evaluated**. Successful change initiatives measure progress. Assessment provides a vital flow of information to guide implementation. The adage that "one attends to what is measured" fits well for intervention programs. Clear measurement of primary constructs is essential both to diagnose the situation and to determine if action has had the desired impact (Moulding et al., 1999).

Case study: the CREW intervention for civility and burnout

A recent program of research on an effective intervention for civility and burnout illustrates many of the arguments we are raising here about a new change model for interventions. It brings together a theoretical perspective, prior research on burnout, and a collaborative partnership with practitioners to implement a long-term group intervention and to assess its effectiveness over time. The Areas of Worklife model (Leiter & Maslach, 2004) has identified a key source of burnout in the area of "community" – which involves the social relationships between people in the workplace. Colleagues are potentially the most effective source of meaningful resources at work, especially when teamwork is a pervasive format. However, people can also be the source of the most distressing demands at work. Social behavior that harasses, excludes, or intimidates colleagues has a major emotional impact. These behaviors not only reduce access to information and expertise resources, they increase the demands that people encounter at work. Further, employees often lack the social skills or the inclination to grapple with the demands of interpersonal conflict and disrespectful behavior. They often consider such behavior as illegitimate demands that Semmer and Schallberger (1996) have shown to have a more insidious impact on burnout than do the legitimate demands at work. A consistent theme throughout the research record on burnout has been the importance of collegial and supervisory relationships in the development of burnout (cf. Greenglass et al., 1997; Leiter & Maslach, 1988). One means through which incivility could affect negative outcomes is through employees experiencing burnout in response to uncivil encounters with colleagues. Withdrawal behaviors, such as absences and turnover, are closely associated with the cynicism dimension of burnout (Halbesleben & Buckley, 2004; Maslach et al., 2001). It has been proposed that employees perceive the workplace as riskier when experiencing incivility from colleagues and supervisors (Leiter, 2012). This perception prompts action to counter such behavior (such as grievances) or escape the situation (absences or turnover).

This identification of a relationship between burnout and incivility among colleagues was then linked to an intervention program that had been developed within health care to address a growing concern about incivility. CREW (Civility, Respect, and Engagement with Work) was originally developed by the National Center for Organizational Development (NCOD) of the Veterans Health Administration (VHA) of the United States (Osatuke et al., 2009), with the goal of improving civility among co-workers. The initiative was developed in response to reports of chronically poor levels of teamwork on some organizational units across the large and dispersed network of over 350 facilities in the VHA system. Although most employees had amicable relationships at work, the units with poor social relationships presented a disproportionally large share of the VHA's management and performance problems. The importance of workplace civility was underscored by the results of the All Employee Survey in which low levels of workplace civility were associated with more frequent absences, grievances, and turnover. These correlations encouraged the development of an intervention to improve workplace civility among members of workgroups.

With the active support of the Veterans Health Administration's National Center for Organizational Development (NCOD) leadership, a research team led by one of us (Leiter et al., 2011) replicated CREW in Canadian hospitals. This study contrasted eight units on which CREW was implemented with control groups from the same hospitals, which participated in other programs designed to improve the quality of worklife. The results were assessed with hierarchical linear analyses to identify interaction effects. The results confirmed interactions in which the intervention groups improved on several measures (including civility, exhaustion, cynicism, commitment, trust, and job satisfaction), while the control groups showed no improvement over the same time interval. In addition to tracking the civility measure from the Osatuke et al. (2009) analysis, we examined CREW's impact on burnout along with other indicators of employees' connection with work. The results demonstrated that improvements in civility mediated improvements in cynicism. Further, these improvements persisted at a one-year follow-up (Leiter et al., 2012) while the control groups continued to remain at the same levels as were assessed at the original baseline. As such, the CREW process served as an intervention to address burnout by way of improving the quality of social discourse among people within workgroups.

CREW's effectiveness is evident in both its immediate impact and in its subsequent implications. That is, the direct focus of the CREW process was on the quality of social interactions occurring among employees. Later on, the impact of the CREW process was reflected in employees' attitudes, feelings of vigor or exhaustion, and other qualities of their experience. Regarding the immediate impact, both Osatuke et al. (2009) and Leiter et al. (2011) demonstrated that participation in CREW improved the quality of social interaction among members of workgroups. CREW is designed to improve workplace civility, and it clearly has that impact. The Veterans Health Administration has continued to implement CREW throughout its system for eight years (at the time of this writing) and has expanded the program into other areas of the US government. In addition, Leiter et al. (2011) also demonstrated that improvements in civility mediated CREW's subsequent impact on other constructs. Workgroups reported improvements in coworker civility, supervisor incivility, respect, cynicism, job satisfaction, and management trust to the extent that they improved their civility. The mediation analysis confirms an active role for collegial relationships in moving employees away from burnout and towards work engagement. It demonstrates that employees can work together to make a difference in the quality of their work environment.

The research demonstrated as well that CREW's effectiveness occurs on the workgroup level. Both Osatuke et al. (2009) and Leiter et al. (2011) assessed all members of participating workgroups, not only those who participated in the CREW meetings (attendance was voluntary for individual employees). The overall improvement within CREW units in contrast to control units indicates that the process changed the social dynamics of the unit beyond the participating individuals.

This broad-based improvement in the workgroup dynamics may be a key to the sustainability of improvements in the one-year follow-up. Participating in CREW did not simply improve the quality of interactions occurring within the structured meetings, but changed how employees interacted with one another throughout their workday. Through processes such as reciprocity or social contagion (Leiter, 2012), colleagues who had not attended the CREW meetings participated in more positive social interactions with their peers.

Intervention qualities of CREW

The CREW intervention encompasses the six qualities of change that we propose as necessary for effective interventions. Detailed descriptions of the CREW process are available in Leiter (2012), Leiter et al. (2011; 2012), and Osatuke et al. (2009), but here we will focus just on how CREW is a good example of the new change model for burnout interventions.

First, CREW brings a sense of **Urgency** in responding to requests from workgroups and organizational leaders to address crises in civility and incivility. Within the VHA system and in the replication study reported by Leiter et al. (2011), CREW was implemented in response to requests from groups that acknowledged a problem with collegial relationships.

Second, CREW is **Goal Oriented** in articulating a constructive objective of improving civility. Osatuke et al. (2009) emphasize the importance of working towards constructive goals, such as increasing the frequency of civil exchanges, rather than passive goals, such as reducing bullying or incivility. In the six months of the process, participants define specific goals for each weekly CREW meeting. The CREW process regards social interaction among colleagues as both essential and inevitable in healthcare work. A passive goal of eliminating incivility fails to address the constructive behaviors that would replace incivility within the ongoing interactions among the employees.

CREW is **Targeted** in that it focuses on a pivot point that is both influential and subject to change. As noted previously, the quality of supervisory and collegial social interactions is closely associated with burnout as well as job satisfaction, commitment, and other psychological connections of employees with their work. These associations suggest that improving the quality of social discourse has the potential to prompt meaningful change. Social behavior is subject to change. Many aspects of social behavior are under conscious control. Although it may be difficult at times to overcome habitual patterns of interaction, there is ample evidence that people can learn rules of comportment when instructed.

The potential for change is more evidenced in CREW's **Collaborative** format. When striving to change the course of social discourse, it helps if the participants in that discourse all share the objective of improving the quality of their social dialogue. It especially helps when all of the employees in the workgroup understand and share the goal towards which they are working. The group dynamics of CREW define a distinct process in which the nature of social interactions among colleagues becomes an explicit topic of conversation. The simple act of putting social relationships on a meeting agenda identifies the strains and slights that employees experience at work, and moves these out of the realm of private complaints among friends into the formal arena of group problem solving. For some groups, this shift may require concerted effort over multiple meetings, as it crosses a boundary to ask people to talk about a topic about which they often avoid explicit conversation. A second important dimension of CREW's **Collaborative** framework is that participants play an active role in setting goals and deciding how to attain those goals. Rather than aspire to an externally imposed ideal of civil behavior, the group process calls upon participants to describe what civility and incivility mean within their work context.

CREW's **Strategic** quality is evident within the overall design of the process as well as in the specifics of the exercises and topics contained within the *CREW Toolkit* that facilitators use to guide the structure of sessions. The structured exercises that guide CREW's facilitators are designed to encourage participants to explore different ways of interacting with one another. The exercises cover a range of situations, such as expressing appreciation, resolving conflict, or challenging a coworker who has behaved uncivilly during a shared interaction with a service recipient.

CREW is **Sustained** over a six-month implementation. Ideally, the CREW process in a milder form persists after the formal CREW process, as the workgroup continues to keep civility and respect on the agenda of the workgroup's meetings and discussions indefinitely. The design of the CREW process recognizes that changes in social behavior are likely to meet resistance when first implemented in the workplace. People have become accustomed to responding to one another in a consistent way, so initial attempts to establish new patterns of social dialogue, even when the new patterns are mutually beneficial, may not meet with immediate success. Colleagues may miss the essential difference in the new behaviors, or may suspect their sincerity. A **Sustained** process encourages change by implicitly confirming the reality and genuineness of the new pattern of interaction.

The **Evaluation** quality of CREW gives it a more credible place within organizational priorities. Contemporary organizations engage in a variety of activities under the general rubric of organizational development or professional development with only the most general indicators of meaningful change. CREW includes an initial survey that serves a diagnostic function in giving facilitators an indication of the workgroup's strengths and weaknesses. The assessment at the end of CREW provides the definitive indicator of progress: have civility, burnout, and other constructs improved over the implementation period?

Effectiveness of the CREW intervention

CREW works as an effective intervention to address burnout by improving the quality of social interactions at work. Work is a highly social activity in an information/service economy where employees with diverse knowledge, skills, abilities, and orientations integrate their work to address complex problems. The quality of collegial and supervisor relationships provides powerful leverage in addressing burnout. Supportive relationships are important for psychological wellbeing as well as for effective workplace performance.

From a motivational perspective, incivility and disrespect from colleagues run counter to core social motivations of autonomy, competence, and relatedness (Deci & Ryan, 1991). By changing the quality of social encounters at work such that they provide more consistent confirmation of employees' sense of agency, efficacy, and belonging, CREW may increase employees' overall motivation to become engaged at work.

Fundamentally, by changing the quality of social encounters among employees on an ongoing basis, CREW has an enduring impact on employees' experience of their worklife. The procedure teaches participants new ways of interacting; it encourages participants to help one another realize these changes. To the extent that these changes assist employees to improve their balance of job resources to job demands and to fulfill their core social motivations, these changes have a potential to sustain.

Conclusion

A vast body of research has confirmed that burnout is prevalent. Research in many countries with many occupational groups have found that employees are vulnerable to experiencing crises in the energy, involvement, and sense of efficacy that they bring to their work. The preponderance of the evidence indicates that burnout does not arise as a personal failing, but in response to mismatches of individuals with the conditions within which they work. These mismatches may pertain to: few opportunities to exert control, lack of recognition for their contributions, or a conflict with core values or fair treatment at work (Maslach & Leiter, 1997). From the perspective of the JD-R model (Bakker & Demerouti, 2007, 2014), job demands overwhelm employees' resources to address those demands. As a result of a mismatch or imbalance, employees feel at odds with the values of their workplace.

The urgency for addressing burnout arises not simply from the discomfort inherent in the syndrome, but from burnout's personal and organizational consequences, as burnout mediates the impact of workplace issues with these consequences. The experience of chronic exhaustion compromises health; cynicism and inefficacy undermine employees' capacity to become engaged and productive in their work.

From this perspective, there are compelling reasons to develop effective, manageable, practical interventions to address burnout. Further, the design, implementation, and evaluation of interventions have the potential to deepen understanding about the connections people develop with their work and how one can deliberately improve those connections. The defining characteristics of burnout – exhaustion, cynicism, and inefficacy – reflect central elements of psychological experience.

Developing and evaluating interventions requires active collaboration of researchers and practitioners (Maslach et al., 2012). Researchers and organizational leaders share an interest in addressing the problems presented by burnout. Partnerships can benefit both parties in many ways. By working together through the design, implementation, and evaluation phases of an intervention project, the parties can adapt the program to the specific needs of the organization while critically evaluating the project through good design, measures, and analysis.

CREW is an example of the kind of research on burnout interventions that we would hope to see more of in the future. It is an organizational intervention that operates in a bottom-up manner with top-down support. That is, implementing the process requires explicit support from organizational leadership and is enhanced by leaders actively promoting respect and civility as organizational values. CREW works from the assumption that persistent problems reside in social relationships, not simply within individuals. The potential for improvements to persist beyond the intervention increases when organizational policies, practices, and professional development priorities align with a core value of respect in the workplace.

References

Bakker, A. B., & Demerouti, E. (2007). The job demands-resources model: State of the art. *Journal of Managerial Psychology, 22,* 309–328.

Bakker, A. B., & Demerouti, E. (2014). Job demands-resources theory. In C. Cooper & P. Chen (Eds), *Wellbeing: A complete reference guide* (pp. 37–64). Chichester, UK: Wiley-Blackwell.

Berg, A., Hansson, U. W., & Hallberg, I. R. (2008). Nurses' creativity, tedium and burnout during 1 year of clinical supervision and implementation of individually planned nursing care: Comparisons between a ward for severely demented patients and a similar control ward. *Journal of Advanced Nursing, 20*, 742–749.

Brotheridge, C. M., & Grandey, A. A. (2002). Emotional labor and burnout: Comparing two perspectives of "people work." *Journal of Vocational Behavior, 60*, 17–39.

Bresó, E., Schaufeli, W. B., & Salanova, M. (2011). Can a self-efficacy-based intervention decrease burnout, increase engagement, and enhance performance? A quasi-experimental study. *Higher Education, 61*, 339–355.

Bridges, W. (2003). *Managing transitions.* (2nd edn). Cambridge, MA: Perseus Books.

Buljac-Samardzic, M., Dekker-van Doorn, C. M., Van Wijngaarden, J. D., & Van Wijk, K. P. (2010). Interventions to improve team effectiveness: a systematic review. *Health Policy, 94*, 183–195.

Butow, P., Cockburn, J., Girgis, A. F., Bowman, D., Schofield, P., D'Este, C., Stojanovski, E., & Tattersall, M. N. (2008). Increasing oncologists' skills in eliciting and responding to emotional cues: Evaluation of a communication skills training program. *Psycho-Oncology, 17*, 209–218. doi:10.1002/pon.1217.

Chambers, R., Gullone, E., & Allen, N. B. (2009). Mindful emotion regulation: An integrative review. *Clinical Psychology Review, 29*, 560–572. doi:10.1016/j.cpr.2009.06.005.

Cohen, M., & Gagin, R. (2005). Can skill-development training alleviate burnout in hospital social workers? *Social Work in Health Care, 40*, 83–97.

Cohen-Katz, J., Wiley, S. D., Capuano, T., Baker, D. M., & Shapiro, S. (2005). The effects of mindfulness-based stress reduction on nurse stress and burnout, Part II: A quantitative and qualitative study. *Holistic Nursing Practice, 19*, 26–35.

De Vente, W., Kamphuis, J. H., Emmelkamp, P. G., & Blonk, R. B. (2008). Individual and group cognitive-behavioral treatment for work-related stress complaints and sickness absence: A randomized controlled trial. *Journal of Occupational Health Psychology, 13*, 214–231. doi:10.1037/1076-8998.13.3.214.

Deci, E. L., & Ryan, R. M. (1991). A motivational approach to self: Integration in personality. In *Nebraska Symposium on Motivation, 38*, 237–288.

DeJoy, D. M., Wilson, M. G., Vandenberg, R. J., McGrath-Higgins, A. L., & Griffin-Blake, C. S. (2010). Assessing the impact of healthy work organization intervention. *Journal of Occupational and Organizational Psychology, 83*, 139–165.

Dierendonck, D., Schaufeli, W. B., & Buunk, B. P. (2001). Toward a process model of burnout: Results from a secondary analysis. *European Journal of Work and Organizational Psychology, 10(1)*, 41–52. doi:10.1080/13594320042000025.

Duijts, S. F. A., Kant, I., van den Brandt, P. A., & Swaen, G. M. H. (2008). Effectiveness of a preventive coaching intervention for employees at risk for sickness absence due to psychosocial health complaints: Results of a randomized controlled trial. *Journal of Occupational and Environmental Medicine, 50*, 765–776.

Elo, A., Ervasti, J., Kuosma, E., & Mattila, P. (2008). Evaluation of an organizational stress management program in a municipal public works organization. *Journal of Occupational Health Psychology, 13*, 10–23. doi:10.1037/1076-8998.13.1.10.

Ewers, P., Bradshaw, T., McGovern, J., & Ewers, B. (2002). Does training in psychosocial interventions reduce burnout rates in forensic nurses? *Journal of Advanced Nursing, 37*, 470–476.

Galantino, M., Baime, M., Maguire, M., Szapary, P. O., & Farrar, J. T. (2005). Association of psychological and physiological measures of stress in health-care professionals during an 8-week mindfulness meditation program: Mindfulness in practice. *Stress and Health, 21*, 255–261. doi:10.1002/smi.1062.

Goodman, M. J., & Schorling, J. B. (2012). A mindfulness course decreases burnout and improves well-being among healthcare providers. *The International Journal of Psychiatry in Medicine, 43*, 119–128.

Greenglass, E. R., Burke, R. J., & Konarski, R. (1997). The impact of social support on the development of burnout in teachers: Examination of a model. *Work & Stress, 11*, 267–278.

Halbesleben, J. R.B., & Buckley, M. R. (2004). Burnout in organizational life. *Journal of Management, 30*, 859–879.

Halbesleben, J. R., Osburn, H. K., & Mumford, M. D. (2006). Action research as a burnout intervention reducing burnout in the federal fire service. *The Journal of Applied Behavioral Science, 42*, 244–266.

Hätinen, M., Kinnunen, U., Pekkonen, M., & Kalimo, R. (2007). Comparing two burnout interventions: Perceived job control mediates decreases in burnout. *International Journal of Stress Management, 14*, 227–235.

Innstrand, S. T., Espnes, G. A., & Mykletun, R. (2004). Job stress, burnout and job satisfaction: an intervention study for staff working with people with intellectual disabilities. *Journal of Applied Research in Intellectual Disabilities, 17*, 119–126

Kabat-Zinn, J., Lipworth, L., & Burney, R. (1985). The clinical use of mindfulness meditation for the self-regulation of chronic pain. *Journal of Behavioral Medicine, 8*, 163–190.

Kompier, M.A.J., & Kristensen, T.S. (2001). Organizational work stress interventions in a theoretical, methodological and practical context. In J. Dunham (Ed), *Stress in the workplace: Past, present and future* (pp. 164–190). London: Whurr Publishers.

Kotter, J. P. (1996). *Leading change.* Boston, MA: Harvard Business School Press.

Lagerveld, S. E., Blonk, R. W., Brenninkmeijer, V., Wijngaards-de Meij, L., & Schaufeli, W. B. (2012). Work-focused treatment of common mental disorders and return to work: A comparative outcome study. *Journal of Occupational Health Psychology, 17*, 220–234.

Le Blanc, P. M., Hox, J. J., Schaufeli, W. B., Taris, T. W., & Peeters, M. C. (2007). Take care! The evaluation of a team-based burnout intervention program for oncology care providers. *Journal of Applied Psychology, 92*, 213.

Le Blanc, P.M., & Schaufeli, W.B. (2008). Burnout interventions: An overview and illustration. In J. R. Halbesleben (Ed.), *Handbook of stress and burnout in health care* (pp. 201–216). New York: Nova Science Publishers.

Leiter, M. P. (2012). *Analyzing and theorizing the dynamics of the workplace incivility crisis.* Amsterdam: Springer.

Leiter, M. P., & Maslach, C. (1988). The impact of interpersonal environment on burnout and organizational commitment. *Journal of Organizational Behavior, 9*, 297–308.

Leiter, M. P., & Maslach, C. (2004). Areas of worklife: A structured approach to organizational predictors of job burnout. In P. L. Perrewe & D. C. Ganster (Eds), *Research in occupational stress and well-being* (Vol. 3, 91–134). Oxford: Elsevier.

Leiter, M. P., Laschinger, H. K., Day, A., & Gilin-Oore, D. (2011). The impact of civility interventions on employee social behavior, distress, and attitudes. *Journal of Applied Psychology, 96*, 1258–1275.

Leiter, M. P., Day, A., Gilin-Oore, D., & Laschinger, H. K. (2012). Getting better and staying better: Assessing civility, incivility, distress and job attitudes one year after a civility intervention. *Journal of Occupational Health Psychology 17*, 425–434.

Lewin, K. (1951). *Field theory in social science*. New York: Harper & Row.

Lindquist, T. L., & Cooper, C. L. (1999). Using lifestyle and coping to reduce job stress and improve health in "at risk" office workers. *Stress Medicine, 15*, 143–152.

Long, C., Collins, L., MacDonald, C., Johnston, D., & Hardy, S. (2008). Staff stress and challenging behaviour on a medium secure development disabilities ward for women: The outcomes of organisational change, and clinical interventions. *The British Journal of Forensic Practice, 10*, 4–11.

Lowe, G. S. (2008). Healthy workplace strategies. Ottawa Canada: Health Canada. Online version: http://www.grahamlowe.ca/documents/93/Hlthy%20wkpl%20strategies%20 report.pdf (accessed 11 June 2013).

Maslach, C., & Goldberg, J. (1998). Prevention of burnout: New perspectives. *Applied and Preventive Psychology, 7*, 63–74.

Maslach, C., & Leiter, M. P. (1997). *The truth about burnout*. San Francisco, CA: Jossey-Bass.

Maslach, C., Jackson, S. E., & Leiter, M. P. (1996). *Maslach Burnout Inventory manual* (3rd edn). Palo Alto, CA: Consulting Psychologists Press. (All versions of the MBI are now published online by Mind Garden, mindgarden.com.)

Maslach, C., Schaufeli, W. B., & Leiter, M. P. (2001). Job burnout. In S. T. Fiske, D. L. Schacter, & C. Zahn-Waxler (Eds), *Annual review of psychology, 52*, 397–422.

Maslach, C., Leiter, M. P., & Jackson, S. E. (2012). Making a significant difference with burnout interventions: Researcher and practitioner collaboration. *Journal of Organizational Behavior, 33*, 296–300.

Matthiesen, S. (1992). *The Bergen Burnout Indicator*. Bergen: University of Bergen Press.

McCray, L. W., Cronholm, P. F., Bogner, H. R., Gallo, J. J., & Neill, R. A. (2008). Resident physician burnout: is there hope? *Family Medicine, 40*, 626.

Melamed S., Kushnir T., & Shirom A. (1992). Burnout and risk factors for cardiovascular diseases. *Behavioral Medicine, 18*, 53–60.

Mommersteeg, P., Heijnen, C. J., Verbraak, M. J., & van Doornen, L. J. (2006). A longitudinal study on cortisol and complaint reduction in burnout. *Psychoneuroendocrinology, 31*, 793–804.

Moulding, N. T., Silagy, C. A., & Weller, D. P. (1999). A framework for effective management of change in clinical practice: dissemination and implementation of clinical practice guidelines. *Quality in Health Care, 8*, 177–183.

Murphy, L. R. (1996). Stress management in work settings: A critical review of the health effects. *American Journal of Health Promotion, 11*, 112–35.

NIOSH (2008). *Essential elements of effective workplace programs and policies for improving worker health and wellbeing*. Cincinnati, OH: NIOSH. Online version: http://www.cdc.gov/niosh/twh/essentials.html (accessed 11 June 2013).

Osatuke, K., Mohr, D., Ward, C., Moore, S.C., Dyrenforth, S., & Belton, L. (2009). Civility, Respect, Engagement in the Workplace (CREW): Nationwide organization development intervention at Veteran's Health Administration. *Journal of Applied Behavioral Science, 45*, 384–410.

Ossebaard, H. C. (2000). Stress reduction by technology? An experimental study into the effects of brain machines on burnout and state anxiety. *Applied Psychophysiology and Biofeedback, 25*, 93–101. doi:10.1023/A:1009514824951.

Peersman, G., Harden, A., & Oliver, S. (1998). *Effectiveness of health promotion interventions in the workplace: A review*. London: Health Education Authority.

Pines, A., Aronson, E., and Kafry, D. (1981) *Burnout: From tedium to personal growth*. New York: The Free Press.

Quick, J. C. (1992). Health promotion, education and treatment. In G. P. Keita & S. L. Sauter (Eds), *Work and well-being: An agenda for the 1990s* (pp. 47–61). Washington, DC: American Psychological Association.

Salmela-Aro, K., Näätänen, P., & Nurmi, J. E. (2004). The role of work-related personal projects during two burnout interventions: A longitudinal study. *Work & Stress, 18,* 208–230.

Schaufeli, W. B., Maassen, G. H., Bakker, A. B., & Sixma, H. J. (2011). Stability and change in burnout: A 10-year follow-up study among primary care physicians. *Journal of Occupational and Organizational Psychology, 84,* 248–267.

Schein, E. (2004). *Organizational culture and leadership* (3rd edn). San Francisco, CA, Jossey-Bass.

Semmer, N., & Schallberger, U. (1996). Selection, socialization, and mutual adaptation: Resolving discrepancies between people and their work. *Applied Psychology: An International Review, 45,* 263–288.

Shapiro, S. L., Astin, J. A., Bishop, S. R., & Cordova, M. (2005). Mindfulness-based stress reduction for health care professionals: Results from a randomized trial. *International Journal of Stress Management, 12,* 164–176. doi:10.1037/1072-5245.12.2.164.

Stenlund, T., Ahlgren, C., Lindahl, B., Burell, G., Steinholtz, K., Edlund, C., & Slunga Birgander, L. (2009). Cognitively oriented behavioral rehabilitation in combination with qigong for patients on long-term sick leave because of burnout: REST – a randomized clinical trial. *International Journal of Behavioral Medicine, 16,* 294–303.

Stragalas, N. (2010). Improving change implementation: Practical adaptations of Kotter's model. *OD Practitioner, 42,* 31–38.

Thomas, J. T., & Otis, M. D. (2010). Intrapsychic correlates of professional quality of life: Mindfulness, empathy, and emotional separation. *Journal Of The Society For Social Work And Research,* 1, doi:10.5243/jsswr.2010.7.

van der Bossche, S., & Houtman, I. (2003). *Work stress interventions and their effectiveness: A literature review.* London: TNO Work & Employment.

van der Hek, H., & Plomp, H.N. (1997). Occupational stress management programmes: A practical overview of published effect studies. *Occupational Medicine, 47,* 133–141.

van Dierendonck, D., Schaufeli, W. B., & Buunk, B. P. (1998). The evaluation of an individual burnout intervention program: The role of inequity and social support. *Journal of Applied Psychology, 83,* 392–407.

van Weert, J. M., van Dulmen, A. M., Spreeuwenberg, P. M., Bensing, J. M., & Ribbe, M. W. (2005). The effects of the implementation of snoezelen on the quality of working life in psychogeriatric care. *International Psychogeriatrics, 17,* 407–427. doi:10.1017/S1041610205002176.

Visser, S. M., McCabe, M. P., Hudgson, C. C., Buchanan, G. G., Davison, T. E., & George, K. K. (2008). Managing behavioural symptoms of dementia: Effectiveness of staff education and peer support. *Aging & Mental Health, 12,* 47–55. doi:10.1080/1360786 0701366012.

Vuori, J., Toppinen-Tanner, S., & Mutanen, P. (2012). Effects of resource-building group intervention on career management and mental health in work organizations: Randomized controlled field trial. *Journal of Applied Psychology, 97,* 273–286. doi:10.1037/a0025584.

Westman, M., & Etzion, D. (2001). The impact of vacation and job stress on burnout and absenteeism. *Psychology & Health, 16,* 595–606.

Index

Note: 'N' after a page number indicates a note; 'f' indicates a figure; 't' indicates a table.

absence from work, among men vs. women 21
active-behavioral strategy 34
active-cognitive strategy 34
aggression 65–6, 70
Ahola, K. 5
alcoholism 12
Aluja, A. 63
Alvaro, C. 128
Andersson, L. M. 67, 70
anxiety disorders. *See* mental disorders
Areas of Worklife Model 60–1, 71–2, 158
Aryee, S. 60
Ashforth, B. E. 34, 45, 105
austerity programs 2
autonomy 156
avoidance strategy 34–5, 41. *See also* withdrawal

Bakker, A. 6, 59–60, 70, 93, 106, 107, 125, 133
Baltes, P. B. 38
Barling, J. 65
Bayer, U.-V. 87
Beal, D. J. 83
Becker, J. A. H. 107
Beck's Depression Inventory 16
belonging 58–9
Bergen Burnout Indicator 152
Beutell, N. J. 46
Billings, A. G. 34
Biron, M. 85–6
Blanch, A. 63
Blau, G. 70
Bliese, P. D. 136
Bono, J. E. 112
border theory 45

Bosker, R. 133
boundaries. *See* inter-role management
boundary theory 132
Bowler, W. M. 59
Breevaart, K. 6, 95, 114
Bresó, E. 152
Bridges, W. 157
Bunk, J. A. 67
burnout: among men vs. women 18; aspects of 58–9; cost of 25; daily experiences of 80–97, 88f; definition of 32, 33, 56–7, 80–1, 145; as fluctuating state 84, 115; as human challenge 1; origin of term 32; overlap with depression 17–20; as predictor of health problems 13–16, 20–3; risk factors for 32; social context of 6; stability of 82, 145; symptoms of 89–90
burnout, collective: definition of 122; and emotional contagion 125–6; and group-level resources 130; shared event approach to 125; temporal aspect of 126. *See also* multilevel models
burnout interventions: change process models 156–8; cognitive behavioral therapy (CBT) 147, 151; CREW intervention 4–5, 68–9, 158–62; employee participation in 155–6; lack of research on 153; literature review 147, 148t–50t; long-term 152, 156–7, 158; mindfulness 151–2; organizational 153; person-centered vs. situation-centered 146, 154–5; public health framework 146; research methodology 153–4; research on 7, 146–53; team/organizational resources for

123–4; work engagement as 3–4; in workplace 152. *See also* CREW intervention; prevention strategies

burnout research: conceptualization challenges 90–1; daily diary method 6, 88–9; episodic approach to 83–4; on interventions 7; measurement-burst design 90; state vs. static approaches to 82; three major foci of 5. *See also* Conservation of Resources (COR) model; daily diary method; Job Demands-Resources (JD-R) model

Butow, P. 151

CBT. *See* cognitive behavioral therapy (CBT)

challenges, seeking 41–2

Chamberlain, L. J. 63

Chambers, R. 151

Chan, D. W. 34

change process models 156–8

Cheng, C. 35

children 46

Chowdhury, S. K. 136

Civility, Respect, and Engagement at Work (CREW) intervention. *See* CREW intervention

civility and incivility: CREW intervention 4–5, 68–9, 158–62; customers 67–8; cyber versions of 66, 67; definition of 66; effect of, on burnout 6, 61, 66; "incivility spiral" 67; and social motivation 59; supervisors and coworkers 67; and turnover 159

cognitive behavioral therapy (CBT) 147, 151

common-method bias 11

community. *See* relationships

compensation 38–9

compensatory hypothesis 44–5

competence. *See* efficacy

competition 124

Composite International Diagnostic Interview 11

confidentiality 116–17

Conservation of Resources (COR) model 60, 70–1; compared to Job Demands-Resources (JD-R) model 127; conservation process 127; as explanation of burnout 126–7; multilevel model of 128, 129f, 130–2; overview of 81–2; resource acquisition process 127

continuous sampling 89

coping strategies 34–5. *See also* prevention strategies

COR model. *See* Conservation of Resources (COR) model

costs 25

CREW intervention 4–5, 68–9, 158–62

Cropanzano, R. 83

crossover 111–12

Csikszentmihalyi, M. 41

cynicism: as aspect of burnout 58–9; and civility/incivility 67; and coping strategies 35; definition of 81; and destructive leadership 116; and inter-role management 46; and passive-avoidant leadership 111; as predictor of disability 21; reduction in, associated with supervisor support 62; and withdrawal 159; and workplace aggression 65–6; and work relationships 70

daily diary method: data analysis of 91–2; and exhaustion research 115; future research 95–6; multilevel modeling 92; overview of 88–9; recommendations for 93–5; research findings from 85–7. *See also* burnout research

Day, Arla, on workplace civility 6

day reconstruction method (DRM) 89

Deci, E. L. 156

Deery, S. 65

DeJoy, D. M. 158

De Leeuw, J. 133

Demerouti, E.: daily diary study 43; and Job Demands-Resources (JD-R) model 59–60; on preventing burnout 7; on Selective Optimization with Compensation (SOC) model 38

Densten, I. L. 108

depersonalization 35, 58. *See also* cynicism

depression 16–20, 25. *See also* mental disorders

detachment: and inter-role management 46; as prevention strategy 37. *See also* recovery

De Vente, W. 151

diabetes 14

disability 21–2

disease 10. *See also* health problems

disengagement 33. *See also* engagement; work engagement

Dormann, C. 46, 67

DRM. *See* day reconstruction method
    (DRM)
drug use 22
Dutton, J. E. 40

efficacy: as aspect of burnout 58–9; and
    civility/incivility 67; and constructive
    leadership 116; daily diary method 91;
    definition of 81; and job resources 86;
    and Self Determination Theory (SDT)
    156
effort-recovery model 87
Einarsen, S. 103, 112
Elo, A. 151
e-mail 67
emotional contagion: and collective
    burnout 125–6; and leadership 6,
    111–12
employees: amount of time spent at work
    56; participation of, in interventions
    155–6; relationship with organizational
    leaders 6
Endres, M. L. 136
engagement: as burnout intervention 3–4;
    Job-Demand Resources model 4; Job
    Demands-Resources (JD-R) model 59;
    Utrecht Work Engagement Scale 4. *See
    also* disengagement
episodic approach 83–4. *See also* daily
    diary method
esteem 58–9
event-based protocols 88
exhaustion: and abusive leadership
    109–10; as consequence of burnout 24,
    33, 58–9; and coping strategies 35;
    daily diary method 91, 115; and
    decrease in proactive behavior 43;
    definition of 81; and destructive
    leadership 116; and detachment from
    work 37; and furloughs 123; and job
    demands 86; Job Demands-Resources
    (JD-R) model 59; and passive-avoidant
    leadership 111; reduction in, associated
    with supervisor support 62; vicious
    cycle of 42–3; and workplace
    aggression 65–6; and work
    relationships 70

Fabregat, Aluja 35
feedback. *See* job feedback
Feldt, T. 92
Finnish Health 2000 Study 11–13, 17, 21
Folkman, S. 34
Fredrickson, B. L. 84

Frese, M. 48
Freudenberger, H. J. 32
Freund, A. M. 38
Fritz, C. 37, 87
furloughs 123

Gibson, J. A. 62–3
Giumetti, G. W. 66, 67
Glasø, L. 112
Global Burden of Disease Study (2010) 10
GMM. *See* growth mixture modeling
    (GMM)
Gonzalez-Morales, M. G. 125, 126, 130,
    135
Grech, M. R. 86–7
Greenhaus, J. H. 46
Gross, S. 85
growth mixture modeling (GMM) 92

Haar, J. M. 47
Hahn, V. C. 46, 48
Hakanen, Jari 5
Halbesleben, J. 91, 123; on collaborative
    interventions 158; Conservation of
    Resources (COR) model 60; daily diary
    method 86; furlough study 130; and
    organizational interventions 153; on
    social context of burnout 6; and social
    motivation 59; on supervisor support 62
Harvey, P. 109
health, definition of 10
health problems: and burnout 5, 63;
    burnout as a predictor of 13–16, 20–3;
    cost of 25; depression 25; diabetes 14;
    exhaustion 24, 33; Finnish Health 2000
    Study 11–13, 17, 21; future research
    25–6; heart disease 14; hospital
    admission 22; infections 14–15;
    mortality 23; musculoskeletal pain 15;
    obesity 24; physical illnesses 13;
    psychotropic drug use 22; and recovery
    87; research methods for 10–11; and
    work disability 10; and workplace
    aggression 65; work recovery as
    reducing 37. *See also* mental disorders
healthy lifestyle, as prevention strategy 39
heart disease 14
Hershcovis, M. S. 64
Hetland, H. 6
Hetland, J. 6, 108, 111, 114
high performance work practices (HPWPs)
    123–4
Hobfoll, S. E. 33, 41, 60, 128
Hockey, G. R. J. 39

Hodson, R. 63
Holman, D. J. 91
hospital admission 22
hostility 65. *See also* civility and incivility
Houtman, I. 147
HPWPs. *See* high performance work
    practices (HPWPs)
Hu, C. 110
Hui, E. K. P. 34
humor 36

Ilies, R. 46, 112
individualism 154–5
inefficacy. *See* efficacy
infections 14–15
inter-role management: border theory 45;
    and children 46; compensatory
    hypothesis 44–5; as prevention strategy
    33, 44–7; role scarcity hypothesis 47;
    segregation (segmentation) hypothesis
    44–6; spillover (generalization)
    hypothesis 44–6. *See also* work-family
    conflict

Jenaro, C. 35
Jerusalem, M. 91
Jex, S. M. 136
job characteristics, changing, to prevent
    burnout 40–4
job crafting: definition of 40; as prevention
    strategy 40–4; and resource acquisition
    process 127–8
job demands: and exhaustion 86; and
    leadership support 114; reducing 41; of
    team or organization 123
Job Demands-Resources (JD-R) model 4;
    compared to Conservation of Resources
    (COR) model 127; and leadership
    103–5; overview of 82; and prevention
    strategies 40–2; and relationships
    59–60, 69–71
job feedback 2
job security 2
Joplin, J. R. 128
justice 123–4

Kalicinska, M. 62
Kanste, O. 108, 111
Karanika-Murray, M. 48
Karatepe, O. M. 70
Klein, K. L. 135
knowledge translation 4–5
Koeske, G. F. 34
Kotter, J. P. 157

Kozlowski, S. W. J. 135
Krasikova, D. V. 109
Kreft, I. G. 133
Kroon, B. 123, 124, 136

Lambert, S. 44, 62, 63
language, accessibility of 4
Lankau, M. J. 107
Lazarus, R. L. 34
leader-member exchange (LMX) theory
    106–7
leaders: burnout of 111–12; employees'
    relationship with 6; role of, in
    followers' well-being 102
leadership: classification of 102–3; future
    research 113–17; and job demands 114;
    and Job Demands-Resources (JD-R)
    model 103–5; moderating effects of
    114–15; multilevel approach 115–16;
    research challenges of 116–17;
    theoretical framework 103–4
leadership, constructive: conceptual model
    for 103; and efficacy 116; and Job
    Demands-Resources (JD-R) model
    104–5; leader-member exchange
    (LMX) theory 106–7; as resource 104;
    supervisory support 105–6;
    transformational 107–8, 113, 114–15
leadership, destructive: abusive 109–10;
    conceptual model for 103; and
    crossover of burnout 111–12; and
    cynicism 116; definition of 109; and
    emotional contagion 6, 111–12; and
    employee exhaustion 109–10, 116; as
    hindrance job demand 103; passive-
    avoidant 111, 114
Le Blanc, P. M. 153
LeBreton, J. M. 134
Lee, R. T. 34, 105
Leiter, M.: Areas of Worklife Model 60–1;
    on burnout interventions 7; civility and
    incivility 67; on coping strategies 34;
    and CREW intervention 160; on
    leverage points 4; and passive-avoidant
    leadership 111; study on civility 69; on
    work engagement 3–4; on workplace
    civility 6
Leon, M. 6
leverage points 4
Lewin, K. 156
Lim, V. K. 67
LMX theory. *See* leader-member exchange
    (LMX) theory
Lopina, E. C. 130–1

Maastricht Cohort 14
Magley, V. J. 67
Mäkikangas, A. 92
Martin, R. A. 36
Maslach, C.: Areas of Worklife Model 60–1; on burnout interventions 7, 68; definition of burnout 56–7; on distancing 96; on improving work relationships 70; interview of human service workers 32; on leverage points 4; on origins of burnout literature 57; on work engagement 3–4
Maslach Burnout Inventory 16, 147
Maslach Burnout Inventory – General Survey 11, 81
Maslach Burnout Inventory – Human Services Scale 58
McCray, L. W. 147
measurement-burst design 90
meditation 39. *See also* mindfulness
Meier, L. 5–6
Meijman, T. F. 36–7
Melamed Burnout Scale 151
men: burnout and depression among 18; and work absence 21
mental disorders 12, 16–20, 25
Merecz, D. 65
mindfulness 151–2. *See also* meditation
mistreatment: by customers/patients 65–6; and intervention research 72; and negative work relationships 64; by supervisors 65–6; and workplace aggression 65–6. *See also* civility and incivility; leadership, destructive
Moliner, C. 123–4, 134
Moos, R. H. 34
mortality 23
Mulder, G. 36–7
multilevel models: aggregation in 133–4; approaches to 135–6; and Conservation of Resources (COR) model 128, 129f, 130–2; and daily diary method 92; ICC(1) vs. ICC(2) 134; measuring variables 133–5; overview of research on 122–4; research implications 132–7; sample sizes for 132–3; and team/ organizational demands 123–4; trend toward 122. *See also* burnout, collective
musculoskeletal pain 15

Nakamura, J. 41
National Center for Organizational Development (NCOD) 159. *See also* CREW intervention

NCOD. *See* National Center for Organizational Development (NCOD)
nurturance 58–9

obesity 24
obstructionism 65. *See also* civility and incivility; relationships
OCBs. *See* organizational citizenship behaviors (OCBs)
Oerlemans, W. G. M. 93
Oldenburg Burnout Inventory 21, 91
optimization 38
organizational change, Kotter's model of 157
organizational citizenship behaviors (OCBs) 86
organizational restructuring 3
organizations: burnout interventions in 153, 154–5; demands of, and burnout 123–4
Osatuke, K. 68–9, 159, 160–1
Ossebaard, H. C. 151

Pearson, C. M. 67
Peeters, M. C. W. 47
pensions 2
Petrou, P. 40–1, 42
Podsakoff, N. P. 40, 41
POMS. *See* Profile of Mood States (POMS)
population-based samples 10
prevention strategies 7; changing job characteristics 40–4; coping strategies 34–5; detachment from work 37; future research 47–9; healthy lifestyle 39; humor 36; for individuals 32–49; inter-role management 33, 44–7; job crafting 40–4; Job Demands-Resources (JD-R) model 40–2; minimizing diminished resources 33–40; recovery from work 36–7; Selective Optimization with Compensation (SOC) model 38–9; and social relationships 43; two-part scheme 33. *See also* burnout interventions
Price, M. S. 112
Prins, J. T. 62
Profile of Mood States (POMS) 91
prospective designs 10–11

recovery: daily experiences of 88f; detachment 87; effort-recovery model 87; as prevention strategy 36–7; role of 87–8; sleep 92 relationships: aggressive 65–6, 70; Areas of Worklife Model 60–1, 71–2, 158; challenges and rewards of 2; civility in 59; Conservation of Resources (COR) model 70, 71; future research 70–3, 73f; improving 68–70; and intervention research 72; Job Demands-Resources (JD-R) model 69–70, 71; leader-member exchange (LMX) theory 106–7; negative, and burnout 64; nurturance of, as prevention strategy 43; quality of, and burnout 56, 58; as resource 59–61; and Self Determination Theory (SDT) 156; and social motivation 58–9; supervisor support 62–3

research findings, sharing with general public 4–5

resources: Conservation of Resources (COR) model 60, 81–2, 126–7; constructive leadership as 104; definition of 60, 127; and efficacy 86; family-friendly 131; and instrumental support 130; and Job Demands-Resources (JD-R) model 104; multilevel model of 128, 129f, 130–2; relationships as 59–61; seeking 41; strategies for dealing with diminished 33–40. *See also* Conservation of Resources (COR) model

risk factors, for burnout 32

role scarcity hypothesis 47

Russell, D. W. 68

Ryan, R. M. 156

Salmela-Aro, K. 152

Sanz-Vergel, A. I. 37

Schallberger, U. 158

Schaufeli, W. B. 57, 106, 113, 153

Schein, E. 156

Schwarzer, R. 91

Schyns, B. 103

SDT. *See* Self Determination Theory (SDT)

segregation (segmentation) hypothesis 44–6

selection, definition of 38

Selective Optimization with Compensation (SOC) model 38–9

Self Determination Theory (SDT) 156

Semmer, N. 158

Senter, J. L. 134

Shilling, J. 103

Shirom, A. 82

Shirom-Melamed Burnout Measure 14

Simbula, S. 85, 91

Skakon, J. 102

sleep 92

Sliter, M. T. 66

Sloan, M. M. 72

Snijders, T. 133

social activities 37

social context 6

social information processing theory 125

social relationships. *See* relationships

SOC model. *See* Selective Optimization with Compensation (SOC) model

Sonnenschein, M. 95

Sonnentag, S. 37, 87, 95, 124, 133

spillover (generalization) hypothesis 44–6

Stogdill, R. M. 102

Stordeur, S. 114

stress inoculation therapy (SIT) 147

supervisors: constructive leadership by 105–6; and leader-member exchange (LMX) theory 106–7; mistreatment by 65–6. *See also* leadership

support: direct effects of 62; emotional 105–6; and group-level resources 130; informational 105–6; instrumental 105–6; mediators of support-burnout relationship 63; as moderator of burnout-outcome relationships 63–4; as moderator of stressor-burnout relationship 62–3; and turnover 64

Swetz, K. M. 39, 43

Sy, T. 112

teams. *See* organizations

temporal aspect: of burnout symptoms 89–90; of collective burnout 126; and resources 130–1

Ten Brummelhuis, L. L. 82

Teo, T. S. 67

Tepper, B. J. 66

Thomas, C. H. 107

Thornton, P. I. 34

time. *See* temporal aspect

time-based protocols 88

Tims, M. 41, 127

Todd, M. 96

turnover 64, 130–1, 159

two-dimensional work stressor framework 40

unemployment 2

Utrecht Work Engagement Scale 4, 67, 95

Van den Broeck, A. 36
van der Bossche, S. 147
Van Gelderen, B. R. 86
van Gelderen, B. R. 115
Van Jaarsveld, D. D. 67, 70
Van Veldhoven, M. 85–6
Veterans Health Administration (VHA)
    159–60. *See also* CREW
    intervention
Vuori, J. 151

Weiss, H. M. 83
Weiss, M. R. 112
well-being. *See* healthy lifestyle
Wheeler, A. R. 86, 91
Whittington, R. 65–6, 70
Wilensky, H. L. 44
Winstanley, S. 65–6, 70
withdrawal: and cynicism 159; and
    workplace incivility 59
women: burnout and depression among 18;
    and work absence 21

work: amount of time spent at 56;
    detachment from 37; lack of closure of
    2; portability of 2; social and economic
    context of 1–3
work absence. *See* absence from work
work engagement. *See* engagement
work-family conflict: and Conservation of
    Resources (COR) model 132; definition
    of 46; role scarcity hypothesis 47; types
    of 47. *See also* inter-role management
workplace civility and incivility. *See*
    civility and incivility
Wrzesniewski, A. 40
Wu, T. Y. 110

Xanthopoulou, D. 5–6, 91, 106–7

Yagil, D. 110
Yela, J. R. 35

Zacher, H. 48
Zapf, D. 67